Restructuring and Resistance
from Atlantic Canada

Restructuring and Resistance from Atlantic Canada

Bryant Fairley
Colin Leys
James Sacouman
editors

Garamond Press
Toronto, Ontario

A publication of Garamond Press.

Garamond Press
67A Portland Street
Toronto, Ontario M5V 2M9

The publishers acknowledge the support of the Canadian Studies Bureau, Secretary of State, in providing a grant to cover development costs for this book.

Cover and design by: Phoenix Productions Intl.
Edited by: Melodie Mayson and Ted Richmond
Typeset by: PageCraft Design Center, Halifax
Printed and bound in Canada

Canadian Cataloguing in Publication Data

Main entry under title:
Restructuring and resistance from Atlantic Cana

Includes bibliographical references.
ISBN 0-9200059-1

1. Atlantic Provinces—Economic policy. 2. Fisheries—Economic Aspects—Atlantic Provinces. 3. Atlantic Provinces—Industries. 4. Populism—Atlantic Provinces. 5. Social classes—Atlantic Provinces.
I. Fairley, Bryant Douglas, 1956- . II Leys, Colin, 1931- . III. Sacouman, R. James, 1948- .

HC117.A8R48 1990   338.09715   C90-094147-2

Contents

List of Tables and Figures

CHAPTER 9

Acknowledgements

This book originated in a conference of invited participants held at Queen's University in September 1985, sponsored by the Social Sciences and Humanities Research Council on the initiative of Bryant Fairley and Colin Leys. The chapters by deMarsh and Cannon, Fairley, Leys, Sacouman, Williams and Theriault, and the first of the two chapters by MacDonald and Connelly, were originally presented and debated at this workshop, and we are grateful to all the participants, and particularly those from the Atlantic Provinces, who gave their time to try to clarify the issues involved in their various areas of expertise. The second chapter by MacDonald and Connelly, and the chapters by Murphy, Overton and Veltmeyer, were solicited subsequently in order to make the volume as broadly representative as possible of the topics and issues involved in the debate. We would also like to express our appreciation of the knowledgeable interest, and prompt and effective editorial input, of Errol Sharpe of Garamond Press. Errol undertook the project after it had suffered a near-fatal delay at the hands of a university press whose interest in it proved to be less strong than the hostile political views of some of their readers. We are also grateful to the board of Studies in the Political Economy of Canada, who have given continuing moral and material support, to Bernice Gallagher and Virginia Smith who efficiently retyped the revised text, and to Melodie Mayson-Richmond and Ted Richmond for their aid with final copy editing.

Chapter One

Restructuring and Resistance in Atlantic Canada: An Introduction

Bryant Fairley, Colin Leys, James Sacouman and Rick Williams

The crisis in the international economy manifests itself in many ways and has a widely varying impact on people in different settings. The ruling class response to the crisis also varies according to local conditions, but certain basic elements are clear: efforts to restructure the state and its role, movements of capital, and a new national and international division of labour.

The dynamics of class struggle are also reshaped by the crisis. In the industrialized countries the working class has been internally transformed by the decline of traditional heavy industries and the growth of the service sector and, particularly, of the female labour force. Independent commodity producers, rather than having been absorbed by wage labour relations, have been perpetuated as a class in ever-more marginalized and economically dependent forms. Resistance to capitalist exploitation and domination is changing in form and focus as the working class increasingly finds common ground with, or is influenced by, the struggles of women and minorities, of popular groups concerned about issues of nuclear war and environmental degradation, and of oppressed people in the Third World.

This book examines the dynamics of crisis, restructuring and resistance in one small corner of the capitalist world. The Atlantic provinces form a region of Canada that has lived largely in the shadow side of the post-war boom. While the central areas of the country have shared in unprecedented growth in employment and material living standards, Newfoundland, Nova Scotia, Prince Edward Island and New Brunswick have seen a dramatic decline of their traditional industrial base, the outmigration of tens of thousands of people, and the perpetuation of widespread poverty and social marginality.

Figure 1
Percentage change in unemployment rates
and in Gross National Product

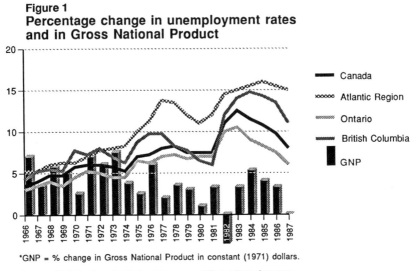

*GNP = % change in Gross National Product in constant (1971) dollars.

Source: Statistics Canada: *National Income and Expenditure Accounts* (Cat. 13-001), *Canadian Statistcial Review* (Cat. 11-003 Monthly), and *The Labour Force.* (Cat. 71-001)

Capitalist expansion nationally and continentally has been accompanied by crisis and collapse in the Atlantic region's economy. The offsetting factor has been the growth of the welfare state, a creature of the redistributive fiscal powers of the federal government. The Atlantic region gradually became a dependency, to the point where economic, social and political stability now all depend on the flow of federal dollars. With the exception of a few multinational corporate enclaves, capitalism within the region is itself largely dependent on state subsidies and transfers, and on the aggregate demand generated directly or indirectly by state expenditures on goods and services (including the wages of state employees).

Figure 1 compares growth in the unemployment rates in the Atlantic region, in Ontario and in Canada relative to overall growth in the Canadian economy, and reveals the profoundly structural nature of unemployment in the region. Within a long-term historical trend to higher unemployment, the Ontario economy can be seen to be responding "normally" to cyclical up-and-down turns. Unemployment in the Atlantic region, however, grows steadily through the peaks and troughs of the business cycle. This apparent autonomy of the regional labour market indicates the weakness of the direct linkages to the central economy and the dependence on secondary or "trickle down" effects through labour force mobility and the compensatory activities of the state. The ever-widening gap between Ontario and the region is clearly evident.

Figure 2 compares business investment in Nova Scotia, New Brunswick, Ontario and Canada on a per capita and constant dollar basis. We focus on these two provinces because they are the most developed of the Atlantic provinces in conventional terms, and because the scale of economic activity is sufficiently large to support generalizations. Housing and direct government expenditures are excluded, but investments by crown corporations and subsidies to industry are included. The severe effects of the 1980 to 1982 recession, and Ontario's strong recovery, are apparent.

While New Brunswick appears not to recover from the crisis at all, the pattern in Nova Scotia, with its very substantial growth up to 1983 and subsequent sharp decline, seems anomalous. The explanation lies in the rapid expansion of offshore oil and gas exploration in the period 1976 to 1983, and the subsequent collapse when world oil prices dropped and the National Energy program was cancelled. Up to 80 percent of such investment was actually state subsidies in the form of Petroleum Incentives Program grants under the National Energy Policy. Such oil and gas exploration spending constituted 34 percent of total "private sector" investment in Nova Scotia in the peak year of 1983. In total, government contributed close to 30 percent of gross fixed capital formation over the 1975 to 1984 period, compared with approximately 17 percent in Ontario and 19 percent in Canada as a whole (housing is excluded

Figure 2
Per capita business capital expenditures
in constant dollars

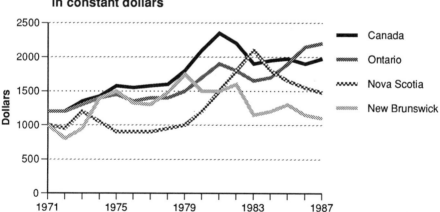

from all these figures). In 1986 in Nova Scotia, for example, federal government expenditure totalled $5.8 billion and was equivalent to 46 percent of the gross domestic product (GDP) in the province. Federal government deficit spending (over and above all revenues from the province) alone totalled $3.5 billion, or 27 percent of provincial GDP.

It is worth dwelling on the dominant economic role of the state in the Atlantic region both because it is a superordinate reality, but also because the dynamics of the current crisis in the region are so shaped by this dependence. The intensifying crisis at the national and international level has dictated the necessity for a restructuring of the state's economic role generally, and of the welfare state in particular. Since the recession of 1980, we have seen the gradual retrenchment of state expenditure in the region and the abandonment of its function as economic stabilizer and investor of last resort.

Such a reversal of the state's role cannot be implemented in a crude or cavalier manner because social and political stability are at stake. Instead, an elaborate ideological rationale, employing such key themes as "de-centralization", "local enterprise", "market driven growth", and "cutting red tape and bureaucracy", is being erected to justify and dissemble the radical "down-sizing" of the state and, by implication, of the regional economy. The effects of this well choreographed transformation are, however, manifold and are reshaping the conflicts and patterns of resistance throughout the region.

Crisis and Resistance

Petty producers and workers in primary industries have occupied a central place in the struggle against economic decline in the Atlantic region largely because of the importance of their industries to what remains of the regional economic base. To some degree, the pre-eminence of primary industries is symptomatic of the underdevelopment of the region: i.e., of the failure of both local and outside capital to generate significant levels of secondary manufacturing activity. On balance, however, these industries are key to the regional economy because they enjoy certain comparative advantages relative to competitors nationally and internationally. The problem of underdevelopment is therefore in large part a function of the failure to build on this base. The fishing and forestry industries, for example, were initially built on very strong resource bases and on ready access to major markets in the U.S. and Europe. The current weaknesses of these industries result from abuse of the resource base and the extraction of economic surpluses by outside capital, and not from any inherent disadvantages, as is often said to be the case with coal, steel and certain sectors of the agriculture industry.

It is understandable, then, that in the long history of the region's struggle against underdevelopment, petty producers and workers in forestry and fishing have played a central part. Three general points can be made about this.

First, in industries based on renewable (i.e., destroyable) natural resources, particularly those which are crown-owned or common-property, overall management of the resource inexorably becomes a focus of class struggle. Capital on one side, labour on another, and petty producers on a third side have quite distinct interests. In a situation of conflict, the hourly wage rate or the price of fish cannot long remain the sole issue when the continued survival of the industry is always in question. Given the nature of these industries, then, class struggle tends to transcend narrow economism and to become more politicized than tends to be the case in other sectors.

Second, with the tendencies towards the politicization of class struggle, the role of the state becomes critical in these industries. To ensure the long-term interests of capital, the state takes on a management function which inexorably grows as the industry expands and as conflicts intensify. In the guise of neutral arbiter, the state becomes the *de facto* "boss" for dispersed and independent-minded petty producers, seeking to impose on them an industrial discipline which aims to integrate their activities within the dominant corporate structure.

Primary producers, however, respond to this encroachment on their autonomy with an inchoate demand that they be the ones to manage their industry through new organs of collective decision- making and action. The politicized struggle for control of the means of production takes the form of conflict over the methods and structures of resource management. In a situation where the state itself is subject to restructuring, and where its role in the economy is being radically constrained, the future trajectory of these struggles becomes a matter of more than usual interest.

Third, while the economic penetration of the state within these primary industries is substantial, petty producers and workers are still not as dependent on the state as the population in general and other industries in the region. Most primary producers know the value of what they do, and still conceive of themselves as productive and self-reliant economic actors. While the most marginalized producers do depend heavily on unemployment insurance in particular, most workers and petty producers in these industries do not suffer the alienation and loss of identity that are more typical of urban industrial or service workers. In their conflicts with both capital and the state, petty producers and workers in these industries therefore tend to be more militant, more prone to believe in their own political efficacy, than other popular groups.

Given this context, two main questions confront those concerned with the future of the region. Will the result of the current crisis be the further marginalization and eventual elimination of the rural economy of small producers in Atlantic Canada, and of the social system underlying this economy? Or can we conceive of an alternative line of development to the capitalist trend which seems to portend sacrificing a further generation or two of Atlantic Canadians who are (it seems) increasingly surplus to capital's requirements? Second, can any such alternative be discerned, actually or potentially, in the ideas and initiatives generated by the resistance to capitalist restructuring?

These are the questions to which the following chapters are addressed. They record the recent evolution of, and some of the main struggles involved in, the main sectors of primary production in the region. Further, they attempt to analyze, in light of current debates, the theoretical and practical significance of such events. A brief word about these debates is therefore also in order.

In *Underdevelopment and Social Movements in Atlantic Canada* (to which the present volume is in some ways a sequel), Brym and Sacouman and their colleagues argued in 1979 that an alternative to the capitalist development of the region was necessary, and was at least embryonically foreshadowed or "inscribed" in the social movements they described. This view relied on an interpretation of the situation that drew substantially on "dependency" theory. Dependency theory stresses the way in which "metropolitan" capital determines development at the "periphery" of the global capitalist economy and extracts the surplus produced by the producers in the periphery's primary sector through a variety of means for enforcing unequal exchange. It also stresses the way in which the peripheral economy is always structured to suit the purposes of metropolitan capital, with the help of the state, keeping the "periphery" dependent on a few primary products, with few or no inter-sectoral linkages, "consuming what it does not produce and producing what it does not consume." The experience of Atlantic Canada seemed to correspond to this model. On this basis it was reasonable to conclude that the region could not expect to develop under capitalism, and that the popular mobilizations that were occurring would be driven by the logic of the situation to adopt an alternative non-capitalist or socialist program.

However, at about this time dependency theory itself came under severe attack. The successes of the Newly Industrializing Countries (NICs) showed that, given certain conditions, it was not impossible for a peripheral country to develop under capitalism. The increasing mobility of industrial capital also suggested that peripheral regions within particular countries might likewise develop. Warren (1980) went further and argued that capitalism always has an incentive to exploit the productive powers of peripheral populations more fully, while peripheral states are steadily acquiring the skills and leverage to make it profitable and even necessary for capital to invest in their economies and not merely extract surplus for investment elsewhere. Warren and others also argued that the alleged mechanisms of underdevelopment did not have the power attributed to them. It was not, they held, unequal exchange that kept the peripheral producers poor, it was their low productivity relative to that of capitalist production. Their elimination through competition with capitalism was ultimately progressive, in the sense of making it possible to produce more with less effort. Reaping the benefits of this process would be the task of a struggle based not on the dying class of independent primary producers, but on the new class of wage workers and unemployed workers.

This line of argument was in turn subjected to equally radical criticism; and today most critical students of development probably incline to a compromise. Dependency theorists have acknowledged that there is no iron law of underdevelopment, while continuing to point to the cumulative handicaps that peripheral countries and regions do experience; they tend to see the NICs as atypical, exceptions that prove the rule. Critics of dependency theory, on the other hand, now seldom endorse Warren's global optimism. They recognize that capital always develops unevenly, with poles of accumulation and pockets of surplus extraction. In addition, they recognize the problematic political factors determining what actually happens in any particular place: the effects of the particular kinds of class forces produced in the earlier stages of capitalist "underdevelopment," the effects of imperialist pressures, and so on.

A similar evolution of ideas has occurred in relation to Atlantic Canada, but with a distinctive emphasis on the nature of the popular movements that have arisen in response to the effects of capitalist development (due, perhaps, to the unusually close involvement of Atlantic Canadian scholars with these movements). Thus, for example, in questioning the dependency interpretation of Sacouman and others who have seen these movements as anti- capitalist in nature, and at least potentially socialist, Fairley argued that the Newfoundland Fishermen's union was not, contrary to appearance, the instrument of anti-capitalist small "inshore" or "independent" fishers, trawler crews and fish plant workers, but rather was more representative of the interests of an emerging class of small capitalist "nearshore" fishers (Fairley 1983, 1985a).

In general, the question was raised of how the political potential of any social movement of this kind is to be assessed. The fact that it enjoys widespread support from small independent producers (farmers, fishers, lumber producers and the like) does not necessarily mean that it is actually or potentially anti-capitalist, let alone socialist. It is at least as likely that it will be *populist*: i.e. defending essentially pre-capitalist values in the name of "the people," but having a very garbled class base, lacking a clear political analysis, and hence being prone to come to nothing (or even to come to serve capitalist purposes). Under what conditions do social movements of the popular classes become socialist and not populist?

This is, in barest outline, the theoretical background of the papers collected in the present volume. It begins with a discussion of the nature of populism and the relevance to the Atlantic provinces of Lenin's critique of Russian populism from almost a century ago. Lenin's trenchant analysis has given populism a bad name, but as Leys points out Lenin assumed with some justification that Russia was on the way to a full transition to capitalism. Today, however, it is not clear that capitalist development will eventually provide later generations of Atlantic Canadians with work and prosperity. In such conditions, it may be wrong to dismiss "populism" too lightly. But it remains an ambivalent force, as Overton's chapter on the neo-populist ideology of "small is beautiful" in Newfoundland clearly shows. Originally propagated by social scientists sympathetic to the plight of primary producers in Newfoundland, the ideology of "small is beautiful" is now being used to legitimize state policies for accelerating the concentration of capital and leaving the majority of small-scale producers and workers to simply tighten their belts.

Subsequent chapters provide an overview of the development of Atlantic Canada and then focus on the main primary producing sectors—the fishery, the potato industry, and lumber. Veltmeyer outlines the evolution of state policy towards the region. Any alternative project for it, he suggests, must start from the fact that its central function has long been to furnish surplus population for Canadian capitalism. State policy in the current crisis has been consistent with this objective. Williams shows how the Maritime Fishermen's Union mobilized New Brunswick and some Nova Scotian fishers to confront the state and the big corporations with a militantly anti-capitalist platform. But he also notes that over time the union has found itself drawn into commercial and other activities, important to its members, that were and are inconsistent with an anti-capitalist stance, leaving the long-run political significance of this mobilization more ambivalent than it had at first appeared.

MacDonald and Connelly first examine the impact of restructuring in the fishery on workers and households in a Nova Scotia community that depends on fish processing. They show how the relations between fishing and processing employment, between men and women, between workers and capital, and between small-scale and large-scale capital have all been radically altered over time, in ways that are quite complex and which have not so far had any tendency to foster a popular anti-capitalist struggle. In a second chapter, MacDonald and Connelly argue more generally for the real analytical and practical gains that arise from combining class and gender analysis with a perspective of change over time. Fairley argues, in his discussion of the Newfoundland fishery, that the class character of both the union and government policy was less fixed or determined than had previously appeared. In the Newfoundland Fishermen's union, the largest and most organizationally successful social movement in their region in the 1970s (Inglis, 1985), the project of the small capitalist "nearshore" fishers was defeated, partly by the federal government's strategy for rehabilitating the bankrupt big companies, but also, Fairley argues, by the provincial government's policy which favoured small local *processors*. The implications of this defeat for the future political potential of the union remain to be seen.

Murphy show that in potato production—virtually the only sector of the region's agriculture to remain competitive—success has been achieved through the inroads of large-scale capitalist production. Murphy believes that it is too late to save the "family farm," but that a strategy of supporting the "family in farming" is not only conceivable but worthy of support. Similarly in New Brunswick lumber, as deMarsh shows, realistic and determined organization among the small woodlot owners has achieved significant gains *vis-a-vis* the large corporations to which they supply their lumber. But there are obvious limits, set partly by the class basis of this sector, and partly by the nature of the product (a constraint that could be more severe for other products, as Cannon's commentary on deMarsh notes).

Evident in all these cases are the ambiguity of the "class impact" of restructuring and, as a result, the problematic nature of the long-run political potential of the popular movements concerned. In the concluding chapter Sacouman argues that this ambiguity is inherent not only to the situation in an underdeveloped region such as Atlantic Canada, but also to global capitalism *and* to all socialist alternatives being forged in the Americas. He maintains that any alternative, socialist form of development must necessarily be the result of clear alliances between quite disparate groups of the popular classes, rather than the self-revealing project of a single class promoted by orthodox Marxism.

Be that as it may, this volume does not attempt to do more than try to describe and honestly assess the movements concerned. Any project for a better alternative than the present path of development in Atlantic Canada must surely begin from this.

Chapter Two

Populism, Socialism, and the Struggles of Primary Producers

Colin Leys

Since the advent of capitalism small primary producers everywhere have been under steadily increasing threat. In Western Europe, where the advance of industrial capitalism came earliest, the "agrarian question" (as the distress of the peasantry was called) was largely resolved by the growth of urban demand for agricultural produce, which led to the extension of capitalist production in agriculture. This forced the pace of differentiation among primary producers. A steady stream of the younger generation went into urban employment; some of the more enterprising or fortunate smallholders evolved into commercial farmers applying capitalist rationality, using small but increasingly permanent numbers of hired workers, and expanding amounts of capital. In the present century, state subsidies have often permitted the older producers to evolve into a stratum of protected, economically marginal "park-keepers" (Franklin, ch. 7, esp. pp. 219-21). Engels' characterization of the peasantry as "future proletarians" was too crude (in Europe even today, in between the "park-keepers" and the emergent capitalistic small farmers there is still a resilient category of worker-peasants, operating in both the urban and the rural economies). Yet in spite of all these qualifications the final disappearance of independent simple commodity production in Europe seemed, to a careful observer at the end of the 1960s (Franklin, 1969), likely to be consummated within the space of perhaps two more generations. A similar trajectory was even more apparent in North America.

But in the late 1980s this looks more problematic. In the most developed areas of Western Europe and North America the rate of growth of industrial productivity means that surplus rural labour can no longer be easily absorbed in industry. On the other hand there is growing opposition in Europe to the accumulating fiscal burden of the Common Agricultural Policy of the EEC, in the U.S.A. to the agricultural price support policies inherited from the "New Deal," and in Canada to agricultural supply management (the marketing boards), i.e. to all the main mechanisms which have limited the erosion of the small producers and cushioned their standard of living. Thus even in these countries a final political solution to the "agrarian question" has still to be found; while in less developed regions of the world, where the prospects for capitalist industrialization are weak, "the agrarian question" tends to become more and more acute and in some places poses the threat of an almost unmanageable human disaster.

Politically, what this has meant is that where the state has not guaranteed living standards to primary producers that are at least distantly comparable to those of urban workers, and where the prices of primary products have fluctuated downwards (because of relative oversupply resulting from capitalist producers achieving rapid increases in output and labour productivity), primary producers generally have been driven to struggle for their survival. The issue then arises, what this struggle is ultimately for—what are, or what might be, its ultimate goals, and how can these goals be accommodated to the goals of the wage-earning working class (a growing proportion of whom are also suffering from growing unemployment and falling living standards as a result of capitalist restructuring)?

This issue has been raised most sharply wherever the "progressive" mission of capitalism (successful industrialization) seemed unlikely to be accomplished, or accomplished at the cost of an unacceptable catastrophe for the primary producers in whose lifetimes it would occur. It has generally been raised in the form of "populism," that is, an approach to the problem based on a critique of the capitalist accumulation process from the standpoint of "the people" (meaning the great mass of the people, of whom the rural producers are seen as the heart and soul); and proposing, broadly, "an alternative to capitalist development, based on small-scale individual enterprise" (Kitching, 1982:19; and cf. Walicki, 1969:9). Populism was first articulated in Russia (the word is a direct translation from the Russian *narodnichestvo*); it has also, of course, been an important political force in the prairies of North America and in Latin America. As Kitching (1982) has shown, it is an influential tendency in much contemporary Third World policy-making. In the Atlantic Provinces of Canada, no political movement *describing* itself as populist has arisen. But as Overton's chapter in this volume shows, it has been an important element in the work of some social scientists concerned with development (or the lack of it) in Newfoundland and the Maritimes. It is now being used, not to protect small producers, but to provide an ideological justification for policies which will accelerate their impoverishment and elimination. The question which this chapter asks, therefore, is what can be learned from the original debate about populism in the country of its origin—Russia—that may help in understanding, and if possible assisting, the struggles of the primary producers in the Atlantic Provinces?

Since it is the advance of capitalist production that eliminates the peasantry, and since Marx was the first to explain this process, and seemed to regard it as inevitable, resistance to this process involved also resisting Marxism. The Russian populists were the first to offer a developed counter-theory. As Mitrany put it, in his book *Marx Against the Peasant*,

> As one travelled eastwards across the Continent factories became scarcer while farms multiplied, until agriculture spread itself out almost without rival on the vast plains of Russia. The revolt against Marxism (in its orthodox version, stressing the primacy of the working class and destining the peasantry to disappear) followed exactly this variation in economic structure. It travelled eastwards in ever widening circles until it struck the shores of Russia; there it encountered intense local currents and the returning tide came back transformed out of all recognition as Populism ... (Mitrany:41)

Lenin, however, pointed out that Russian populism, although formulated by the anti-Czarist intelligentsia, was really a utopian "protest against capitalism from the point of view of the small immediate producers ... being ruined by capitalist development" (Walicki:6), and *not* from the viewpoint of *all* "the people." Lenin argued that the majority of the Russian people were destined to be proletarianized, and an analysis from the standpoint of the proletariat yielded a very different strategy, the "revolutionary-democratic dictatorship of the proletariat and peasantry," which was not utopian, and could not be turned to advantage by reactionary forces, as populism could. Some Russian populists, for example, advocated support for the Czarist autocracy, notwithstanding its utterly backward character, seeing it as being more likely to preserve the Russian peasant commune than a constitutional state would be, since the latter would necessarily be dominated by the capitalist middle class. This position was dubbed by the revolutionary populists as "police populism" (see Walicki:175).

Lenin's critique of Russian populism has tended to be adopted on the left as a universally valid critique of populism, both because he correctly analyzed its class character, and because Russian populism indeed put forward no practicable alternative to capitalistic development, given the Russian political situation. What is less widely recognized, however, is that it was the gradual acceptance, among the Russian populists, that *capitalism was successfully developing Russia*, that made Lenin's position seem more and more correct. In situations where it is not unreasonable to have radical doubts about the likelihood of capitalism expanding the productive forces in return for the people's suffering, populist ideas are less likely to be abandoned. This is the case in many parts of the Third World, especially in Africa, and may also be true for "peripheral" sectors or regions in advanced capitalist economies (such as the Atlantic provinces today).

More speculatively, "populism" of some kind may tend to become even more generally appealing in the context of increasing international mobility of capital. In this situation capitalist competition on a world scale increasingly seeks to force the conditions of labour everywhere down towards those of the cheapest and most oppressed workforces in the world, and the rate of increase of productivity through technological change progressively reduces the demand for labour power. Thus the modern utopian socialism of writers like Andre Gorz (1982), for example, can be seen as representing a kind of "global populism" arising from the prospect of the marginalization and pauperization of a growing proportion of the workforce in advanced capitalist economies, and from the belief that the means of production created by capitalism are becoming less and less suitable for appropriation and use under any form of democratic socialism. Of course, if this is "populism"—i.e. a critique of capitalism and a program advanced in the name of all "the people"— it is not so from the standpoint of the petty commodity producer, but rather from that of the increasingly marginalised wage worker. And if its utopianism is rather transparent—relying, as Gorz does, on the "non-class of non-producers" for its implementation—this is a weakness it shares with most populism of a more familiar kind. Whether this weakness is inherent in populism, or only in some of its particular expressions, is one of the issues to be resolved. If there is a case for rehabilitating populism (let alone as the "highest form of socialism," as Laclau [1977] has recommended) it seems important to be as clear as possible about this issue. We must continue to be on guard against the familiar dangers of idealism and opportunism. One such danger is idealism: supposing that it is enough to "articulate" a promising alliance of interests for it to be capable of being realized. Another is opportunism: articulating interests because they *can*, perhaps, be articulated, with too little attention to the implications of doing so—as in the case of "police populism."

1. Classical Russian populism

Walicki dates the beginning of classical populism from 1869, eight years after the emancipation of the privately-owned serfs, three years after that of the state-owned serfs. Its precursors were Herzen, who criticized capitalism from an "aristocratic" standpoint, i.e. for producing a mass consumerist culture, and argued for a direct transition to socialism based on the peasant commune; and Chernyshevskii, who criticized feudal institutions from an "enlightenment" (universal-rational) standpoint, and accepted the necessity of a capitalist phase. The latter also argued that Russia could avoid the worst of its social costs by protecting and fostering the peasant commune, which was still the pivot of rural life, even if it was being undermined by the "redemption" debt (the ex-serfs were saddled with a crippling debt to "compensate" their former owners) and the inroads of capitalist competition, proletarianization, and the rise of the kulaks.

The classical populists inherited both these elements (critique of bourgeois values, and celebration of the commune as the ultimate manifestation of Slavic identity) but went further and created a comprehensive doctrine in conscious response to the Marxist theory of capitalism.

The Marxism they encountered was, above all, the version presented by Engels in his application of historical materialism to Russia. Engels held that capitalism would inexorably advance there, and this could be avoided only if there was a proletarian victory first in Western Europe. This position was endorsed by the Russian Marxist Struve, and ultimately also by Plekhanov (himself a former populist). They both held that socialism was impossible until capitalism had developed the productive forces and created a proletariat capable of seizing power. Therefore Russia must undergo the vicissitudes of capitalist development, and socialists must support and accelerate the development of capitalism. This fatalistic view, and the passive political conclusion that seemed to follow from it, was naturally rejected by the populists, whose whole aim was to alleviate, and if possible prevent, the suffering of the peasant masses. Mikhailovskii expressed their reaction when he wrote that according to Marxism,

All this "maiming of women and children" we still have before us, and, from the point of view of Marx's historical theory, we should not protest against them because it would mean acting to our own detriment; on the contrary, we should welcome them as the steep but necessary steps to the temple of happiness. It would be, indeed, very difficult to bear this inner contradiction, this conflict between theory and values which in many concrete situations would inevitably tear the soul of a Russian disciple of Marx. He must reduce himself to the role of an onlooker, who ... writes in the annals of the two-edged process. He cannot, however, take an active part in this process. He is morally unable to push forward the wicked side of the process and, on the other hand, he believes that activity motivated by his moral feelings would only contribute to make the whole process longer and slower. His ideal, if he is really a disciple of Marx, consists among other things, in making property inseparable from labour, so that the land, tools and all the means of production belong to the workers. On the other hand, if he really shares Marx's historico-philosophical views, he should be pleased to see the producers being divorced from the means of production, he should treat this divorce as the first phase of the inevitable and, in the final result, beneficial process. He must, in a word, accept the overthrow of the principles inherent in his ideal. This collision between moral feeling and historical inevitability should be resolved, of course, in favour of the latter. (quoted in Walicki, 1969:146)

Similar sentiments are frequently expressed today in relation to Third World peasants (e.g. Beckmann 1981:10-11), and in relation to primary producers in the Atlantic Provinces (e.g. Sacouman, 1980).

The Russian populists' response took several forms, all of them readily recognizable in contemporary replays of the debate. They attacked the idea of "objective" social science (then called scientific "positivism") and argued instead for a "subjective sociology," based on the "ethicism" of the researcher and on the historical effectiveness of the individual (Lavrov, Mikhailovskii). They challenged the material criteria of progress proposed by Marxism (which in this respect was in complete harmony with classical political economy), and proposed instead that progress should be defined as "the development of consciousness and the incorporation of truth and justice in social institutions, by the critical thought of individuals who aim at the transformation of their culture" (Lavrov, in a passage that like certain passages in Mikhailovskii, actually resembles some of the *young* Marx's then unpublished thought). Mikhailovskii looked to the restoration of human "wholeness" after the fragmentation of men by the division of labour. He saw this process as a "conservative" reversal re-establishing craft-like production, rather than the establishment of a higher level of collective labour, based on the full socialization of labour resulting from the division of labour and machinery, that was envisaged by Marx. In general, the populists romanticized pre-capitalist Russian communal life (compare the voluminous literature on "the 'real' Newfoundland" such as Overton, 1980).

Eventually two failed attempts to mobilize the Russian peasantry on the basis of a populist program (in 1873-74 and 1876-78) led to a crisis; active populists finally realized that the autocracy was indeed an insuperable barrier to any project for saving the commune (because it defended the privileges of the landed class, and was actually encouraging capitalist modernization). The radical wing turned to terrorism: following the assassination of Alexander II in 1881 they were effectively liquidated. Plekhanov and others turned towards Marxism, and founded Russian Social Democracy.

At this point Vorontsov and Danielson produced economic analyses designed to prevent other populists from following that route. Vorontsov argued (in *The Fates of Capitalism in Russia*, 1882) that it was not merely a question of capitalism being undesirable, but of it being *impossible* in Russia. This was because already developed capitalist countries had dominant positions in foreign markets which a newly-industrializing country could not hope to penetrate. Therefore it depended on its "home" market; but this was being reduced, not expanded, by the impoverishment of the peasantry by taxation and debt, and by the competition which its handicrafts were now experiencing from new capitalist industries which, using technology developed elsewhere, were increasingly capital-intensive and hence also did not generate their own consumer market (cf. contemporary "dependency theory"). Vorontsov thought that the statistics showed that state-sponsored large-scale industry was already employing a *decreasing number of workers and concluded that in spite of massive government subsidies, capitalism was collapsing due to the basic inhospitality of Russian conditions* (Harding, 1977:83). Danielson, who actually considered himself a Marxist, argued his views in a series of articles beginning in 1880 and culminating in *Outlines of our Social Economy after the Enfranchisement of Peasants* in 1893. He called for an immediate socialist revolution to carry out a program of industrialization for social ends rather than profit. In his view such a revolution would be both socially beneficial and capable of succeeding where capitalism could not. Vorontsov also advocated reforms to ease the lives of the peasants (cheap credit, lower taxes, extension services) (Kitching:38).

2. Marx and Engels and Russian populism

Perhaps only Marxologists need be greatly concerned about what Marx and Engels thought about populism, but as Shanin (1983) has recently raised the issue as one which sheds a new light on Marx's conception of his own analysis of capitalism, it is worth discussing briefly here.

Engels' position is fairly clear. In 1881 he wrote a preface for a Russian edition of the *Manifesto* (with Marx, though Wada [in Shanin, 1983:70] speculates that Marx did not pay much attention to it), which said that if there were a proletarian revolution in the West following a revolution in Russia, the Russian commune *might* serve as a "starting point" for a "communist development." But in 1894, in a postscript to his 1875 essay *On Social Relations in Russia*, Engels asserted that the commune could not survive the further capitalistic development of Russia. In this he came close to the position of the "evolutionist" wing of Russian Social Democracy, led by Plekhanov.

Marx, however, seems to have been influenced by the Paris Commune of 1871, and by his extensive reading of Russian literature and contacts with Russian populists, to veer more towards the populists' position. In 1877 he wrote a letter to a Russian populist journal (*Fatherland Notes*) commenting on Mikhailovskii's anguished rejection of the "Marxist" vision of Russia as doomed to undergo a capitalist development, according to which it was utopian to dream of saving the peasant masses from their suffering until they all became proletarians. In his letter Marx disclaimed any such vision. His theory was, he said, not a universal model of the development of all countries in the world: national historical conditions determine the outcomes of the struggles that take place around the potential that is present in new economic forces and relations. Wage-labour had been introduced in Rome, he wrote, but did not lead to capitalism. In relation to Russia, this meant that all he contended was that *if* Russia became capitalist it would mean it had succeeded in proletarianizing its peasantry, and *then* it would be subject to capitalist laws of motion and "lose the finest chance ever offered by history to a people" and undergo all the vicissitudes of capitalist development. In referring to this historical opportunity he made no mention of the condition that there must be a supporting proletarian revolution in the West. As Walicki points out, this statement was ambiguous. The populists saw it as endorsing their call for immediate revolution, before capitalism became more entrenched. Plekhanov later said, that since Russia after 1877 had indeed followed a capitalist path, Marx's text meant that it must now suffer all the consequences. Lenin said that in this text Marx had avoided giving a definite answer (Walicki:187).

But in 1881 Vera Zasulitch put Marx on the spot, explaining very lucidly in a letter that the issue was critical for revolutionary populists in Russia—did Marx's theory, which they greatly respected, mean that they should try to make the revolution now, or should they first support the development of capitalism? Marx eventually sent her a very short reply, to the effect that if the commune was to be the basis for socialism, it must be assured "normal conditions" for development (i.e. not be taxed to death, etc.). But in the long second draft of his reply out of the four that he wrote (the first three were never sent), Marx can be seen as far more inclined to accept the populists' ideas than his final reply indicated (Wada, in Shanin:64). In particular, he noted that the Russian commune was a nation-wide institution, that its structural features were propitious for collective production and appropriation, and that capitalist technology could be adopted to facilitate the transition to co-operative labour on the land. He also accepted the view that what the commune was suffering from was state policies that were undermining it, not the unfolding logic of capitalist production. Noting what he called the "fatal crises" that capitalism was then undergoing in Europe, he said that the time was ripe for a socialist form of production. Shanin, and Sayer and Corrigan (in Shanin, 1983), speculate that Marx's confrontation with the imperfect reality of an actual revolutionary situation, in the shape of the Paris Commune, and his emerging idea (in the drafts for *The Civil War in France*) that the socialist revolution must involve abolition of the state as an independent power, led him to take more seriously the Russian commune as also a potentially prefigurative form for the ultimate emancipation of labour (Shanin, 1983:15 and 91).

However, Marx did not write the pamphlet on the subject that he had promised Vera Zasulitch. It is difficult not to agree with Walicki that the most likely reason is that he was not sure of his argument. As Sayer and Corrigan note, he also said nothing about the rather important question of whether capitalism was necessary in order to develop the forces of production prior to the establishment of socialism, as the *Manifesto*, the 1859 *Preface*, and the 1867 first volume of *Capital* all seem to assert. His sympathies were always with those who acted in a revolutionary spirit (including the Peoples' Will terrorists who were executed for assassinating Alexander II) and he was sensitive to the moral dilemma which "evolutionary" Marxism presented to the populists. It cannot be said, however, that he resolved it. Lenin, living in Russia, was able to grasp the contradictions of both capitalist development in Russia and its feudal integument much more accurately and profoundly.

3. Lenin's critique

Lenin replied to populism with a comprehensive historical materialist analysis of the development of capitalism in Russia, culminating in his book of that title of 1899. He showed—with the aid of the excellent household and market data on rural Russia collected by the populist statisticians who went to work in the provinces from the late 1870s onwards—that Russia was not a dual economy, with a modern sector or "corner" (as the populists represented it) artificially implanted and sustained by state subsidies, alongside a traditional peasant economy. Rather, the modern capitalist factory was only *the most fully developed expression* of a mode of production which had already begun to establish itself throughout the whole economy, including agriculture. The emergence of the successive forms of capital—usurer, merchant, and manufacturer, preceding the emergence of mechanized production—was traced by Lenin in the Russian data. The peasantry had become more and more dependent on the kulaks for whom they worked as, in effect, wage labourers, in order to pay off the debts they incurred in order to meet their tax and indemnity payments. Gradually more and more of them were forced to sell their own plots and become fully proletarianized. At this point, of course, they also became *mobile*, for the first time, migrating over large distances in search of work, supplying the labour force for the new factory system in the towns, and in the process acquiring a new sense of class solidarity and a non-parochial, non-deferential outlook. The relationship of these ex-peasants with capital changed immediately, and insofar as the industrial plants they worked in were largely archaic, relying primarily on absolute surplus value, an often brutal and degrading relationship arose. These ex-peasant proletarians were thus the "natural" representatives of *all* the exploited (and increasingly also semi-proletarianized) masses:

> Natural because the exploitation of the working people in Russia *is everywhere capitalist in nature* ... but the exploitation of the mass of producers is on a small scale, scattered and undeveloped, while the exploitation of the factory proletariat is on a large scale, socialised and concentrated .... That is why the factory worker is none other than the foremost representative of the entire exploited population. (Lenin 1960a (1894):299)

As for the home market for capitalist production, which Vorontsov said was shrinking due to the impoverishment of the peasantry, the proletarianization of the peasantry was a *precondition* for it. It was true that the impoverishment of the peasant meant that he consumed less, but it did not mean that he *spent* less on capitalistically produced goods, because he now had to buy more and more of what he consumed:

> [T]he "impoverished" peasant who formerly lived by his own farming now lives by "earnings", i.e. by the sale of his labour-power; he now has to purchase essential articles od consumption (although in a smaller quantity and of inferior quality). (103)

"Lenin could point to an impressive volume of Russian evidence ... that while the level of consumption of the peasants and artisans had declined, nonetheless the quantity of goods purchased on the market had increased" (Harding, 1977:99). Consequently there was no absolute barrier to the capitalist development of Russia.

Lenin thus did not challenge the populists' argument concerning the sufferings of the 82 percent of the Russian population who were peasants, but put it into a radically different analytic context, with different political implications. The contrast can be seen very clearly by comparing the interpretation of Stepniak (real name S. Kravchinskii), for example, a revolutionary populist, who described the sufferings of the Russian peasantry in 1871 as having two prime causes: (a) lack of land, due to the retention of 73 percent of the cultivable land by the Czarist state and the nobility, so that when the serfs were "freed" they and their families received only minute allotments; and (b) taxation plus redemption payments, extracted from them on pain of flogging, which in 1871 amounted on average to 92.75 percent of the net value of the produce of the land held by the roughly 50 percent of the peasantry who had been state-owned serfs, and who had much *larger* allotments; and 198.25 percent of the net value of the produce of the land held by the former serfs of the nobility (Stepniak, 1888). This of necessity meant that the peasants became semi-proletarian "debt peons" working for their former owners, or for the kulaks who emerged (through luck, usury, superior farming practices, etc.) among the peasantry.

Stepniak's idea—in fact the key idea of Russian populism in fact—was that if "the nation obtain(ed) control over the political powers" (i.e. if "the people" were in power) there would be a painless universal land redistribution, on the basis of need. The traditional process of periodic redistribution of peasant communal land would simply be extended to all the land, with the landlords receiving their due family shares, but no more than this. And then co-operative production, organized in "artels" (traditional voluntary work co-operatives), would "give to Russia a splendid start on the road to social progress." (Stepniak, 1888, II:634)

> Why should they be unable to till the communal land with improved implements on the co-operative system, which would be so immeasurably more profitable? Why should not they in the natural course of their intellectual and economical growth pass from communal and local cooperation to general national cooperation, gradually embracing all the branches of "national" industry, which is nothing but socialism?

Stepniak rejected the view that this was utopian: on the contrary, he believed that the national culture would not allow Russia to become great on the basis of individualistic principles.

> Russia can be great otherwise than by her size, if only political freedom walks hand in hand with the growth of those ideas of labour which spring from the collective aspirations of her people. We are not European enough to successfully initiate a progress based upon the fruition of individual interest. (643)

It was this that Lenin's analysis challenged, both by tracing the process of the actual and growing entrenchment of individual interest as the motor of economic change in Russia, and by his assertion of the necessarily leading and representative role of factory workers, in the struggle to give "the nation ... control over the political powers." Stepniak's analysis pointed forward to the Socialist Revolutionaries' program of 1905, which called for land redistribution and the reunification of the peasantry as a classless force for agricultural cooperation and development. Lenin's analysis pointed to a process of accelerating rural differentiation, which *could* not be stopped so long as a reactionary Czarist state resisted land reform, and which would be actually accelerated (he believed) if landlord and state land were distributed to the land-hungry by a revolutionary regime, as the Socialist Revolutionaries wanted. Only class struggle could clear away the mystification and personal bondage in which the mass of the peasantry were in reality ensnared (Harding, 1977:217).

4. What happened to Russian populism?

As is well known, the Socialist Revolutionary party, the main vehicle of populism after 1900 (it was formed in 1902), was the single largest party in the constituent assembly elected in November 1917 and forcibly dissolved in January 1918. But it was Lenin who had correctly understood the strategic and tactical situation before and after the February revolution, and whose Bolshevik party seized and retained political power. The populists had established themselves as the wing of the intelligentsia most sympathetic to the peasants, but their lack of political judgement was matched by a continuing naivete about agricultural policy.

Had they come to power, they would have faced an obvious dilemma. As Lenin insisted, "no state decrees could 'legislate' an equalisation of land tenure or an advance into socialism for, so long as commodity production and the hiring of wage labour prevailed in the countryside, any paper equalisation would swiftly be eroded just as all the elaborate restrictions on renting or alienating of communal allotment land had been ignored wholesale" (Harding:256). Lenin, in fact, considered that an equalising measure of land redistribution such as the populists called for would in practice be "a highly consistent and thoroughgoing *capitalist* measure" (Lenin, 1960, Vol. 18:357 italics added). To secure a harmonious socialist agrarian policy, therefore, would have required not just credit and advice, etc., but the elimination of commodity production and wage labour. It is very doubtful if the Socialist Revolutionaries could have enforced this, even if they had seen the necessity of doing so; and if they could have enforced it, it is even more doubtful if they could have produced and implemented a successful alternative strategy of rural development, with appropriate incentives, management, inputs, price policies, marketing arrangements, etc. Most likely, they would have shared power with the liberals, and become merely a party of agrarian "reform," destined perhaps to be polarised into two, one representing the kulaks, and the other the rural proletariat and semi-proletariat.

Intellectually, it does not seem as if Russian populism advanced significantly beyond the theses of Vorontsov and Danielson, which Lenin had effectively demolished. Chayanov, as Banaji (1976) has shown, although often represented as a "neo-populist" economist, was really only a theorist of the smallholder "sector"; and Chernov, the Socialist Revolutionary leader, largely repeated Vorontsov's and other earlier populists' ideas of capitalism as a state-imposed artificial corner of the economy that did not yet deeply affect the countryside (Utechin, 1963:142-43).

The situation following Lenin's critique seems to have been as follows. Russian development was already in the grip of the laws of motion of the capitalist mode of production. Moreover Russia seemed capable not merely of developing under capitalism, but also of appropriating the rewards of such development. Its size and potential wealth (i.e. the scale of its potential internal market, and its natural resource endowment), its favourable balance of visible trade during the period 1880-1914, its strong centralized state and Westernised intelligentsia, and its vast Asian hinterland to serve as an "open frontier" on the North American model or as a colony for primitive accumulation (or both), all this meant that an "American" or "German" growth path was possible in Russia. As Shanin points out, this was not *assured*; mounting external debt and declining terms of trade would most likely have led to a post-war balance of payments crisis, and the scale of foreign ownership resembled latter-day Canada's (though it was more diverse) (Shanin, 1972:15-17). The point is rather that Russia was a very large, unevenly developed, potentially rich country which *could* be driven forward to modernity, once the handicaps of its agrarian backwardness could be overcome. Both Lenin and his adversaries assumed that *the whole Russian empire was the unit of analysis* and the more it was clear that, in fact, it was rapidly undergoing a transition to capitalist relations of production, the less anyone seriously doubted that Russia would become a productive economy and, in consequence, a wealthy country and a strong state internationally. The populists, in effect, gave up trying to maintain that capitalism *could not* develop Russia, but argued only that there was a more desirable alternative (within a capitalist development) which, however, their analysis did not enable them to implement, and which probably could not have been implemented.

Lenin, by contrast, was able to synthesize theoretically the contradictions of Russia's capitalistic development, and the politics of the contradiction between this development and the feudal social and political order, so as to produce a political strategy responsive to both. He built a strongly-organized party based on the most acutely oppressed section of the factory working class, appealing to them on a policy of uncompromising opposition to capital. He appealed to the peasantry *qua* peasantry on a program of nationalization and distribution of the landed estates, and to both workers and peasants, as soldiers, on a policy of peace. He could rely on the feudal autocracy to block land and constitutional reforms; and the reactionaries obligingly discredited, and then connived at the assassination of, Stolypin, the one Czarist minister who threatened to resolve the all- important agrarian question by giving freehold tenure to the peasants, and letting a class of capitalist farmers form and rapidly raise productivity. Lenin correctly forecast that the liberals and the mensheviks would be paralyzed by conflicting concerns: on the one hand the need to abolish the autocracy, so as to secure legitimacy through constitutional and representative government, and on the other their fear of the revolutionary left and popular radicalism, and their reliance on the Czarist state and army to protect them from both. His tactical reading of the situation from April 1917 onwards flowed from his overall analysis and its success was largely due to this.

5. Russian populism and contemporary issues

The conclusion of scholars who have studied Russian populism from a contemporary perspective is that the populists raised issues that have come to seem more and more pertinent in the post-colonial era. We see "the problem of an 'asynchronic development, the peculiar privilege of backwardness', the role of cultural contact and demonstration effect in a telescoped, epitomised evolution, in a word, the problem of the non-capitalist way of overcoming economic and social backwardness" (Walicki:194). Other issues made visible are the general problem of uneven development, the character of backward capitalism in a global framework, how a major "periphery of capitalism" could follow a road different from that taken by Europe, the importance of state power in development, the significance of incentives, the social psychology of development, and the analysis of alliances between classes (Shanin 1983:270).

While one can agree with this, it does not follow that the questions were raised in a useful form, and on balance it is hard to see that they were. On the other hand, neither does Lenin's critique provide an acceptable general model. He assumed (along with the populists) that capitalist development is essentially national in character, although he naturally also stressed that national development paths are hierarchically ordered by the imperialism of the most advanced capitalist countries. Given that the state served the interests of capital accumulation, then if a country had a strong enough sovereign state and adequate resources including human resources (skills, technology, etc.), then the capitalist accumulation process would tend to proceed without any necessary limit except that of the proletarian revolution itself.

But as was suggested at the beginning of this chapter, there are at least three standpoints from which some of these assumptions cannot be made, and which therefore tend to generate "populist" arguments that remain somewhat immune to Lenin's critique. These include the standpoint of a small, poorly-endowed national economy with a weak, dependent state in a backward continent (the African case), the standpoint of the majority of the population of a backward *region* in a large but no longer dynamic national economy (the Atlantic Provinces, or the U.S. "rust belt"), and possibly the standpoint of the popular majority in any advanced capitalist country. In the latter case capital has become increasingly mobile and moves in search of the least expensive and most effectively disciplined labour forces. This leaves formerly-employed workers unemployed, while simultaneously increasing capital-intensity in the metropolitan country as capital seeks to further lower its costs of production.

In the first case, labour frequently cannot cross national boundaries in search of employment elsewhere, while the state may be incapable of creating "a regime of accumulation" that can play any role (beneficial to the country concerned) in the international division of labour. This is roughly the case for many African countries. The second case resembles the first: in principle labour-power can migrate out of a region, although this presents serious political problems; on the other hand the regional state may be weak, or even non-existent (as in underdeveloped regions of unitary states such as the Italian south or the English north), so that no regional regime of accumulation can be constructed, even if one can be imagined. The Atlantic Provinces correspond approximately to this case. The third case is roughly that represented by Lipietz's scenario, calling for strategies short of revolution, to create insulated regional trade and production "blocs," setting barriers to the mobility of capital out of the bloc and preventing the competitive lowering of the price of labour power within it (Lipietz, 1987). Gorz's scenario of a post-capitalist, increasingly leisure-based society would presumably require a similar international framework (Gorz, 1982).

What all these cases have in common, what makes them liable to give rise to populist analyses and projects, is the tendency to marginalization of the direct producers, without readily perceptible useful employment alternatives within the framework of a continuing capitalist accumulation process (in a context, however, where *some* alternative is believed to exist). Even an evolutionist model of capitalistic accumulation on a global scale does not seem to hold out the prospect of any real compensation, however distant, for many or even most of the direct producers in some of these situations. The moral dilemma articulated by Mikhailovskii is even more absolute in these cases; any committed person is likely to feel compelled to support a project that is directed to the needs of these victims of the accumulation process. However, the shortcomings of populism are not thereby neutralized. The need seems to be, rather, to establish the terms of a progressive approach to these situations which avoids the weaknesses of populism, but without relying on the optimistic assumptions of Lenin's critique of populism. Of course the fact that this is what is needed does not mean that it is possible.

6. Kitching's analysis

Kitching's study, *Development and Underdevelopment in Historical Perspectives*, covers most of the ground reviewed above and concludes that:

> the central weakness of populism in theory and practice is that *it is unable to provide any coherent account of how a continuing process of rising material productivity and living standards is compatible with the maintenance of an economy in which peasant agricultural producers are the dominant social force* (1982:180).

Perhaps this is a little too strong. Populism, as we know, can be adapted to a rather wide variety of settings in some of which the peasant producers need not be the dominant social force (for example in Denmark after 1870 a peasant sector was *created*, or at least greatly enlarged, by a nationalist policy developed by a largely urban middle class). But Kitching's general conclusion is surely correct: although populism and "neo-populism"[1]

> draw attention to the desirability of going about industrialization in a manner which does not simply sacrifice millions of peasants to "market forces" or some state-directed process of crash industrialization, *in themselves* they do not provide a coherent or practicable way to do it. (p. 180)

Some populists argue, of course, that raising living standards should *not* be an object of policy. This seems worthy of consideration, at least in a region like the Atlantic Provinces, if not in Africa (Kitching's main focus), even if those who advocate this view seldom would be content with the existing living standards of most primary producers. However, it is important to recognize that even if people are willing to abandon material ambitions, a "zero-growth" policy is a chimera unless economic autarky is potentially feasible. Otherwise, products must be traded at prices which will reflect the rising productivity achieved by capitalist production elsewhere, i.e. at falling real prices, unless productivity can be raised *pari passu* by the small independent producers too. So, even to *maintain* living standards, rising material productivity is indeed necessary, which means (as Kitching argues) new technology and a movement of labour out of primary production; and hence, an integrated development of primary production and manufacturing, for which populists must have a plausible program. Whether this involves a centrally planned economy (as Kitching argues), or a system of co-operatives much more reliant on markets, Kitching is surely right to insist that it is essential to think clearly "about what, precisely, socialist industrialization implies, and how it can be made as 'humane' as possible." In particular, Kitching argues that such socialists must be able to believe that "socialist industrialization in one country" *can* occur "without even greater costs than those incurred in industrialization under international capital," and that they must be able to produce models of an "open socialist industrialization process" (p. 179).

Kitching's criticism of the populist tradition in development studies—that it fails to show a coherent alternative route to rising productivity—applies to some of the literature on development in the Atlantic Provinces, in which unemployment and dependency, and the subordination of traditional community values to the dictates of international corporate capital, are accurately described and rightfully deplored. In this literature the culprit is seen as the nature of the "ownership" of corporate capital (e.g. Carter, 1983:3 and *passim*) or its bigness, or its "inappropriate" technology, or the intervention of the state in favour of large capital. There are proposals which, as Kitching says, tend to be romantic or utopian, looking towards the bolstering up or reintroduction of small-scale capitalism and independent production. There is also a silence, possibly symptomatic, concerning what is to be done (Carter, 1983, is a case in point). Meanwhile, the rhetoric of populism is meantime appropriated by capital to produce an accommodation to the accumulation process by its victims, as Overton clearly shows in Chapter 3 of this book.

7. Political implications for underdeveloped regions in advanced capitalist countries

Given a competitive party system with elections, *and* a federal system, two general options within a capitalist process of development seem to be available for areas such as the Atlantic Provinces: compensation, or the creation of new regional "regimes of accumulation."

By "compensation" is meant exacting, through political pressure, measures to mitigate the suffering of those who are victims of the accumulation process. An obvious example is the extension of unemployment insurance to the self-employed East Coast fishers. Significantly, this right was denied to the primary producers of the Northwest Territories, who were faced with a very similar crisis (Clancy, 1985:420). Other measures may be less purely compensatory, involving state support for independent or household production in competition with capitalist production (subsidies for equipment, cheap state-provided credit and infrastructure, etc. such as the French state extensively provides to smallholders). Given the central role of the state in promoting large-scale capitalist production, the latter's victory over small-scale producers is by no means purely the result of the inherent superiority of such production. Depending on the nature of the commodities produced, the rate of decline of independent production may be slowed down, or even partly reversed, by state action. The populist analysis of the role of the state acting in the interests of large-scale capital deserves respect (as Marx realized) and indicates a "terrain of struggle." In this respect it is also a mistake to dismiss in advance the possibilities of collective economic action by small-scale producers, even if these initiatives are rarely "pre-figured" in traditional practices in the manner that populists have often tended wishfully to believe. Some Inuit carving co-operatives for example, like Danish dairy co-operatives, have proved to be effective institutional forms for sustaining independent producers.

A new "regime of accumulation" may also be a regional option. Such a regime may be based on a fully open regional economy in which case it is likely to have an extremely right-wing character, as in the so-called "right to work" laws of the southern states of the U.S.A., which effectively minimize unionization of the workforce, and are complemented by a battery of investment incentives for capitalists. Or it could, in theory, be more closed. This would be possible only in an area where there was a rather homogeneous regional culture (to sustain the degree of austerity that would be involved in reducing external trade), and a large degree of autonomy on the part of the provincial state or states, to protect the regional market from external market forces. This option, while implicit in the nationalist/populist literature of, for example, Newfoundland in the 1960s, and even more in the 1970s, does not seem very realistic, and has so far been unsuccessful as a political project even in areas of the world with a strong cultural base for sub-nationalism (e.g. Scotland and Wales).

In practice, a strategy based on an open regional economy is usually pursued by the provincial or state governments of most underdeveloped regions, *together with* a strategy of compensation. The main measures have been anti-union legislation, and "incentives" (tax holidays, investment allowances and direct subsidies) for corporate investors and small businesses. But as the element of labour costs in the final value of commodities with high value added falls below about 10 percent, access to merely cheap (non-unionised) labour appears to become of little concern to corporate capital, and access to highly-trained labour and other externalities becomes more important. Consequently the least prosperous regions may not be particularly well placed to compete in the establishment of new competitive regimes of accumulation via such "tax spending." The level of wages and the degree of labour discipline required, therefore, to offset these other disadvantages in the competition for investment by multinational capital may be politically unacceptable. The real competition for regions pursuing this strategy comes in the end from the NICS, or from the "candidate NICS" such as China's "special economic regions," where manufacturing wages in 1978 were one-fortieth of U.S. wages (Chossudovsky, 1983:80). As is now becoming more widely understood, the ultimate logic of a "market" solution to the problems of regional underdevelopment in Canada or any other industrial country is to push down consumption levels, and to raise the intensity and amount of labour towards Chinese (or Indian, etc.) levels.

A more plausible alternative therefore seems to be a *national* strategy to create a *national* regime of accumulation which provides both for internationally competitive rates of productivity growth and for transitional compensation and protection for disadvantaged regions. These measures must be specifically targeted to primary producers and to wage workers, who will increasingly be exposed to comparable sacrifices. Such measures should include unemployment pay, shorter hours on full pay and a guaranteed minimum income. They must be combined with retraining, re-housing and re-employment packages, and include plans to control the effects of these processes on the regions. This implies a "social-democratic" state-led capitalist development strategy with regional dimensions in the case of Canada it seems hardly less utopian than a socialist alternative. It is certainly as remote as can be imagined from the market-oriented thinking of the Liberal and Conservative establishment as reflected in the Report of the Macdonald Commission of 1984, or the policies of the governments in the Atlantic Provinces in the 1980s.

8. Conclusion

The social costs of the national, and now international, processes of capital accumulation through periodic "restructuring" have long borne particularly heavily on the Atlantic Provinces. Out of this experience has arisen a distinctive tradition of struggle, and a distinctive school of analysis on the part of regional scholars engaged in the effort to secure the region's recovery and emancipation. In both processes populism has played some part and is likely to continue to do so. The occupational and political structure of the region is such that any project for radical change must rest on a definition of the "popular interest" which includes primary producers as much as the wage-earning class. The aim of this chapter has been to clarify some of the conditions which need to be met by a populist project (in this sense of the term) if it is to be both successful and genuinely popular.

The most important lesson to be drawn from the debate about populism in Russia is the necessity of analyzing clearly the *tendencies* of the development that is actually occurring. Lenin's analysis was in this respect demonstrably superior to that of the Russian populists, and it is this that needs re-emphasis today. In particular it is not generally an "inappropriate choice" of technology, nor the "wrong" owners, nor the *scale* of big companies, nor even state intervention on behalf of big companies that are the *ultimate* cause of the hardships of primary producers. Rather it is the fact that they are producing in a global economy that is expanding under the imperatives of the law of value, which imposes constant pressure to raise labour productivity in order to stay competitive, and hence to use less labour-intensive technology, and in many fields to enlarge the scale of organization for productive efficiency, monopoly power, financial strength, and other reasons. The agents of this process are not its cause, although they cannot escape personal responsibility for being its agents.

In this regard, the complex class relations of the Atlantic Region to which Brym and Sacouman and others have drawn attention need to be clearly grasped as an aspect (both effect and cause) of the historical developments occurring in the relations of production. The complexity derives partly from the incomplete destruction of precapitalist production relations, but also from the nature of capitalist development which does not, contrary to a vulgar orthodoxy, have an immanent tendency to *simplify* the class structure, except in the general sense of a tendency to drive independent producers into the ranks of the waged or unemployed labour force. The manifold differences within the wage labour force need to be analyzed in detail, as do the complex processes of differentiation among farmers or fishers (mediated by relations of credit, price regulation for some products, etc.). It is necessary to be clear about the conflicting class interests that populist discourse often articulates as non-conflictive, and to be clear which interests are promoted in the chosen political strategy.

Finally, a democratic-socialist project (or socialist-populist—the label is not important, if the project's content is clear) must propose solutions to the problems of economic organization and productivity growth. The possibility of fusing the goals of the primary producers with those of the working class in a new project for long-term social reconstruction in which both groups, constituting the great majority of the population, can see their interests potentially reflected—must rest on a sober material basis. Perhaps the most general lesson of hitherto-existing populisms is that they have failed, and among the reasons has been the fact that they did not adequately confront this question.

Notes

1. "Neo-populism" refers to twentieth-century populisms that unlike classical populism in Russia accepted both capitalist development in the wider economy and the need for technological transformation in agriculture but sought to preserve the precapitalist agrarian social system through co-operatives and other protective measures.

Chapter Three

Small is Beautiful and the Crisis in Newfoundland

James Overton

1. Introduction

In 1973 E.F. Schumacher, in his book *Small is Beautiful: A Study of Economics as if People Mattered*, proposed a solution to many of the problems of underdeveloped and decaying rural areas. The promotion of small businesses and communal enterprises, using local resources and intermediate or alternative technology, would help restore the declining economic bases of such areas, and by being labour-intensive would reduce unemployment. He also emphasized new values and alternative patterns of consumption as an aid to solving the problems of poverty and outmigration.

The "small is beautiful" approach to development was promoted in Newfoundland in the 1970s as an alternative to the large-scale industrialization efforts of the 1950s and 1960s. Since then it has gained a degree of acceptance, and in 1986 elements of it were taken up by the Royal Commission on Employment and Unemployment in the Province (Newfoundland and Labrador, 1986). This chapter explores the ways in which this development alternative is being reconstituted as part of a new economic orthodoxy during capitalism's present crisis.

Interest in the "small is beautiful" approach to development emerged in Newfoundland in the late 1960s and early 1970s, when there was a growing awareness that the development strategies of the previous twenty years had failed to eliminate poverty and unemployment in rural areas. There was disenchantment with modernization, and a lament for what became known as Newfoundland's traditional way of life. A diffuse populism, characterized by a ready sympathy for rural dwellers and the problems they face, emerged in intellectual circles. Urban bias and inappropriate development strategies were identified as the main cause of Newfoundland's problems. The province, it was argued, had been led down the wrong development path, a path which had led to the destruction of the way of life of the small rural producer and which threatened rural existence. What was needed was a new approach which would serve the interests and meet the needs of the small producer in rural areas. If Newfoundland was characterized by a dual economy and society, then a dual development strategy would be appropriate. It was in this context that Schumacher's ideas gained favour. In the 1970s a widespread and influential rural revitalization movement developed armed with elements of the "small is beautiful" philosophy.

But its proponents never provided an adequate understanding of the problems facing Newfoundland. Like the orthodox modernization school of development theory, they subscribed to the idea that Newfoundland has a dual economy—there supposedly exist, in the province, two separate economic spheres, the "traditional" and the "modern," which are worlds apart. While modernization theory and practice attempts to move the traditional economy towards modernization by removing barriers and diffusing growth, the advocates of alternate development promote separate development strategies for each sphere.

But the dual economy model is a totally inadequate intellectual tool for understanding Newfoundland's economy and society, past or present. Newfoundland's so-called "traditional society" was never a peasant, subsistence economy—a body of self-sufficient, independent producers who marketed their surplus. It was never an economic system which operated according to its own, relatively unchanging, logic outside of the "modern," capitalist sector. The past and present class structure and the dynamics of rural Newfoundland can only be understood in terms of the broad processes of capital accumulation, national and international. What is called Newfoundland's "traditional society" can indeed be understood as an adaptation to a peculiar or distinctive niche in the overall economy, but we have to understand the forces which first produced and have subsequently been changing this niche.

It cannot be understood if it is considered as a separate sector, essentially independent of the rest of Newfoundland's economy and society. On that analysis, for example, it is impossible to explain why the "traditional economy" collapsed in the 1930s, and in many areas survived only thanks to public relief. Similarly today, the idea that rural Newfoundlanders would solve their problems by changing their technology or lifestyles is misguided for the same reason. It is to ignore the broader context which determines the overall changes in the economy, and the policy decisions made by governments (including the technology that is favoured).

2. Origins and background of the "small is beautiful" ideology

E.F. Schumacher's attention was drawn to the problems of underdeveloped areas during a visit to Burma as an economic advisor in the 1950s (Wood, 1985:240-253). In the wake of his Burmese visit, Schumacher became increasingly critical of approaches to development which were formulated in terms of W.W. Rostow's notion of a "take-off" to economic development (317). For Schumacher, patterns of growth in underdeveloped countries were "pathological" (1974:56-57). All attention was devoted to modernization, while the disintegration of economic activity in rural areas was overlooked. Yet, the decay of the traditional sector in such countries was causing poverty and unemployment on a massive scale, while out-migration threatened to "poison economic life in the modern sector as well" (139).

The solution to this complex of problems, Schumacher argued, was to create employment in rural areas: "intermediate technology" could be used in "millions of workplaces" in order to "maximize work opportunities for the unemployed and under- employed" (1974:145). People would at least be provided with some work, the assumption being that "for a poor man ... even poorly paid and relatively unproductive work is better than idleness" (145). The use of "intermediate technologies" in small rural enterprises was the key to creating "full employment in developing countries" (159). This technology could be adapted to conditions in rural areas—that is, be culturally acceptable and be compatible with the human, financial and material resources found in rural areas (small scale and low cost); it could create jobs rather than destroy them, serving the people where they are (labour intensive not capital intensive); and it could produce goods at prices which were competitive with other technologies.

A "small is beautiful" approach to development was viewed by Schumacher as being complementary to large-scale development in the modern sector. A dual approach to development would help build a balanced economy and thus strengthen the overall economic system. But, to succeed, the new approach also required new values and attitudes amongst the rural poor. For his plan to work, people would have to be prepared to accept lower wages and a lower standard of living than they desired (1974:246).

Schumacher's approach to development was taken up in Newfoundland in the late 1960s by academics associated with Memorial University's Institute of Social and Economic Research (ISER). Links were made with Schumacher's Intermediate Technology Development Group, and several books were published promoting "intermediate" or "marginal adaptation" (Freeman, 1969; Wadel, 1969; Brox, 1972). Similar ideas were soon taken up by other academics, as well as by civil servants, Memorial University Extension Service workers, and others (Matthews, 1977; McCracken and MacDonald, 1976; McCay, 1979; Briton, 1979; Peterson, 1977:31-39). During the 1970s, the "small is beautiful" approach to development found widespread acceptance as a program for revitalizing Newfoundland's rural areas.

This approach to development is not particularly new, as Kitching (1982:93) points out. It is similar to that suggested by William Booth of the Salvation Army (1890) and to the land settlement and community development efforts which were popular in the 1930s. In particular, it is remarkably similar to the rural rehabilitation efforts undertaken in Newfoundland during the 1930s under Government by Commission (which, in turn, built on earlier initiatives).

In the early 1930s the fishing industry in Newfoundland collapsed and employment in the other major sectors of the economy was severely curtailed. The servicing of debt and the provision of relief consumed practically all of the country's shrinking revenue and by 1931 bankruptcy was looming on the horizon. Retrenchment was undertaken, but efforts to cut relief met with violent opposition and were not particularly successful (Overton, 1987). It was in this climate that many middle-class people began to show a great interest in schemes which would foster self-sufficiency amongst the population. A large body of propagandists took up the task of instructing the population as to their responsibilities during the crisis. A flood of sermons, songs, poems, speeches and fables which lauded the virtues of self-help, thrift and discipline was released. From prime minister to priest, from police constable to adult educator, from newspaper editor to "concerned citizen," all enthusiastically embraced the patriotic task of re-educating the long suffering population for austerity.

The flavour of the movement of the 1930s is conveyed by a call for "New Standards for Old" made by "Observer" in 1932 (*Evening Telegram*, October 28, 1932). According to this writer, the depression provided a great opportunity to "discard old ideas and old standards." Hard times might not be popular, but they had valuable "lessons to teach." In the future the country would have to "cut its garment according to the cloth": the population would have to expect less and become more self-reliant. Put simply, the message was: in the future "only those who work will eat." It was in reality a call for the state to cut relief (which provided about 50 percent of the average person's basic food requirements in rural areas) to force the unemployed to become self-sufficient. Many thought the unemployed should be encouraged to cultivate the soil. Thus, in 1932, a concerted effort was made to provide the unemployed of St. John's with allotments and the middle-class worthies of the Land Development Association began to press for land settlement (in 1984 there were calls to revive these schemes). This, they thought, would cut unproductive expenditures on relief, make work, and remove the "wilfully idle and troublesome" from the capital (*Evening Telegram*, July 29, 1932).

Following the financial and political collapse of the country, Government by Commission was introduced in 1934. The Commission soon realized the enormity of the task of refloating the foundering economy. Reform proved difficult, not least because the Commission was unable or unwilling to challenge powerful vested interests. During the second half of the 1930s, however, the Commission forged a relatively coherent and comprehensive plan for rural reconstruction which built on many of the initiatives of the early 1930s and previous periods (Wilfred Grenfell's activities in Northern Newfoundland and Labrador in the 1890s and early 1900s were one model). It assumed that reforming the fishery would be a slow and difficult task and that in the foreseeable future neither the fishery nor other established industries would provide employment at even minimal incomes for those who needed it. Rural rehabilitation was also seen as a way of dealing with the spectre of permanent mass pauperization (what is nowadays called welfare dependency). Rural development, it was hoped, would prevent wholesale moral collapse and also cut relief expenditures in the long run.

In 1936 a Department of Rural Reconstruction was established and a program for the encouragement of co-operatives initiated, these being regarded by the parsimonious Commission as a "social welfare measure" (McKay, 1946:185). The promotion of land settlement also became official government policy and by 1938 five schemes were operating (Newfoundland, 1938). The government's plans for rural rehabilitation were set out most clearly in two reports by J.H. Gorvin in 1938 (Newfoundland, 1938a; Newfoundland, 1938b). The aim was to create "a class of fishermen-farmers" in rural Newfoundland, an independent peasantry able to support themselves by "following a combination of occupations" (Newfoundland, 1938b:21 and 40). Existing agriculture and fishing would be improved and the introduction of small-scale farming activities encouraged. Small rural industries would be set up (craft production for local use and for the tourist trade, for example). Thrift, mutual aid and household economy were to be promoted by co-operative study groups. Education would be for responsible action and would be a cornerstone of the Commission's village development efforts.

Rural rehabilitation was given a distinct regional focus by Gorvin (Newfoundland, 1940). The Special Areas Development Bill of 1940 allowed for the establishment of Regional Development Councils and Corporations as well as Special Area Boards for marketing. In order to facilitate the new approach to development, the administration of public relief would be transferred to the Department of Natural Resources in regional development areas so that these funds could be used for the "rebuilding of old and the development of new industries" rather than simply supporting the destitute (10).

These rural rehabilitation efforts of the late 1930s, which amounted to a comprehensive program of rural containment, were largely abandoned at the outbreak of the Second World War. The War brought many changes to the country and something close to full employment was achieved. Then, as Newfoundland entered Canada in 1949, and unemployment was again becoming a serious problem, the Liberal government of J.R. Smallwood initiated a fairly intensive program of state-directed economic and social development in an effort to address the related problems of out- migration, rural decline, poverty and unemployment (Alexander, 1974; Matthews, 1976, 1979; Overton, 1978, 1979; Bassler, 1986). The cry was "develop or perish" and the promotion of progress became almost a cult movement as the population was mobilized for modernization. Attempts were made to establish small manufacturing plants producing for the local market (cement, shoes, chocolate, clothes, etc.), but exploitation of the province's primary resources was also encouraged. The mines of Labrador were opened and hydro-electric schemes developed in an effort to attract industry with cheap power. Considerable attention was paid to improving the province's infrastructure. New roads were constructed, transportation upgraded and education revolutionized. In the period 1953-75, some 6,000 families were resettled from small communities of less than 500 people, mostly into "growth centres" (Hoggart, 1979). A phosphorous plant, a linerboard mill and an oil refinery were built, and funds were directed towards fresh fish production (Bassler, 1986:99-100).

The modernization and industrialization of the 1950s and 1960s was, however, uneven and often contradictory. There was considerable emphasis on large-scale development schemes and funds were used to stimulate a substantial movement of labour power from rural to urban areas, these being justified as attempts to eliminate or ease regional disparities. Many people left Newfoundland altogether to find employment in expanding areas of the mainland. At the same time, however, programs such as Unemployment Insurance (UI) for those engaged in catching fish, and the new sources of employment in the province, gave those remaining in rural areas a much higher standard of living. Similarly, road and park construction helped attract visitors to rural areas and stimulated a small but valuable tourist industry.

Despite the relative affluence of Newfoundland in the 1950s and 1960s, the period was not without problems. In the late 1950s the province's unemployment rate rose to almost 20 percent (the Canadian rate also rose sharply) and as a result a Royal Commission on Unemployment was established (Palmer, 1986). The Commission thought that the unemployment crisis would be short-lived and would "probably not occur again." It suggested dealing with it by emergency spending, but cautioned that "in normal times expenditure of public monies should not be made merely to give jobs." State efforts to "create the atmosphere in which private enterprise will provide employment" were to be encouraged, but the provision of "public relief" for "prolonged periods" might destroy "the self-reliance, the independence and the initiative which are the traditional traits of Newfoundlanders." The crisis stimulated Senator C.C. Pratt to issue a caution that attention be devoted not just to "the development of big industry," but also to the encouragement of "a greater self-sufficiency among Newfoundlanders" (1959). This was a recognition that "the many social security measures" available "are only as dependable as the national ability to pay," and that this "varies with times and conditions" (7). He urged Newfoundlanders to eat more fish, pick berries, revive kitchen gardens, build more hen houses and use more needles and cotton. This program for individual and community self-sufficiency was presented as a "realistic" alternative to "more and more dependence on public welfare services and less and less independence of life and spirit" (10).

Such voices as these were, however, dissenting ones in the 1950s and early 1960s. The idea that an "orderly transition" from Newfoundland's "semi-subsistence way of life to a modern monetary economy" should proceed apace was the dominant ideology. This was confirmed by the *Royal Commission on the Economic State and Prospects of Newfoundland and Labrador* in the mid-1960s. It would take much hard work and the crisis of the 1980s before the "small is beautiful" alternative could once again be dominant.

3. The present crisis:
from dependency to self-reliance

With the economic crisis of the 1970s and 1980s "small is beautiful" appeared as a new set of ideas whose time had come (Athanasiou, 1977a; 1977b; Harris, 1983; Mattera, 1985). What many regarded as a radical alternative to the development orthodoxy of the 1950s and 1960s has since been not only "readily accommodated" as Raymond Williams put it (1986:61), but enthusiastically embraced by the state and capital. Elements of the "small is beautiful" ideology have been worked into a new regional and rural development policy. They have been used to justify and facilitate state-imposed austerity measures and the abandonment of the state's responsibility for creating employment. "Small is beautiful" has also become a rallying cry for small business. How and why has this happened?

By the late 1960s and early 1970s state policy was beginning to change. As growth faltered in the late 1960s it became increasingly obvious that the growth centre/diffusionist approach to regional development would have to be reworked. Planners concerned with regional and rural development began to discuss a dual development strategy for traditional and modern sectors of the economy, with "balanced" development between these dual spheres (Poetschke and Shevciw, 1974:7). It was recognized that the state might have to intervene in the traditional economy in order to affect some improvement in its productivity.

From about 1972 there was a noticeable shift in the policy of the Department of Regional Economic Expansion (DREE), the main federal agency dealing with regional problems (Storey and Hayter, 1978). The new policy direction allowed provincial government to set general development policy, while DREE became a funding agency for approved projects. In 1972 there was a change of government in Newfoundland. The Progressive Conservatives came to power and a new development policy, supported by DREE, began to emerge.

The extent to which the policy of the Progressive Conservatives represents a significant shift away from the policies of the Smallwood era is open to debate (Overton, 1985a, 1986a). The government embraced, at least rhetorically, a dualistic approach to development. There was to be an emphasis on developing industries in which Newfoundland was regarded as having a comparative advantage—forestry, mining, oil and gas, hydro-power, fishing—into a modern, efficient export sector. At the same time there was to be a policy of promoting small businesses in order to create jobs. The modern sector of the economy, largely in the hands of multinational corporations, was to provide the general buoyancy for the economy. Small businesses would be less concerned with economic efficiency and export markets and more concerned with employment creation. Local entrepreneurs were to be encouraged to set up businesses, especially in rural areas, so as to provide work opportunities. Some of these businesses would find niches in the "modern" sector, but others would take advantage of opportunities arising from state encouragement of tourism, agriculture, handicrafts, etc. In addition, there was to be an effort to improve the social and economic viability of rural communities through investment in roads, sewer systems and wharves. In fact, this "new" approach to development proved to be a rather familiar and somewhat jaded set of policies to further the interests of Newfoundland's existing and budding entrepreneurs.

In the four years after 1974 some sixteen DREE subsidiary agreements were signed between the federal government and the government of Newfoundland (Newfoundland and Labrador, 1983:82- 83). DREE spending in the province of Newfoundland under the General Development Agreements reached a peak of $76.2 million in 1979-80. After that expenditures fell drastically and eventually the GDAs were allowed to lapse. This was part of a shift in regional development policy in the early 1980s, a shift in which the federal government attempted to gain more control over this policy area (Lithwick, 1982:362). According to the report of the Senate Standing Committee on National Finance, *Government Policy and Regional Development* (1982:80), the policies which had been developed in the 1960s and 1970s, and in particular the GDA system, were weak and inconsistent. They were "not tight enough" to prevent the financing of projects which did not offer good long term payoffs. The creation of the Economic Development Ministry in 1982 was an attempt by the federal government to exert greater control. Funds were to be directed towards promising new industries and towards economic adjustment for declining industries in order to make them more competitive and efficient. For the future, the emphasis was to be on aiding "winners" within a general strategy that was to emphasize "economic policy" rather than "social development" (Collison, 1982). Aid might be given to industries in crisis where this was politically unavoidable, but generally this aid was to be used to ensure that such industries become more competitive. The trend since the early 1980s has clearly been towards what Courchene (1981) calls a "market perspective" on regional problems, inducing the removal of "labour bottle-necks." The Economic Council of Canada argues that a wide range of state programs "subsidize residency" in areas such as Newfoundland and prevent labour mobility (1981:5-7). This observation has since been repeated by numerous analysts, with the Unemployment Insurance system as it applies in areas like Newfoundland coming in for most criticism in this regard.

In the last few years the federal government has taken a much tougher attitude towards the poorer regions of the country. The changes in regional development policy are but one manifestation of this. If it proves politically feasible the federal government is also clearly interested in modifying the Unemployment Insurance Program by cutting support to those catching fish and by eliminating regionally extended benefits. Established Program Financing and equalization payments to the poorer provinces have already been cut. This may not mark the end of the "redistributive state" (Collison, 1982:37), but it does indicate an attempt to "downgrade" both interpersonal and interregional income redistribution, or at least "seek its relegation to a distant and vague priority" (Bickerton and Gagnon, 1984:88). But it is important to appreciate that this tougher attitude on the part of the federal state is not simply the expression of efforts to exercise financial restraint during a period of fiscal crisis. The redistributive policies of the era of the "Just Society" which are attacked by analysts like Thomas Courchene are presented as part of the *cause* of continued regional disparity (Courchene, 1981). They are seen as having led the poor provinces into a "welfare trap" where they languish with "no real incentive to get 'off the dole'" (McNiven, 1986:81). The removal of support will, it is argued, stimulate efficiency and personal and provincial initiative (Courchene, 1984:16).

In the light of this, the emphasis placed on fostering self- reliance makes sense. The message is simple and it was very plainly stated in early September 1986 by John Crosbie in Moncton. The same day that he defended the closure of the Canadian National Railways repair shop in that city he announced that the Atlantic region is "not have-not" when compared to nations like Bangladesh and Jamaica and that Atlantic Canadians should stop comparing themselves with Ontario. The message was: get used to expecting less (*Chronicle-Herald*, September 3, 1986). Fostering self- reliance means throwing much of the responsibility for development and relieving unemployment onto the shoulders of the governments of the poorer provinces of Canada, and ultimately onto the shoulders of their inhabitants. In this context the "small is beautiful" ideology has been enthusiastically embraced by the state. It had already been realized in the late 1970s that during a period of greater "realism" in government policy such an approach might be useful. In 1978 Judith Maxwell of the C.D. Howe Research Institute examined the options open to a government faced with the erosion of a region's economic base (Maxwell, 1978). She argued that during a period when efforts were being made to "redirect massive flows of support money into activities that can pass the test of the market," it might be wise to follow a "small is beautiful" approach to regional development, encouraging small-scale projects using "inherent resources and skills" (109). A similar suggestion was made by McAllister (1980). He urged that in order to "achieve a greater degree of balanced development" across Canada a policy position between "the extreme positions" of "small is beautiful" and "big is beautiful" should be traced (39): "A greater degree of regional self-sufficiency would quite reasonably provide a more secure basis for future economic development." He outlined the rationale for this new direction:

The argument for greater regional self-sufficiency is here made in the context of degree of compromise, of hedging of bets, of concern for flexibility and balance in future political and cultural as well as narrowly economic growth, as opposed to short-term efficiency based on the existing pattern (39).

In fact, his argument was that:

Regional specialization, along the lines of potential and not merely "frozen historical" comparative advantage, should be the core framework for national economic policy (41).

This regional specialization would, however, have to be supplemented with other policies designed for those sectors outside the "mainstream":

There is a very strong case for the encouragement of a fabric of smaller scale activities. The North American economy has always been so constructed. Given the economic experiences of the past six years or so, the regions of Canada might be prudent to concentrate much attention on the welfare of small farms, small businesses and the semi- subsistence activities that people can fall back on in times of inflationary pressure. Such activities can provide a far more socially meaningful and economically productive cushion than broad social programs such as unemployment insurance and family allowances. This is not to argue for the eradication of such broad social programs, but to emphasize the importance of fostering small scale activities of a business and semi-subsistence nature (41).

This new set of attitudes towards regional problems has also quickly become an important part of federal government practice, as well as being enthusiastically embraced by some groups in the poorer regions of the country. In 1986, for example, the Atlantic Provinces Chamber of Commerce (APCC) proposed a program called *Operation Bootstraps* which: "encourages Atlantic Canadians to pull themselves up by their own bootstraps and to move towards greater regional prosperity through self-reliance and self-initiative" (*Chronicle Herald*, September 2, 1986). In explaining the scheme, the Chairman of the APCC argued that: "the Atlantic Provinces are addicted to government spending and we want to take actions to wean us from the habit" (*Chronicle Herald*, September 3, 1986). Fifty million dollars would be allocated by the federal government to "wean the private sector from government support" on the assumption that "the regional economy is not strong enough to go cold turkey," according to the Chairman of APCC. New activity programs will lead to lower dependence. In fact, the $50 million program would be administered by "the business community" rather than the government. The plan is to use the money to turn "100 local chambers and boards into 'one-stop shopping centres'" to provide support for small business. The fund would also be a source of venture capital for small business. Here we have the business people of Atlantic Canada using the image of a region addicted to state support to argue for funds for a rehabilitation program under *their* control.

4. The state, the crisis and small business

> From the stately halls of Parliament Hill to the bank towers of Bay Street, there is a growing sense that "small is beautiful" after all. The Conservative government is pinning much of its hopes for job creation on the small business sector; financial institutions are eagerly courting entrepreneurs as a vital market for future growth; and an increasing number of university and college graduates are walking past the doors of the majors and setting up shop on their own (Steward-Patterson, 1985).

Since the mid-1970s there has emerged in Canada as in other countries the phenomenon of "small business revivalism" (Rainnie, 1985:166). Small business and the entrepreneur have been allocated the task of saving the crisis-ridden Canadian economy and creating jobs. The hero of the 1980s is the entrepreneur, the risk-taker, who as far as possible will be given encouragement and a free field of action in which to operate. A whole mythology has grown up around small business a good part of which is, according to Rainnie (1985:148), "derived (and distorted) from Schumacher's ... catch phrase 'small is beautiful'" and "widely accepted."

By 1978 Anthony Abbott had been appointed Minister for Small Business in Canada (*Evening Telegram*, June 14, 1978), and a host of programs and policies were introduced at both the provincial and the federal levels in Canada to aid small business. The federal Ministry provided advice, and tax concessions and various forms of financial assistance were given, including subsidized labour (the Job Employment Training Program, for example). The small business lobby also had some impact on federal policy concerning unemployment insurance, pressing for tightening up the regulations. Small businesses were also one of the main forces behind efforts to keep minimum wage levels down. The Newfoundland and Labrador Development Corporation launched a campaign in 1978 to publicize the virtues of small business and to encourage entrepreneurs to come forward. A government "Action Line" was established to help potential entrepreneurs cut through red tape and get government loans. Meanwhile citizens were informed of their duty to "Buy Newfoundland" in order to aid local business.

All this occurred at a time when small business was starting to experience more problems than at any time in recent history. In Newfoundland, as in Canada, the problems identified by those speaking for small business were high taxes, slow sales, competition from big business and the difficulties of obtaining investment capital (*Evening Telegram*, March 16, 1978). The problems of obtaining adequate labour at low wages have also continued to be stressed by small business lobbyists. It was in this context of economic difficulty and rising bankruptcy rates for business in general and small business in particular—2,976 in 1976, 4,131 in 1977 and even higher in 1978 (*Financial Post*, October 14, 1978)— that small business in Canada began to weld itself into a formidable lobby group.

The most visible organization is the Canadian Federation of Independent Business (CFIB) founded in 1970. Led by John Bulloch, it had a membership of 45,000 and a budget of $3 million in the late 1970s and a membership of 78,000 in 1986 (*Financial Post*, March 11, 1978; December 29, 1986). A variety of other business organizations have also developed a strong political presence at local, provincial and national levels in recent years. Rarely a day passes when the St. John's Board of Trade does not issue a statement which finds its way into the *Evening Telegram*. Often using the slogan "small is beautiful," part of the aim of such organizations is to create a public awareness of the importance of small business and to give entrepreneurs a positive image in society. The small business movement has a quasi-religious character. It is, in part, involved in a consciousness-raising exercise and, in part, a demonstration of the power of positive thinking. It is also an exercise in how to win friends and influence people. Business people are urged to become "Castenada-like warriors of the market-place" in promoting "counterculture capitalism" (Gerzon, 1977), and with the formation of such groups as Business Warriors (*Financial Times*, September 11, 1978) apparently such advice is not falling on deaf ears. Obviously the movement grows out of the real problems of small operators in the present economic crisis and is an attempt to do something about them. Afraid of being eliminated by competition, it issues a plea for small business to be allowed to exist, for a national strategy which will maintain a *balance* between small, medium and large operations (the first being largely Canadian owned).

The small business lobby is distinctly populist in nature. It draws to some extent on the "small is beautiful" ideas of the 1960s and 1970s. It lauds the "old" virtues of self-help, thrift, independence and self-sufficiency, and opposes the faceless bureaucracy, big government and big unions.

> [T]he sterile old formulations of "right-wing" and "left- wing" have become increasingly irrelevant. The old battlelines between business and government are changing. The new divisions are between smallness—which means people—and bigness, wherever it occurs. And smallness is winning (Ross, 1977:48).

Thus, small business is presented as something to be supported by all those who are interested in humanity ("Man is small, and, therefore, small is beautiful"—Schumacher, 1974:133) and in helping the ordinary person against the large and powerful forces which shape our lives.

There are important economic and political reasons for the current interest in small enterprise. The crisis of capitalism is a world crisis in a system dominated by transnational corporations and an international division of labour (Harris, 1983). Individual nations, even with the use of tax concessions, subsidies, free enterprise zones, and various means to hold down wages, are able to have only a limited influence on international capital. They react to the crisis in an *ad hoc* fashion, so that the problems of mass unemployment and poverty are dealt with, if at all, in a totally inadequate fashion. In a period of rising unemployment and of state withdrawal from responsibility for direct job creation, the promotion of small business is grabbed at as *the* potential solution to unemployment. Because small businesses are generally more labour-intensive than large ones they appear to have good job-creating potential for low capital inputs (an important factor in what are regarded as capital- scarce regions). The emphasis on small business in job creation is also partly a result of a recognition that current efforts to provide a national solution to economic problems will not solve Canada's unemployment problem. In fact, the current emphasis on export-led growth in Canada's major areas of comparative advantage means that key industries will be streamlined, becoming less labour intensive in the process. But whether or not the new "conventional wisdom" associated with the job-creating potential of small business will prove to be even partially valid remains to be seen, because as Rainnie (1985:148) notes, this is an area which is still largely unresearched.

The growth in interest in small business is also related to the economic crisis in another way. In recent years there has been a tremendous growth in what is variously called "decentralized production" (Mattera, 1980), the "sweated trades" (Harris, 1983:134-167) or the "underground" or "submerged" economy (Mattera, 1985). These studies, and that of Rainnie (1985), document the growth in small scale enterprise during the current economic crisis, and offer some insights into its causes. One of the main causes appears to be capital's quest for flexibility, and in particular for a means of undermining the organized power of labour. As Elliott and McCrone (1982:128) put it:

> It can pay large companies to subcontract some of their activities to small businesses, especially those making use of cheap immigrant labour or relying on the exploitation of family labour to produce their goods. In some instances smaller firms appear more efficient than larger ones; not only do they have lower labour costs, they also have lower levels of unionization and lower strike rates than big concerns. Encouraging small business may also mean weakening or slowing the advance of unionism. For these reasons we may well see considerable encouragement of small firms by the large enterprises—especially in the form of subcontracting and franchising.

Thus a strategy of promoting small business may well be a means of extending that sector of the economy which provides part-time, low-paid work for women, young people, immigrants and the unskilled—the depressing world of the working poor.

The enthusiasm with which the cause of small business has been embraced in recent years is also due to the fact that the small business lobby has played a key role in supporting monetarist trends and agitating for free market conditions. In many ways the new values which various Conservative governments are promoting are those which are central to the small business movement. When writers such as Brown (1976) point to the importance of small business as representing the essential values on which society has been built it is clear that they see this social group as providing a strong base of support for policies of a conservative nature.

In fact, the small business lobby has, since the early 1970s, been attempting to push governments to the right. One area in which they have been particularly active is in lobbying for a more restrictive Unemployment Insurance system. Unemployment Insurance is seen by small business as one of the key obstacles to their being able to get the labour they require *at as low a price as possible.* Hence they have mounted a sustained campaign to persuade Canadians the that existing Unemployment Insurance setup provides a "dis-incentive to work" (*Evening Telegram*, November 2, 1985). This argument was made by the Newfoundland and Labrador Employers' Labour Relations Council in a brief to the Royal Commission on Employment and Unemployment. The Council suggested that UI benefits were too attractive and too easily available and that this has "contributed to an attitude problem in that there is decreased incentive for recipients to search for work." At the same time the Council attacked the Peckford government in Newfoundland for being "pro-labour" and suggested that full employment was not a "legitimate goal" in Newfoundland since it might "never be possible." Essentially the same argument was made in the same month by the St. John's Board of Trade to the Forget Commission (*Evening Telegram*, November 23, 1985), when it suggested that Unemployment Insurance undermines the work ethic.

But small business is not only concerned with Unemployment Insurance because they see it as limiting their supply of cheap labour. The direct cost of maintaining the system is also a problem. When Michael Wilson announced in January 1985 that the federal government was considering stripping what he called "social benefits" from the UI program, he made the argument in terms of the potential benefits to small business. Trimming the UI system would reduce the contributions of small business to the UI fund, while the programs hived off would be paid for out of general revenue. Thus part of the cost of maintaining the unemployed would be shifted from business to Canadian taxpayers generally. Pressure to do this has been maintained by groups like the St. John's Board of Trade, which argues for a two-tiered program which would separate the "insurance" and the "social" aspects of UI and in the process relieve some of the financial burden which falls on their shoulders (*Evening Telegram*, October 22, 1986). The Newfoundland and Labrador Employers' Labour Relations Council has also suggested that any funds saved by cutting UI could be given to small business (*The Metro*, March 16, 1986). It is significant that the Report of the Royal Commission on Employment and Unemployment in Newfoundland was launched in October 1986 with the cry that "UI is crippling the work ethic in Newfoundland" (*Globe and Mail*, October 7, 1986), echoing comments which had already been made in the MacDonald Report, and which would soon be made in the report of the Forget Commission. Returning UI to "insurance principles" is clearly a way of forcing people into low-wage employment, or at least creating a low-wage environment for capital, and it conforms to T. Courchene's "market-oriented" vision of social policy as being subordinate to "the pursuit of industrial flexibility and adjustment," and to the need to "fuel the failing engines of economic growth" (1984:16).

The idea that Newfoundland's underdevelopment (poverty, unemployment, etc.) is to a significant degree due to lack of entrepreneurial effort and talent, and to a failure of imagination and skill, on the part of the Newfoundland elite, is well established in the work of people like David Alexander (1974:180). It follows from this analysis, that conditions can be greatly improved by prodding reluctant entrepreneurs into action. Since the 1970s the idea that state encouragement is needed to overcome the "cultural" factors which are a barrier to entrepreneurial activity has been widely expressed in Canada in general, and in Newfoundland. It is usually argued that people are poor risk takers and that, for many, business activity has not been respectable. Ignoring the fact that there has never been any shortage of persons willing and even anxious to take entrepreneurial initiatives in Newfoundland *if there seemed to be a chance of reasonable profit*, and ignoring the fact that the bloated tertiary sector of today testifies to the continued efforts of people to engage in small trading activity (spurred on partly by lack of alternative ways of earning a living), these arguments have emerged as a key element in conservative thinking in the 1980s.

The previously mentioned Operation Bootstraps launched by the Atlantic Provinces Chamber of Commerce seeks to provide the Atlantic region with a network of "enterprise centres." This idea has recently been endorsed for Newfoundland in the report *Building on our Strengths* (Newfoundland and Labrador, 1986:393). For the purpose of nurturing small businesses a "$2.9 million incubator mall" is being developed near Corner Brook, Newfoundland (Roche, 1985). This will provide companies with subsidized space until they mature. Other locations for "incubating small business" are planned for Newfoundland. Creating entrepreneurs is almost seen as a patriotic duty, a way of saving Newfoundland and providing the unemployed with jobs while making money. Groups like the YM-YWCA have become involved in a program (via the Canadian Job Strategy) to create young entrepreneurs (*Evening Telegram*, January 22, 1986). After a short course and a lesson in the power of positive thinking, a squad of young people will be ready to start their own fish selling or house painting operations.

One of the obstacles identified by the YM-YWCA in its efforts to create entrepreneurs is the fact that young people are brought up with the notion that they have to be employees. Similarly, John Bulloch (1984:7) has focused on the weakness of "entrepreneurship culture":

> Entrepreneurs are not born; they are made. Entrepreneurship is a cultural phenomenon and with it comes flexibility, risk-taking, and innovation. Societies can develop strong beliefs in the desirability of self-employment, entrepreneurship, and small business ownership if governments make special effort to develop and strengthen their entrepreneurial culture.

Building on our Strengths (1986:384-388) argues that Newfoundlanders have "an attitude problem" when it comes to starting business enterprises. Too many look towards other people and the state to provide them with jobs rather than going out and creating their own employment.

Both the Royal Commission report and the statements of Douglas House (its Chairman) suggest that business activity has a bad name in Newfoundland. *Building on our Strengths* (384) links this bad attitude to "the old merchant system" and to the fact that people in small communities are "frowned on if they become too ambitious and try to 'get ahead' of other people." House's explanation is more comprehensive. In a talk to the St. John's Board of Trade he suggested that the Newfoundlander's distrustful attitude towards small business results from: "... the legacy of an oppressive merchant class, traditional dependence on government and the left-leaning politics and climate of earlier decades" (*Evening Telegram*, October 24, 1986).

House, Bulloch and many others all make the argument that Canada should educate for entrepreneurial activity. Business activity needs to be made respectable. People have to be encouraged to make money and take risks (which will of course be minimized by the state). Thus, when House argues that economic development should be "one of the primary goals of the education system" (*Evening Telegram*, April 9, 1986) he is making a case for greater effort to be devoted towards encouraging a business mentality. Thus, Harold Lundrigan, one of the Royal Commissioners and Chairman of the Economic Council of Newfoundland and Labrador, calls for education for entrepreneurial spirit (*Evening Telegram*, January 9, 1986), a call which is echoed constantly by other Commissioners. Independence has to be promoted, not dependence on government:

> If we as a province are going to take seriously our responsibility of becoming more self-reliant and to cease relying on continual government support, all sectors of society must see that our children are educated to know more about the economic side of the world we live in.

A positive set of attitudes towards business activity would presumably also imply a more pliant and appreciative workforce. A St. John's journalist, Mark King (*The Metro*, December 8, 1985), suggests that "our educational system is currently gutterized by a left-liberal frame of thought" and is "failing our young people because it doesn't adequately prepare them for the real world." The new education will help change people politically:

> Instead of voting for higher taxes and government intervention, they'll start voting for lower public spending and less regulation, realizing that the government is stifling their chance to expand, make money and maybe even hire some people.

In fact, King sees the new education as putting into practice the lessons learned by young people who rejected the "tired drivel" of social democracy and found their own way out of unemployment and into a new set of attitudes which meant that "they ... began to resent unbridled government waste":

> Some of the unemployed went out and started looking for some way of taking care of themselves and their families without relying on a government cheque. They made muffins in their kitchens and sold them down the street. They went back to school and picked up some new skills. Some, laid off from their jobs, took a new look at freelance writing and editing and found some remarkable things about it....

Those who have promoted small business as a vital element in the "small is beautiful" response to unemployment and underdevelopment have, thus, helped pave the way for the government's retreat from responsibility for providing employment, or adequate support for those who are unemployed.

5. "Small is beautiful" and austerity: the "informal economy"

> One of the major changes in western societies during recent years has been a dawning realization of the limits of the welfare state. We now know that the state is simply not able to satisfy all the needs of all its citizens. People have to become more self-reliant: they have to rely more upon themselves, their households and their communities to meet their economic and social needs (*Building on Our Strengths*, 1986:314).

Part of the "new" philosophy is a lessening of government commitment to deal with a variety of social problems. In the future, "entitlements" are to be even more subordinate to "efficiency" than in the past (Courchene, 1984). This is "bad news for Atlantic Canada," as Kerans (1986) points out, because of the region's heavy dependence on state spending. What will take the place of state responsibility? By all accounts a "do- it-yourself" approach to income support, job creation, etc. According to Employment and Immigration Minister Benoit Bouchard, "we must change our mentality" to facilitate the government's new philosophy (*The Globe and Mail*, October 8, 1986). Individuals will have to take more responsibility for "their social problems, their pensions and their job training." The message that Atlantic Canadians should reduce their expectations and their dependence on government comes in a variety of forms; bluntly from federal politicians like John Crosbie, or in a slightly less aggressive form, from Don Jamieson shortly before his death. The latter told the Atlantic Provinces Economic Council that people living in small communities would have to be told that they could not continue to enjoy that lifestyle *and* expect the same kinds of services available to people living in "a different region and under different circumstances" (*Evening Telegram*, September 26, 1986).

The "small is beautiful" model of development is proving very useful in this context. As already noted the "small is beautiful" and "alternatives" movement of the 1960s and 1970s placed a great deal of emphasis on self-reliance, self-help, thrift and making do with less. The energy crisis of the 1970s led to serious attempts by the state to explore alternative energy technology and to promote conservation ideas. By the mid-1970s the Conserver Society arm of the Science Council of Canada (1977) was heavily involved in a "small is beautiful" approach to development within their general "limits to growth" philosophy. Experiments with alternate lifestyles and technologies were sponsored by groups as well as by various provincial governments in Canada. The construction of the Ark in Prince Edward Island (which subsequently failed) was one such experiment.

With cash in short supply the "underground" or "subterranean" economy was also more and more talked about (*Financial Post*, October 6, 1979). People (mainly from the middle class) became very interested in becoming more self-sufficient. Building on the ideas of Schumacher and Ivan Illich (1973) an interest developed in "networking" and do-it-yourself. Keeping expenditures and demands down (living lightly on the earth) was also seen as a political statement for those concerned about the future of the planet. For writers like Paul Hawken (1980) the "mass economy" was in crisis and a new kind of economy was needed. The new emphasis was to be on "economy"; that is, "careful management ... frugality, thrift, saving" (56). Hawken subsequently invented the term "disintermediation" (1981). The call was for businesses to by-pass institutions and cut out the middleman, and for people to grow their own food. Buying food, according to Hawken, is an example of "intermediation"; growing your own is "disintermediation." As such he describes gardening as "an economic act that clearly recognizes the geopolitical reality and acts upon it" (1981:7). For Hawken, "disintermediation is the natural and appropriate activity in a steady or contracting" economy (8). It is appropriate to hard times, but it also is a way of subverting the mass economy. That disintermediation is appropriate to economic stagnation, is confirmed by Bryce and Margaret Muir's discussion of the Maritimes (1981). They claim that a fully disintermediated society already exists.

> In traditional maritime society every man is a jack of all trades, able to cut his own firewood; build a house and a boat; make and mend fishing gear; fish and hunt; keep animals for meat and dairy products; do his own boat and auto mechanics; plumb and wire. In a pinch he can do a little smithing in the parlour stove, some rough doctoring offshore, and put down a wellpoint by hand. Each maritime woman is a respected master at the arts of child rearing and housekeeping. Raising, gathering and preserving; making and mending clothing; and keeping the social gears greased are all in her days work.
>
> When cash is abundant, Maritimers may hire out some or all of the subsistence chores: buy California lettuce, take the car to a garage, send away for a new dress. So long as cash work, or good fishing, produces surplus income, beyond present needs and subsistence maintenance for the off season, specializations proliferate. When the fish are running, there's lots of work for carpenters. When the catch is off, I can pound my own nails, thank you.
>
> The uncertainties, and seasonality, of maritime cash flow mean that no specialist can depend on continuous employment. Carpenters cut pulp in the winter. A grocer may own a truck for hauling gravel. Anthropologists call this diversified pattern of employment "seasonal pluralism," and it is an appropriate adaptation to the ebb and flow of a resource-based economy (75).

The virtues of the "culture of patching" as against the "Cult of the Purchase" have also been celebrated recently by Burrill (1986). Patching, he argues, is a "time-honoured tradition" in the Maritimes and one which may have considerable survival value during an economic crisis.

For some, the "informal economy" is seen as a realistic adaptation to hard times, and as a kind of challenge to corporate-consumer culture. The virtues of thrift, neighbourliness, pioneer values and the family are lauded: these values will help people survive. But as one author claims, "a work force ... that had learned to live with reduced expectations would be far less willing to jump through the corporate hoop" (Simoni, 1982:678). This observation comes in an article which calls for a reduction of work time to about twenty hours a week as one step towards a "no-growth economy." A second step would be a "guaranteed basic income" which would be set at such a low level that "there would still be a strong incentive to work—the more so if the work-week was only twenty hours, for the minimum-base-income scheme would actually complement the reduced- work-time program rather than serve as an alternative to it" (678). People's spare time would be used "to compensate for the reduction in ... standard of living" (677). One of the virtues of the scheme, according to Simoni, would be that "with the dismantling of the whole welfare and unemployment-compensation apparatus, the monster of government would shrink to close to manageable size" (678). Simoni's proposal would free labour for "production for personal consumption" and "backyard entrepreneurialism" (678). Thus, in the guise of a radical proposal, we are presented with a scheme to provide small enterprise with a cheap and flexible labour force, and governments with a less dependent populace. The self-styled radicals who call for "disintermediation" are making essentially the same argument as those who urge people to rediscover the sort of hard-working lives their grandparents lived and to strengthen the family rather than forge exotic new relationships (Ross, 1977:42).

The promotion and institutionalization of the informal economy also plays a key role in the recent Royal Commission's report on Newfoundland. Efforts to construct a "post-industrial Newfoundland" will build on existing strengths (1986:18-35). The traditional economy of Newfoundland is described in the report very much in the same way as Margaret and Bryce Muir describe Maritime culture:

> Flexibility, adaptability, occupational pluralism, home production, the rhythm of a seasonal lifestyle, household self-reliance—these are catchwords that capture the traditional culture of outport Newfoundland (24).

They note that in most "blueprints offered us for industrialization" these characteristics "have been seen as barriers to economic development." In spite of this, and although "ignored, battered or deprecated, Newfoundland's small communities have stubbornly persisted." Outports, "have persisted despite neglect and discouragement rather than because of official support," while their "inherent strengths ... have not ... been appreciated or built upon." For the future, however, those interested in development should build on these strengths. The Commissioners say that they don't want to return to the past, assuring us that they "have promised not to be rural romantics"; they want to "revitalize" rural Newfoundland, producing "the kind of social and economic development that is in keeping with the spirit of the twenty-first century" (24).

For the Royal Commission, the viability of the traditional outport has been undermined by inappropriate development schemes and the welfare state:

> Since Confederation, as a result of government preoccupation with large-scale industrialism along with the rapid growth of the Canadian welfare state, Newfoundland outports have been in danger of becoming rural welfare communities (19).

In one of the background technical/consultation papers produced for the Royal Commission (Thornton, 1986) the destructive effect of inappropriate development schemes and the welfare state is explored in detail. Citing Canning's work (1974:22), Thornton (1986:18) makes this comment on the Newfoundland outport:

> After Confederation, the household and community resources included not only the "local" renewable resources of old but also "an overdose of *ad hoc* subsidies, welfare payments and L.I.P. grants ... brought in as stop-gap measures." These, and especially unemployment insurance—predicated upon a misconception of the nature of employment in the outport—had the effect of increasing the "cash component" in the economy out of proportion to its cash requirements.

According to this view, it is government policy which has "eroded the peasant way of life" of the outport and "external" forces which have upset the "highly adaptive, innovative and ecologically balanced community" (22). If wrong government policies have been responsible for the demise of the outport, the corrective is obvious:

> It is time to discard imported solutions, to build on the strengths of the traditional economy and society, particularly those aspects which made it adaptive, innovative, ecologically balanced and economically stable and which enabled it to survive for so long (23).

Similar themes are taken up in the Report of the Royal Commission. The task of rehabilitating rural Newfoundland is outlined thus:

> From fishing outports we have to create, not welfare ghettoes, but modern communities which use up-to-date communications, intermediate technology and modern forms of enterprise, so as

to achieve a new kind of self-reliance appropriate to the post-industrial age. If we are to achieve this, these modern villages will need to experience a revolution in the education of their citizens, be linked into provincial research and development schemes which are geared to their needs, enjoy a newly designed income security system, gain greater control over the decisions that affect them directly and receive the active support and encouragement of both federal and provincial government agencies in their efforts to achieve self-reliance (*Building on Our Strengths*, 1986:19).

The "non-cash or domestic part of the economy continues to play an important role in rural Newfoundland," according to the Commission, "contributing significantly to people's standard of living" (26). This, together with "occupational pluralism" and some government assistance suggests to the Commission that unemployment is not such a serious problem in rural Newfoundland as "official statistics imply" (113). Accordingly, the Commission suggests that for the future "policies that enhance home production could play an important role in alleviating poverty and low productivity" (26). But any improvement, it is suggested, must rest on the removal or modification of policies which undermine or destroy traditional adaptations. It is assumed that rural survival will depend on Newfoundlanders being willing to gear their expectations to the "realities" of living in a "small, remote, open and highly dependent economy" (23). Newfoundland's "post-Confederation affluence has been bought at the high price of dependency upon international resource markets and the fiscal largesse of the federal government" (22). If expectations are lowered, then people can be happier with less. A well-established theme in Newfoundland ("we may be poor, but we're happy") is thus reworked by the Commission and presented as common sense in the conditions of the 1980s.

Revitalizing rural Newfoundland's traditional adaptation to unemployment, insecurity, isolation and poverty will, however, require more than simply the lowering of expectations. A few comments about education and income support will make this clear. According to the Royal Commission (1986:229), Newfoundland's education system has "never been geared to the kind of society we really are, and to the kind of society *we should reasonably aspire to be in the future*" (emphasis added). The argument appears to be that past and current educational practices are inappropriate to Newfoundland's reality. They have played a part in the breakdown of traditional society and in promoting the industrial dream. They have led to a high drop-out rate from high school, because "for poorer families ... and particularly for those living in small communities, there is little connection between what goes on in the class-room and what goes on at home or in the community" (313). To improve the situation, the Commission suggests that the education system, and in particular the curriculum, "must be made more relevant to the lives and experiences" of rural inhabitants (314):

> The Department of Education, in consultation with the Newfoundland Teachers' Association, should redesign the primary, elementary and secondary school programmes so that they provide instruction in, and give credit for, skills that contribute to greater self-reliance and successful adaptations to life in rural Newfoundland (315).

Education, it is argued, "must begin with the child in his or her own setting." In Newfoundland outports,

> [t]his setting is typically one where fishing is the main industry, men build and repair their own houses and boats, women work as homemakers and as seasonal fish plant or service-sector workers and people of all ages spend much time household production— cutting firewood, fishing, hunting, berry-picking and perhaps some gardening and animal husbandry (314).

Courses "geared to rural life-styles" and "self-reliance" would therefore be of a "practical, applied nature." They would include "carpentry, small-engine repair, animal husbandry, and fish harvesting and processing" as well as "more sophisticated programmes in such things as home insulation, automobile repairs, and furniture making," according to *Education for Self-Reliance* (Newfoundland and Labrador, 1986a:116-117). The teaching of "practical life skills" would, however, not mean the neglect of "basic academic skills," which are "just as important to successful rural, as to successful urban, living in the late twentieth century" (117). Such basic skills should be learned because they are useful to rural Newfoundlanders "not simply because they are part of an *alien* school curriculum" (117, emphasis added). The Commission subscribes to the "ideals of universal education," but apparently this education should be a bit less universal than hitherto (Newfoundland and Labrador, 1986:313). It seems that people should be educated according to their place in society. What the Commission appears to be suggesting is a *dual* education system to fit Newfoundland's *dual* society, at least at the primary and elementary levels. They suggest that this will not prevent people from moving on "in search of work and new experiences," but clearly the main thrust is to educate people for rural life and for a "post-industrial" era in which the limits of the welfare state have been realized. This thrust has an openly ideological slant:

> People ... have to become more knowledgeable about the way our economic system works and the roles played by its constituent parts: big corporations, banks, co-operatives, small companies, labour unions, development associations and various government agencies. This learning should begin at an early age, continue throughout each child's school career and include basic training in personal financial and household management. And it should instil the spirit of entrepreneurship—the idea that people can initiate small enterprise for themselves—into young people (1986:314).

The Commission also recommends that labour relations be taught "at all levels in the education system" (315). This essentially very conservative and even reactionary vision of education owes much to the suggestions of the small business lobby and to the ideas of journalists like Mark King (discussed above): an education which would fit people for their slots in society and prepare them for austerity.

Another element in the undermining of Newfoundland's traditional way of life is what the Royal Commission terms the "UI make-work system." That such programs have undermined rural independence and initiative is a long-established "fact" in populist writing about the province, dominating the thinking of writers like Stratford Canning (1974) and Pat Thornton (1986). It is significant that the Commission links Unemployment Insurance with make-work programs. They do this in spite of "recognizing that most people qualify for UI through means other than make-work projects," because they argue that the linking of the two "captures the essential spirit" of the income security system in rural areas (*Building on Our Strengths*, 1986:406). According to Christopher Palmer, the Commission's research director, the main problem with the "UI make-work system" is "the undermining of serious efforts towards economic development and long-term employment enhancement" (*The Globe and Mail*, October 7, 1986). The "system," according to the Commission, "undermines the intrinsic value of work ... good working habits and discipline ... [and] personal and community initiatives." It "discourages self-employment and small-scale enterprise" and "distorts the efforts of local development groups." Above all, it is "a disincentive to work" (1986:406-8). The "ten-week syndrome" is not natural and inevitable; it is the unfortunate and artificial consequence of a scheme that has become distorted to serve a purpose for which it was never designed (417).

The system should be dismantled so the natural process of development can occur. The Royal Commission suggests that UI should "revert to its intended function of providing income maintenance for people in transition between permanent jobs or on short-term lay-off, sick leave or maternity leave" (417). For the rest of the population (those outside the permanent labour force) a new income security system would be set in place:

> The proposed system would provide basic income support for all individuals and households through a Guaranteed Basic Income (GBI) set at half the minimum income level established by Statistics Canada's low income cut-off lines. This level would be roughly equivalent to what households in Newfoundland now receive on Social Assistance. The GBI would be based on household income (411).

The low level of support would prevent the GBI "from becoming a financial disincentive to work" (412). Because the level of support would be so low, however, those unable to work "and genuinely destitute" would be provided with social assistance. For those capable of working, and Earned Income Supplementation (EIS) scheme would "subsidize earned income ... up to an agreed upon limit" (412).

This scheme would have many benefits, according to the Commission. It would "eliminate the need for useless make-work projects" and free up funds for "longer-term economic development." It would "encourage people to work, even for a low wage" and "reward all work for earned income." It would "allow for the reinstatement of good work habits and an appreciation of the intrinsic value of work." It would provide "at least minimal income security," while encouraging "self employment" and "flexible forms of economic adaptation, including occupational pluralism and household production" (414-6). In short, the new system would encourage people to fend for themselves and to work for whatever wages were offered by local employers.

Without doubt this is a scheme for lowering the general standard of living for people in rural Newfoundland. It would mean the virtual end of Unemployment Insurance and of make-work projects. Both of these provide low incomes, but provide them to *individuals*, and probably at a higher level than the proposed *household* GBI. Able-bodied workers, even with the GBI but without social assistance), would be at the mercy of potential employers, whether small businesses or co-operatives. No doubt subsistence production would increase! The whole scheme seems a blueprint not for rural revitalization, but rather for reinforcing and institutionalizing a low-wage, marginal existence for rural people— with an income security system appropriate to this type of existence.

6. "Small is beautiful" and make-work

> Canadians do not want the old make-work projects. These projects
> not only offer old solutions, they were wasteful and they diminished
> the dignity and self-respect of the individual. Canadians deserve
> better.
>   I would like to stress this element. Each region will have to
> find its own answer to the problems of employment. The Minister
> of Employment and Immigration will stand behind them to support
> them (Benoit Bouchard, quoted in the *Evening Telegram*, October
> 8, 1986).

The above statements were made by Employment Minister Benoit Bouchard
in the course of announcing that the old days of make-work projects
funded by the federal government are over. Presenting his views as
decentralist and anti-bureaucratic, the Minister declared that: "Global
bureaucratic planning in Ottawa does not relate to the problems faced
by an unemployed woman in Ontario, a laid-off miner in Manitoba or
a Newfoundland fisherman." In the future, we are told, the responsibility
for creating jobs will be a shared one. The provinces will have to play
a part, as will the unemployed as well. To mark this new direction in
policy the federal government announced the creation of the Atlantic
Canada Opportunity Agency, a body intended to coordinate job creation
efforts by industry, governments and individuals in the region. The
formation of a new agency was not intended to signal that any new
job creation money would be put into the region. If anything it seemed
to indicate that, in the future, funds would be tighter and federal spending
more market-oriented. This represents a confirmation of the federal
government's retreat from responsibility for direct job creation—a retreat
facilitated by the promotion of "small is beautiful" ideas.
    Federal employment creation programs have quite a long history in
Newfoundland. From the mid-1970s to the mid-1980s some eighteen
different program were in existence and over 335 million dollars were
spent in the province (Montgomery, 1986:40). Spending rose from about
ten million dollars in 1974-75 to more than fifty-five million in 1982-83
(18). In the 1970s the names of different programs such as OFY, LIP, LEAP
and Canada Works became widely known in Newfoundland and their
development merits were the focus of considerable discussion (Overton,
1977). Beginning in 1977 the provincial government also got involved
in short-term make-work schemes through the Department of Social
Services (*Building on Our Strengths*, 1986:284).
    During the expansionist post-war period there was much outmigration
from rural areas in Canada. In Newfoundland the government became

involved in schemes to centralize the population, in part to provide an accessible labour force in economic growth centres. As unemployment mounted in the late 1960s and early 1970s, the federal government focused its attention on means to reduce unemployment among certain target groups. Youth was one of the first targets for direct job creation; other targets soon followed. Areas with high rates of unemployment began to receive federal funds for short-term work-projects according to their levels of unemployment. In many respects these initiatives were simply the old familiar public works projects of the 1920s and 1930s. They were labour-intensive projects clearly intended to ease unemployment, prevent alienation and keep people's commitment to work at least alive if not intact; they were also presented as a means by which the chronically unemployed might be returned to the work force. In a situation of rising unemployment, the state took on a degree of responsibility (however inadequate) as employer of last resort.

The make-work schemes of the 1970s adopted some of the ideas of the "small is beautiful" philosophy (which had, in turn, taken up and elaborated many of the ideas associated with rehabilitating the unemployed current in the 1930s and even earlier). As noted, projects were labour-intensive; for example local timber was cut in the woods and hauled for wharf construction rather than purchased. The projects were community-oriented, using local resources where possible. They emphasized the intrinsic value of work for motivation, for maintaining skills and for discipline. The name of the largest project—"Canada Works"—implied that, in spite of unemployment, the country was still working. The community orientation of the projects suggested they were also intended as a form of development. In spite of the numerous problems associated with these make-work schemes, they did provide income for many people in both rural and urban areas, and they did allow some people to qualify for Unemployment Insurance, even if at a very low rate.

The introduction of make-work schemes was part of an *ad hoc* response to rising unemployment. These projects were seen as part of a short-term "holding operation" designed to "give people something to do" (Employment and Immigration Canada, 1981:35). As such the projects were consistent with well-established counter-cyclical responses to economic downturns. By the end of the 1970s make-work had become well established in Canada:

Direct job creation measures have now been in place for a decade. After a sharp increase in scale early in the decade, they have varied in size depending on economic conditions and on the perceived need of the federal government to engage in expenditure-cutting exercises.

> Although these programs ... were designed and considered as short-term measures to reduce unemployment in periods of temporary slack in the economy, they have in fact become a permanent feature of the labour market policy landscape (1981:34).

By the end of the 1970s, however, the make-work approach was coming under attack at the federal level, along with Unemployment Insurance and various forms of regional development:

> A process which allocates short-term job creation and training funds to the eastern regions on the basis of their share of national unemployment is virtually guaranteed to produce an orientation towards simply absorbing the excess labour supply with very little impact on output and income per worker over a longer-run horizon (1981:35).

It was argued that make-work programs were "impeding desirable longer-run adjustments in the labour market" and that a new orientation for government policy should be devised (35). At a time when more emphasis was being placed on "structural unemployment problems," programs designed for counter-cyclical purposes should be abandoned. It was suggested that a new, structurally-oriented program would direct effort towards skill training, rehabilitation and job creation for those most likely to suffer from long-term unemployment.

By the early 1980s, make-work schemes were widely regarded as *a barrier* to any long-term solution to unemployment. The arguments against these projects were essentially the same as those about unemployment insurance. The report *Unemployment Insurance in the 1980s* (Canada, Employment and Immigration, 1981a) suggested an extensive program of cuts in unemployment insurance to facilitate "labour market adjustment" and to "encourage job attachment." The report proposed that the government move away from using income maintenance as a means of dealing with chronic unemployment towards programs which would address the causes of unemployment (84). Cuts in UI would force people to move from areas like Newfoundland to places where they could find work. Short-term public works might be needed to offset the "adverse impact" of changes in UI regulations while "adjustment" took place.

Similar suggestions were later made by the MacDonald Royal Commission and by the Forget Commission. The St. John's *Evening Telegram* (September 6, 1985) reported that the MacDonald Commission described the UI system as "an unwieldy $11-billion-a-year giant that actually keeps people out of work." The call was to change the system in order to make it "less like welfare" and to "destroy the disincentive to work." Forget make similar suggestions, arguing that UI needed to be brought closer to insurance principles. Benefits would be reduced selectively, while a universal income supplement would be used to offset the impact of this on "the losers" (*Evening Telegram*, October 17, 1986). Any savings made by cutting UI might, according to Forget, be used for economic development and job training. Presumably the benefits of this spending would at some stage be expected to trickle down to "the losers." Forget also attacked make-work schemes as leading to dependency and inhibiting long-range development (*Evening Telegram*, December 6, 1986).

Much of the effort to get government to end make-work schemes has come from the owners of small businesses. In 1977 a sawmill operator in Dover, Newfoundland complained that his business was "touch and go" due to competition from cheaper lumber imported from the mainland (*Evening Telegram*, March 12, 1977). He suggested that make-work money might be better spent if the government paid his former employees to cut logs for his mill. With a cheap supply of raw material he might be able to survive and to keep the employees working for the rest of the year without any government handouts. Other complaints have come from businesses engaged in work similar to that of the make-work projects, such as wharf and marina construction. In one case employers complained that they had to hire labour at $6.00 per hour while people on a Canada Works project were paid $2.50 to do similar work (*Evening Telegram*, February 3, 1978). In another case a Boyd's Cove businessman, head of the local Employment Committee, preferred to see federal funds used to clear 200 acres of land for blueberries. His company would be able to buy the blueberries picked by local residents (*Evening Telegram*, May 16, 1986).

The system of make-work has also been attacked by rural development associations in Newfoundland and Labrador for some time. From the Newfoundland Association of Social Workers, which attacks make-work as leading to dependency (*Evening Telegram*, October 18, 1986), to Newfoundland's Social Services Minister, the message is the same: "we are looking for ways to break the welfare cycle" (*Evening Telegram*, September 20, 1985). There appears to be a consensus that make-work projects are bad, and there is a strong current of thinking which supports the channelling of state job creation funds away from make-work and towards small business.

Building on Our Strengths (1986) provides a bridge between the attacks which have been launched on make-work in Newfoundland and those at a national level. Under programs like the Canada Job Strategy the job-creating efforts of small business will be aided in an attempt to get people to "work their way off welfare" (*Evening Telegram*, September

19, 1985), while some young people will be absorbed into programs designed to create entrepreneurs. "Entrepreneurial activity provides one of the most valuable outlets for the ambitious, under-privileged and non-conformist" (Brown, 1976:15).

The Royal Commission calls for "practical community development" to replace existing initiatives in Newfoundland, and sees this as a means of attaining "full employment":

> We have to take the eradication of unemployment and the commitment to full employment as a societal and political goal to be sought by all means possible. By "full employment" here we do not mean that everyone would have a permanent, year-round job, but rather we mean full employment in a Newfoundland sense. Many people, particularly in rural areas, would continue to pursue a seasonal round, with periods of self-employment, paid employment, house-hold production and, when necessary, some income supplementation. But there would be more work, more earned income and less dependency upon government transfers than at present, and even the "official" unemployment rate would decline significantly (1986:35).

But is this anything but a way of declaring that the state will no longer be responsible for supporting people in the face of continued hight levels of unemployment? Does this scheme for "full employment in a Newfoundland sense" really mean anything but hospitalizing rural Newfoundlanders in a poverty-ridden state while they provide cheap labour for any local employers who care to exploit it?

7. Conclusions

Towards the end of the period of capitalist expansion which followed the Second World War, it was possible for many to see the "small is beautiful" ideology as a kind of opposition to industrial capitalism. However this ideology did not challenge the structural causes of the problems to which it was reacting. In practice the neo-liberal, market-oriented conservatives eventually came to exploit the ideology most effectively. The "small is beautiful" chickens which have come home to roost in the 1980s are very different from those which took wing in the late 1960s and early 1970s. This is seen most clearly in the report of the Royal Commission on Employment and Unemployment in Newfoundland published in 1986.

During the late 1970s and early 1980s, as we have seen, many of the ideas associated with the "small is beautiful" philosophy became popular in Atlantic Canada. Elements of this philosophy found their way into regional/rural development thinking, and then became part of a rationale used by the state—with the strong support of small business and other interests—to divest itself of responsibility for the poorer regions of the country. We should not be surprised that the state would try to unload responsibility in a time of crisis. What is more noteworthy, however, is that the ideas used to justify this retreat have been largely developed and propagated in the first instance by radicals, who thought they were working towards an alternative and more humane society.

Royal Commissions, as Mallory (1986) notes, serve an important educational role. By means of their hearings, their published reports and research studies, and the statements and presentations made by the commissioners and their support staff both before and after the publication of reports, these commissions play a part in "the process of engineering consent so that the public and the political actors will come to accept what has already become the conventional wisdom among elites" (597). *Building on Our Strengths* takes as its main them the need to adopt a "small is beautiful" approach to solving the problems of rural Newfoundland. Following "advanced thinking" in Scandinavia which "seeks to 'leap-frog' the industrial age," it suggests that Newfoundlanders should "become leaders ... in building a pluralistic post-industrial Canada" (1986:20). All the background research and reports of the Commission are geared towards supporting the program for a "post-industrial" Newfoundland which is outlined in the final report. All the items selected from the Commission's hearings are fitted into its populist frame of analysis. The Commission's blueprint for a "revitalized Newfoundland" (18) has received widespread support. One journalist thought that the report of the Commission "might be the frog that became a prince" (Moores, 1986:18). A representative of the Canadian Federation of Independent Business described it as a "watershed report" (on CBC's *Sunday Morning*, October 19, 1986); a community development worker as "a Bible, a new testament" (*Evening Telegram*, November 15, 1986). Gene Long of the New Democratic Party described Douglas House, the Chairman of the Royal Commission, as "genuinely trying his creative best ... to open a space through which small victories might be squeezed" (*Sunday Express*, November 16, 1986). Even Miguel Figueroa of the *Canadian Tribune* (1986), the newspaper of the Communist Party in Canada, described the report of the commission as having the "right diagnosis" and suggesting "much needed reforms," even if it did have the "wrong prescriptions."

But a critical look at the findings of the Royal Commission reveals anything but a new approach to Newfoundland's problems. In fact, the whole scheme for rural revitalization is depressingly like the community development schemes of the 1930s in Newfoundland. Then, as now, a failing economy and widespread pauperization stimulated a great interest in small industry, co-operatives, crafts and agriculture. The "dangerous" unemployed were resettled on the land, and people were forced into self-sufficiency by setting poor relief levels at about one-half of what the authorities considered necessary to meet basic food requirements. Then, as now, practical community development was part of an attempt by the state to relieve itself of the burden of supporting the poor.

The talk of realism and pragmatism is all about accepting the emerging policy direction of the state. The lesson of hard times is wrapped up in a small but beautiful package labelled "the post-industrial society." Inside the package there is an income support system which would mean "guaranteed poverty," to use a phrase applied by Pat Kerans to the MacDonald Commission's Universal Income Security Program (Kerans, 1986:16). It is a system which by supplementing low wages and encouraging people to take any job under any conditions would drive down real wages, undermine organized labour and provide a willing and subsidized workforce for Newfoundland's small capitalists. Inside the package are also instructions on how to stand on your own two feet while pulling yourself up by your bootstraps (made, of course, from moosehide you cured yourself). We should not be surprised that we are being handed this package at the present time. What is disturbing is that so few see the package for what it is, and that those who considered themselves to be critics of capitalism have played such an important role in continuing to represent the package as an *alternative* to industrial capitalism, rather than as a painful and humiliating surrender to its global logic.

Song of the Simple Lifers

Why don't you get back to your outports,
Forget about colour TV,
To a life with more psychic income,
You don't want to end up like me.

For we have all been through it,
And we know that it's just a sham,
But now we're hooked on consuming,
And the lifestyle of old Uncle Sam.

After all you have *real* culture,
And benefits of a spiritual kind.
Just knit some mitts and whittle a boat,
To keep your pockets lined.

There's a splendour in the simple,
In keeping essentials bare.
And a dignity in labour,
Why don't you stay right there.

Don't you know that the city is evil.
You never know those you meet.
While salvation lies in nature,
Satan stalks the streets.

Not for you the crowded sidewalks,
Nor the robot assembly line,
But the tangy salt sea breezes,
Washing away the grime.

And you just have to curb your passions,
And keep expectations down,
Accept what life doles you out,
And refuse to move to town.

Don't you see that the tide is turning,
So of dependency beware.
Our civilization's crumbling.
You're better off out there.

Why don't you get back ...

(Source Unknown)

Chapter Four

The Restructuring of Capital and the Regional Problem

Henry Veltmeyer

1. Introduction

Atlantic Canada has been the focus of a protracted debate on the regional discussion of capitalist development. Among the central questions in this debate are the following: What is the root cause, and what are the structural sources, of what appear to be entrenched regional disparities in income and employment? Can we identify regional conditions of capital accumulation, and corresponding dynamics of regional class relations and struggles? More generally, is there a regionally specific form of capitalist development—on the periphery of a nation-wide (and to an extent global) process of capital accumulation?[1]

On the one side (in the radical tradition, which has tended most consistently to pose the problem in a national or global context) are those who argue that capitalism in its development penetrates all branches of production and displaces all alternative forms of production; and, in the process, converts the means of production into capital and the direct producers into proletarians. On the other side (within the same tradition) are those who see regional limits to this process of capitalist development, and draw attention to the specific forms that capitalist development tends to take in peripheral social formations. The latter position is argued in this chapter.

An early expression in the Maritimes of the orthodox Marxist view can be found in the writings of Colin MacKay who, as far back as 1913, argued with respect to the fisheries that "there is every reason to expect that the evolution of capitalism within the ... industry will follow the course it has taken in the other industries [and that] ... the workers in the fishing industry will find themselves in the same position as the workers in all capitalistic industries." As MacKay saw it, "unless the fishermen organize an extensive system of co-operative societies, typically capitalistic methods [will] be applied to the fishing industry and ... eventually, the fishermen will find themselves in much the same position of dependence as the city workers ... the prices paid the fishermen will only yield a living wage" (*Eastern Labour News*, September 13, 1913).

This type of analysis and prognosis was not restricted to the fisheries, which at the time was second only to agriculture in terms of both production and employment in the region. Capital had already penetrated most regional branches of manufacturing and virtually extinguished all other forms and method of production. Agriculture, accounting for 43 percent of employment in the region, and forestry, dominant in New Brunswick, were, in the view of many commentators, subject to the same forces and would develop in the same way. In this view the Atlantic provinces were fully participating in a nation-wide transition towards monopoly capitalism, a spectacular wave of mergers in 1909-1913 having consolidated major units of capital in the region's leading industries, restructuring them on a national scale. After World War I, and throughout the 1920s, the concentration and centralization of these capitals proceeded apace, facilitated and furthered by various political actions that resulted in the virtual collapse of industry in the region, cut off from its central Canadian markets. The consequences of this collapse gave rise to one of a series of Royal Commissions (Canada, 1926) into "the economic problems of the Maritime provinces" as well as another round in "the great debate" between capital and labour within the region,[2] ahead of the general slump of the 1930s. In the late 1930s and 1940s the centralization and concentration of manufacturing capital was renewed, but the rate of accumulation in Central Canada, and especially Ontario, was more than three times that in Atlantic Canada, increasing the already pronounced dependence of the region on natural resource industries, with their relatively low levels of capitalist development, seasonal production cycles, and associated problems. Tables 1 to 3 below provide some data on these developments.

In the 1950s a low rate of investment and capitalist development (reflected in low productivity rates) was diagnosed by the Royal Commission on Canada's Economic Prospects—the Gordon Commission (Canada, 1957)—as the primary cause of widespread regional disparities in income and employment. On the other hand, other more recent studies suggest a more complex picture, with quite large accumulations of capital and productivity growth in some sectors, and strikingly low levels in others, notably agriculture. One study of Maritime agriculture found a 7 percent *decline* in the total value of all functioning capital over the

Table 1

New Capital Investments* per capita by regions, in selected industry groups, 1949-56 (constant 1949 dollars)

	Atlantic	Que.	Ont.	Prairies	B.C.	Canada
1949						
primary	23	22	39	115	38	46
manufacturing	19	42	55	15	57	40
1950						
primary	28	19	42	124	36	49
manufacturing	14	37	47	16	56	35
1952						
primary	28	25	32	138	42	50
manufacturing	23	45	82	30	82	55
1954						
primary	21	27	32	102	30	42
manufacturing	13	37	65	26	52	43
1956						
primary	32	31	52	140	44	58
manufacturing	21	52	81	0	104	61

* figures are based on gross expenditures on new durable physical assets. They exclude outlays of repair and maintenance on purchase od existing assets.

Source: constructed with data supplied by the Department of Trade and Commerce and compiled by Howland (1957:92-97).

period 1961-1971, during which the value of all capital in agriculture had risen 23 percent for the country as a whole (Jones and Tung, 1977:25, Table 3). This was manifested in a pronounced tendency towards stagnation in agricultural output in the Maritimes, and in the very large number of farms that disappeared. Anthony Winson in a comparative study of Maritime and Ontario agriculture (1985:427-431), found that over the entire post-war period (from 1946 to 1971) 87 percent of all farms in New Brunswick and 85 percent of all Nova Scotia farms failed or disappeared (compared with 54 percent of Ontario farms). As a result, large numbers of producers were separated from their means of production and abandoned agriculture (and to some extent, the fisheries) altogether,

Table 2

Population, New Capital Investment, New Manufacturing Plants and Employment, Regional Percentage Shares, 1946-53

Region	Population	Investment	Plants	Employment in new plants
Atlantic	12	4	5	5
Quebec	29	27	38	32
Ontario	33	50	38	49
Prairies	18	8	9	7
B.C.	8	11	10	8
	100.0	100.0	100.0	100.0

Source: based on data supplied by Howland (1957:11).

Table 3

Percentage Increase by Region in gross value of production in resource and manufacturing industries, 1926-53

	Resources Industries %	Secondary Manufacturing %
Maritime Provinces	69.0	31.0
Quebec	40.5	59.5
Ontario	28.5	71.5
Prairies Provinces	70.7	29.3
B.C.	74.7	25.3
Canada	43.2	56.8

Source: Calculated from various D.B.S. bulletings in Howland (1957,80).

in many cases with the direct assistance of the federal and provincial governments.[3] In this connection, the Gordon Commission found a 34 percent decline in the labour force of these branches of production in the decade leading up to its study, compared with a 23.7 percent decline for Canada as a whole (Howland, 1957:106). When added to the large numbers of workers who were expelled from declining manufacturing industries, the agricultural producers and workers dispossessed from their means of production and livelihood fuelled a massive outmigration, leading by 1951 to the loss of over 20 percent of the region's 1921 population (Howland, 1957:196-7).

But developments in subsequent years clearly indicate that this outmigration does not reflect so much a simple lack of capitalist development in the region's industries, as varying conditions of capitalist development. Rather, recent studies have drawn attention to developments associated with increasing levels of capitalist penetration: a growing differentiation of independent and capitalist producers, leading to a protracted—and losing—struggle of independent producers against expanding forms of monopoly capital; and the rapid and growing proletarianization of many direct producers, with their subsequent conversion into workers (in the industrial and service sectors of the region).

Thus Bryant Fairley (1983), in an analysis of post-Second World War developments in the Newfoundland fisheries similar to that of MacKay seventy years earlier, emphasizes the growth and increasing penetration of capitalism in the industry, with a growing tendency for capital to directly subsume the labour of the remaining producers. The "near-shore" sector of medium-sized boats is seen as an emergent capitalist sector of the fishery; declining numbers of fishers pursue the logic of independent production and the fishermen's union's struggle against big capital is seen as "populist" (enlisting the small independent fishers but in reality serving mainly the interests of small capitalist fishers). On this view, any potential for a politics of radical change and socialism is increasingly restricted to fish plant workers and crewmen working for wages.

In taking this position, Fairley took issue with a set of arguments advanced in the 1970s by exponents of what has been termed "Maritime Marxism" (Clow, 1984a). Members of this school have generally focused on the limits of capitalist development and the political and economic conditions associated with these limits. They argue that under regional conditions the monopoly form of capital confronts not only the successful resistance of independent producers but various structural obstacles to both the expansion of capital and the direct subsumption of labour. These obstacles (the capacity for self-exploitation, ground rent, the discrepancy between production time and labour time, etc.) are found in the harvesting or extraction sectors of agriculture and fisheries— and, to an extent, forestry and other resource industries. But, given both the low capacity of the Atlantic region's declining manufacturing industries to absorb labour, and the region's dependence on increasingly capital-intensive resource industries, they have a considerably greater regional impact.

These structural obstacles lie behind (and thus explain) the formation in the region of a distinctively variegated set of class relations and political struggles, formed under conditions both of capitalist development and the lack of it, including the formation of both a sizeable *semi*-proletariat, and politically significant scatterings of small- scale "independent" producers who are dependent on capital for their inputs and markets, (and in a growing number of agricultural sectors), for access to the means of production such as seed and harvesting machinery. In addition, many if not most of these small producers tend to calculate the return to their labour in wage-equivalent terms.[4] In effect, they constitute a distinct class, a form of proletariat with an antagonistic relationship to capital under the conditions of its regional expansion, and, arguably, with some potential for socialism in its populist if not statist form. Various authors in Brym and Sacouman (1979), myself included, argued this point.

This chapter expands on this line of thought in the context of the latest crisis in the conditions of capital accumulation. This crisis has given rise to a series of renewed efforts to restructure capital on a national scale, with a corresponding impact on the regional conditions of production and employment—and politics.

To put these developments in their context, various efforts by the federal government to provide the ideological and political conditions of the restructuring process will first be referred to. It will be argued that official government thinking, like orthodox Marxist thought, fails to provide an analysis that is adequate to the economic situation of so many producers and workers in the region or to their politics.

2. The regional problem and "official" thinking

The Royal Commission on the Economic Union and Development Prospects for Canada (Canada, 1985) begins its limited discourse on regional development by noting that "few of the issues in [its] mandate proved more perplexing," and that "relatively little is known about how and why regional economies grow" (Canada, 1985:111-198). "Many theories abound," the Report adds, "but none has gained wide acceptance." Although the point is debatable—the Commission's "canvas of the research community" excluded all those theories that connect the conditions of regional development to the dynamics of capital accumulation—the "regional problem" undoubtedly has been "a hornet's nest for [the] Commission as for governments" (199).

In the form that the Commission and various governments over the years have confronted it, "the regional problem" has various dimensions but is most often posed in terms of income and employment disparities. In these terms the problem has had a long history, dating back at least sixty years when relevant data were systematically collected for the first time and the first of several Royal Commissions (Canada, 1926) was set up to examine and report on "the economic problems of the Maritime provinces" ("Atlantic Canada" after 1949). Although there has been a slight narrowing of regional disparities in income and employment opportunities in the post Second World War period (see Tables 4 to 6), this is almost exclusively attributable to inter-regional income transfers by the federal state, which by 1981 accounted for 26 percent of total income for all individuals in Atlantic Canada (compared to 15 percent for Canada as a whole, and up from 17.8 percent in 1971), and federal government expenditures, which by 1981 accounted for over 80 percent of the Gross Provincial Product.[5]

Allowing for cyclical swings in production and periodic crises, the pattern of relatively lower incomes and higher rates of unemployment in the Maritime provinces and Newfoundland has resisted all attempts of the federal government over the past twenty years to change it. Tables 4 to 6 illustrate this point, as well as showing that the trend towards a narrowing of relative income shares stopped in the mid-1970s and that the disparity in employment opportunities worsened, and continues to worsen.

Before taking a closer look at the structural conditions and forces that underlie these trends, we will first review various efforts by state ideologists to conceptualize the problem. Key points of reference for these efforts are the Royal Commission on Canada's Economic Prospects (Canada, 1957) and the 1985 Royal Commission on the Economic Union and Development Prospects for Canada (Canada, 1985). A brief review of the thinking behind these two Royal Commissions is followed by an analysis of the way in which the recent world-wide economic crisis has led to another restructuring of certain forms of capital in the Atlantic region, with a corresponding (although as yet unanalyzed) impact on the regional conditions of production and politics.

The Gordon Commission's Solution
In 1951, per capita earned incomes in the Atlantic Provinces averaged 52 percent of those in Ontario (Howland, 1957:157). The Gordon

Table 4
Provincial distribution of gross value added, 1890-1910, and personal income, 1927-1983, Canada (As a percentage of the national total)

Province	1890	1910	1926	1931	1936	1941	1946	1951	1956	1961	1966	1971	1976	1980	1983	Change 1926-83
Newfoundland	—	—	—	—	—	—	—	1.2	1.4	1.5	1.5	1.5	1.7	1.5	1.6	—
P.E.I.	1.8	0.8	0.5	0.4	0.5	0.4	0.4	0.4	0.4	0.3	0.3	0.3	0.4	0.4	0.4	-0.1
Nova Scotia	8.1	5.6	3.7	3.8	3.9	3.9	4.2	3.1	3.1	3.1	2.8	2.8	2.8	2.8	2.8	-0.9
New Brunswick	6.2	3.7	2.7	2.6	2.7	2.5	2.9	2.5	2.3	2.2	2.1	2.1	2.2	2.1	2.1	-0.6
Quebec	26.3	23.2	23.3	26.3	26.0	25.0	24.0	24.3	24.6	26.0	25.8	24.8	25.2	24.9	24.2	+0.9
Ontario	49.3	41.1	38.3	42.3	41.3	42.6	38.4	38.8	39.7	40.6	40.5	41.8	39.3	38.4	38.7	+0.4
Manitoba	3.8	6.5	7.3	6.1	6.0	5.9	6.0	5.6	5.1	4.8	4.4	4.3	4.2	3.9	3.9	-3.4
Saskatchewan	1.2	5.9	8.8	4.0	4.9	4.6	6.5	6.3	5.1	3.6	4.4	3.4	4.0	3.7	3.7	-5.1
Alberta	—	4.8	7.3	5.5	5.4	5.5	7.0	7.4	7.3	7.3	7.3	7.5	8.2	9.7	10.2	+2.9
British Columbia	3.3	8.1	7.9	8.6	9.2	8.8	9.6	9.9	10.5	10.3	10.5	11.0	11.7	12.3	12.0	+4.1
Yukon & N.W. Terr.	—	—	—	—	—	—	—	0.1	0.1	0.2	0.2	0.3	0.3	0.3	0.3	—
Canada	100.0	100.0	100.0	100.0	100.0	100.0	100.0	100.0	100.0	100.0	100.0	100.0	100.0	100.0	100.0	

Source: Statistics Canada, Provincial Economic Accounts, for 1926-1983 data, and Allan Green, Regional Aspects of Canada's Economic Growth, 1971, University of Toronto Press for 1890-1910 data.

Table 5

Personal income per capita, by province, 1926-1983
(relative to the national average: Canada = 100)

Province	1926	1931	1936	1941	1946	1951	1956	1961	1966	1971	1976	1980	1983
Newfoundland	—	—	—	—	—	48.2	53.5	58.2	59.9	63.6	68.5	64.0	67.6
P.E.I	56.1	51.4	55.6	46.9	58.2	54.4	58.7	58.8	60.1	63.7	68.6	71.0	74.3
Nova Scotia	67.8	75.9	79.6	77.1	85.9	69.1	71.9	77.5	74.8	77.4	78.8	79.1	80.4
New Brunswick	64.8	67.2	67.4	63.9	75.2	67.0	65.9	67.8	68.9	72.2	75.6	71.1	74.2
Quebec	84.6	94.9	92.1	86.6	81.5	83.9	86.1	90.1	89.0	88.8	93.0	94.5	92.5
Ontario	114.4	127.9	125.5	129.4	115.7	118.3	117.8	118.3	116.9	117.0	109.0	107.0	109.2
Manitoba	108.4	90.7	92.4	92.8	102.9	100.8	96.9	94.3	91.9	94.0	93.7	89.5	93.0
Saskatchewan	101.8	44.9	58.0	59.3	96.1	107.1	93.5	70.8	92.9	80.3	99.6	91.0	93.7
Alberta	113.7	77.9	76.3	80.0	107.8	111.0	104.6	100.0	100.0	98.9	102.6	111.6	108.4
British Columbia	122.1	129.9	131.9	120.9	114.9	119.2	121.1	114.9	115.9	109.0	109.1	111.3	106.0
Yukon & Northwest Terr.	—	—	—	—	—	86.7	129.8	96.6	80.7	86.8	91.9	102.9	105.9

Source: Statistics Canada, Provincial Economic Accounts

Table 6
Rates of unemployment by province

Year	Nfld.	P.E.I.	N.S.	N.B.	Quebec	Ontario	Manitoba	Sask.	Alberta	B.C.	Canada
1966	5.8	—	4.7	5.3	4.1	2.6	2.8	1.5	2.5	4.6	3.4
1967	5.9	—	4.9	5.2	4.6	3.2	3.0	1.7	2.7	5.1	3.8
1968	7.1	—	5.1	5.7	5.6	3.6	3.9	2.4	3.3	5.9	4.5
1969	7.4	—	4.9	6.7	6.1	3.2	3.2	3.2	3.4	5.0	4.4
1970	7.3	—	5.3	6.3	7.0	4.4	5.3	4.2	5.1	7.7	5.7
1971	8.4	—	7.0	6.1	7.3	5.4	5.7	3.5	5.7	7.2	6.2
1972	9.2	—	7.0	7.0	7.5	5.0	5.4	4.4	5.6	7.8	6.2
1973	10.0	—	6.6	7.7	6.8	4.3	4.6	3.5	5.3	6.7	5.5
1974	13.0	—	6.8	7.5	6.6	4.4	3.6	2.8	3.5	6.2	5.3
1975	14.0	8.0	7.7	9.8	8.1	6.3	4.5	2.9	4.1	8.5	6.9
1976	13.3	9.6	9.5	11.0	8.7	6.2	4.7	3.9	4.0	8.6	7.1
1977	15.5	9.8	10.6	13.2	10.3	7.0	5.9	4.5	4.5	8.5	8.1
1978	16.2	9.8	10.5	12.5	10.9	7.2	6.5	4.9	4.7	8.3	8.3
1979	15.1	11.2	10.1	11.1	9.6	6.5	5.3	4.2	3.9	7.6	7.4
1980	13.3	10.6	9.7	11.0	9.8	6.8	5.5	4.4	3.7	6.8	7.5
1981	13.9	11.2	10.2	11.5	10.3	6.6	5.9	4.7	3.8	6.7	7.5
1982	16.8	12.9	13.2	14.0	13.8	9.8	8.5	6.2	7.7	12.1	11.0
1983	18.3	12.2	13.2	14.8	13.9	10.4	9.4	7.4	10.8	13.8	11.9
1984	20.5	12.3	13.1	14.9	12.8	9.1	8.3	8.0	11.2	14.7	11.3
1985	21.3	12.9	13.8	15.2	11.8	8.0	8.1	8.1	10.1	14.2	10.5
1986	20.0	13.0	13.4	14.4	11.0	7.0	7.7	7.7	9.8	12.6	9.6

Source: based on data from Statistics Canada, *Historical Labour Force Statistics* (various issues)

Commission attributed the source of this disparity to four factors: the size of the labour force relative to the total population, the relative intensity in the use of labour-power as measured by the number of weeks worked per annum by part-time workers, the distribution of occupational and industrial categories, and the rates of earnings.[6]

In the Commission's view these four factors together accounted for the observed disparity in earned income. However, as the MacDonald Commission would note thirty years later, to list the core factors of income disparities is not to explain the problem. To do so (to identify the major structural source of these disparities) the Gordon Commission focused on differences in productivity, as measured by the net value of production (or value added) per worker. In 1953, the productivity of workers in the Atlantic provinces was 52 percent of that of Ontario workers, which corresponded precisely to the disparity in income (Howland, 1957:171). The productivity gap was particularly pronounced in agriculture, forestry and fishing, which together accounted for 56.1 percent of gross production and 26.8 percent of the labour force in the region.

This difference in productivity was reflected in the regional share in Canada's net value of production and total employment. Whereas Atlantic Canada's share in manufacturing was 2.4 percent of net value and 3.1 percent of employment, the comparable figures for agriculture were 3.6 percent and 6.4 percent, and for fishing 47.7 percent and 59.9 percent (Howland, 42). This significant productivity gap not only reflected a significant under-capitalization of Maritime farms and other production units, and a pronounced tendency to retain labour, but it pointed towards what the Commission regarded as the most striking feature of the regional economy, namely "the disproportionately large number of people engaged in marginal or submarginal activities in these provinces" (Howland, 5-6). And these figures on the marginally employed excluded the large numbers of people who had been compelled to abandon agriculture or fishing altogether in search of wage-labour employment in Central Canada.

The Gordon Commission's solution to the disparity problem took two forms. First, it identified the slow rate of capital investment in the region as a major problem. Over the years studied by the Commission (1946-1953) the region attracted on a per capita basis only one-half to one-quarter as much new capital as was invested in Ontario. Per capita investment in manufacturing was only 38.4 percent of the national average (versus 143.2 percent for Ontario). And in the primary resource-extraction sector, the per-capita rate of capital formation was only 54.3 percent of the national average (compared to 253 percent for the prairies). In this context, the only "long-term and ultimately effective solution" for the region's problems was to create conditions which would attract capital to its resource industries and "to improve the environment in which capital has to operate" (Howland, 1957:6,192).

As the Gordon Commission saw it, the trend towards the concentration of manufacturing in the more populous areas of Ontario and Quebec (which together received 80 percent of all new manufacturing plants over the 1946-1953 period) was inevitable and necessary, the result of a drive to achieve cost efficiencies in the national market (Howland, 1857:141). As for Atlantic Canada, its only future was a "further development of the resource industries." This would entail improved productivity, requiring increased capitalization and rationalization; that is, the replacement of labour with capital. There was already an exceptionally low rate of labour force participation (48.6 percent versus 56.2 percent for Ontario) and a loss of population through outmigration. Notwithstanding this, the Commission argued the need for greater "flexibility in the labour force, including job transfers and in some instances geographic relocation" (Howland, 1957:192).

This was the nub of the Gordon Commission's solution: to create and improve the workings of the market so that the region's producers and workers could adjust better to the requirements of capital organized on a national basis. This solution would soon be tried by the Newfoundland government in its program to resettle the inhabitants of outport fishing communities in various urban centres, and to encourage their outmigration.

Closing the circle: The MacDonald Commission
In November 1982 the Federal Government appointed a Royal Commission, chaired by Donald MacDonald, a well-known Liberal and former Minister of Finance in Pierre Trudeau's government, to inquire into and report on the "long-term economic potential, prospects and challenges facing the Canadian nation and its respective regions." In August, 1985 this Commission submitted its three-volume 699 page report, including twenty-four pages on regional economic development (Canada, 1985 (Vol. III):198-221).

To provide the context for this Commission's view of regional economic development it is necessary to make reference to federal regional policies with respect to the "regional problem" over the previous twenty years. The federal government's basic response to this problem had been a program of equalization payments introduced in 1957 and set up as a comprehensive regional development program in 1967. Soon thereafter (in 1968), the Department of Regional Economic Expansion was established and the Unemployment Insurance Program was revised (in 1971) with a significant regional effect: a shorter waiting period and larger entitlements in places with lagging employment rates. Also, in this period most of the federal government's welfare-related income transfer programs took form. By 1985, over 40 percent of the gross provincial product was based on such transfers (Statistics Canada, 1985:14, 16).

What has been the impact of these and other federal programs designed to provide "development" in depressed regions and to lessen regional disparities in income and employment opportunities? It can be summed up in one word: negligible. The most that can be said of the federal government's regionally specific development programs is that, in the words of the MacDonald Commission, "[W]e may have prevented the less-developed regions from falling further behind." As noted above, although the rankings of particular provinces have occasionally altered, the general pattern in the regional distribution of income and employment opportunities has changed little over the sixty years for which data are available. In 1981 Newfoundland's per capita market income was only 53.8 percent of the national average, while Alberta's was 114.1 percent (see Table 5 above). If we take into account government transfers to individuals, the poorest province stood (and still stands) at 65 percent of the national average, while the richest stands at 110 percent. If we further add the effects of income tax, the disparity would be further narrowed, but not significantly.

Why have regional disparities in income and other measures of disparity resisted all of the programs introduced and implemented by the federal government over twenty years? The MacDonald Commission identified two factors. One was regional differentials in wage rates and employment rates, which, according to the Commission, account for about one-half of the observed income disparity—paralleling precisely the conclusion of the Gordon Commission thirty years earlier. The remaining differential reflects the smaller proportion of people actually working; that is, the lower participation rate which is widely (and correctly) viewed as an indicator of under-employment or disguised unemployment. In 1985 the participation rate in Atlantic Canada remains eight percentage points below the national average, virtually the same as in 1957.

One obvious cause for regional disparities in per capita income is that occupational structures vary by region. As the MacDonald Report sagely observed, "fishermen do not make as much as corporate vice-presidents," and there are relatively more fishers in Nova Scotia and relatively more corporate executives in Ontario. However, like the earlier Gordon Commission, the MacDonald Commission acknowledged that earnings per job, rather than differences in the types of job available, account for most of the income differential. The explanation for *this* is a gap in "productivity," reflecting the lower level of capitalist development in Atlantic Canada and other hinterland regions. The identified conditions of lower productivity in the Atlantic region are (a) lower capital-to-labour ratios, (b) fewer workers in prime age groups, (c) less education of the work force, (d) slower adoption of new technologies and poorer management, (e) smaller urban centres, and (f) greater distance from important markets (MacDonald, 203). These factors of regional disparity are virtually identical to those identified by the Gordon Commission twenty-eight years earlier and by the Economic Council of Canada in its various studies and reports over the years (Economic Council of Canada, 1977; 1980).

However, as already observed, the Commissioners recognized that to list these conditions of regional disparity is not to explain the problem. To do so, they turned to ideas associated most often with Thomas Courchene (1978) and other neo- conservative economists to conclude that regional disparities in per capita income and employment opportunities are the result of distortions created by well-intentioned but misguided economic policies—minimum wage legislation, financial aid to declining industries, unemployment insurance and other forms of transfer payments to governments, businesses and individuals (Canada, 1985:213). What such transfers do, the Commissioners argued, is send out false signals to economic actors, blocking adjustment in the form of restructuring, outmigration, or a fall in real wages. According to this analysis, unemployed or marginally employed individuals should migrate or accept lower paying jobs. Without such adjustments, the region cannot hope to regain its former economic standing, as its wage rates will remain out of line relative to its labour productivity (or the locational characteristics of the region). Transfer payments not only inhibit mobility but they support unviable economic operations and discourage workers from accepting lower paying jobs, leading them to either price themselves out of the market or permitting them to remain unemployed (Polese, 1985:22). In other words, the problem of high unemployment and low incomes is the product of inflexible labour markets and government interference, a point made by Thirsk (1973:129) and other neo-classical economists on whom the MacDonald Commission relied. The reliance by individuals and provincial governments on these transfers has created what Thomas Courchene (1978; *interalia*) has termed "transfer dependency," a vicious circle in which "economic misfortune begets transfers which, in turn, further poor economic policies which beget further economic misfortune" (Canada, 1985, Vol. III:213-214). This situation, the Commissioners add, "causes increasing expense to the economic region [Canada] as a whole." To relieve this national burden and resolve the regional problem the Commissioners recommended the elimination of all such inappropriate incentives, to both facilitate the redeployment of labour from declining industries in depressed communities to expanding sectors of the economy, and recommended the government to "generously subsidise any large-scale exit from a community of workers and their families" (Canada, 1985, Vol. II:215).

The restructuring of capital and the regional crisis

Both the 1957 and 1985 Royal Commissions regarded the mobility of labour and the relocation of workers and producers to centres of capital accumulation as the solution to the regional problem. On this analysis, state intervention, in the form of Unemployment Insurance payments and other transfers, has worked to reinforce "the concentration of seasonal industries" associated with conditions of low productivity and marginality (Cousineau, 1979; cited by Canada, 1985, Vol. III:214).

Some other studies suggest that this view is partially correct. The sociologist Robert Hill (1983), among others, has found that Unemployment Insurance provides a critical material support for households in small fishing communities which, it is estimated, sustain more than one-quarter of the total population in Atlantic Canada and over 50 percent in Newfoundland (Canada, Task Force on Atlantic Fisheries, 1982:64,70). However, a closer look at this question suggests that the role of Unemployment Insurance payments is more complex (and different) than suggested by the neo-liberals and neo-conservatives. For one thing, it is closely tied to a complex system designed to reproduce the critically important relations of independent and capitalist production in the fisheries and other regional industries characterized by seasonal production cycles and other discontinuities in the production process. Other elements of this system include wage labour, other forms of transfer payments and vestiges of subsistence production, which all help to reproduce and maintain an adequate supply of labour-power and other material conditions for both independent and capitalist production.

Table 7 provides some data on this point, with reference to the 34,316 households in Atlantic Canada which in 1981 had at least one member involved in commercial fishing. What these data show is that wage labour is critical for maintaining the viability of independent production in the fishing industry. In 1981 over 75 percent of part-time fishers relied on wage labour, working part of the year for wages in construction work, processing plants, logging, mechanical, maintenance or teaching (Canada, Task Force on Atlantic Fisheries, 1982:54). This reliance on wage labour is particularly pronounced among part-time fishers, most of whom are former full-timers who turned to other sources of employment as the only way of ensuring that they could continue to own the means of independent production, and sustain their families. As noted by the federal Task Force on Atlantic Fisheries in 1982, without wage labour the majority of East Coast fishers and their households would fall below the recognized poverty lines (1982:58). What the Task Force could have added is that most of these fishers would also have lost their remaining property in the means of production and hence fallen fully into the proletariat.

Table 7

Income sources of fishers and their households, Atlantic Canada, 1981

	Full-time	Part-time
Households with members who fished commercially	20,028	14,288
Fishing household members	84,558	56,663
Active producers (by use of commercial licence)	23,434	17,445
% households with fish plant workers	21.5%	18.5%
Av. weeks of fish activity	23.5 wks	11.8 wks.
Av weeks of plant employment	2.5 wks	15.3 wks
Av. individual annual income by source		
• **fishing**	$11,907	$2,783
• **non-fishing wage-labour**	$927	$2,910
• **UI**	$2,466	$1,483
• **Other transfers**	$444	$723
• **All sources**	$15,791	$11,182
% of fishers receiving UI	83%	52%
Total household incomes (before taxes)	$21,900	17,607

Source: Kirby (1982: 48, 53-4, 61, 63, 66, 69).

As for Unemployment Insurance payments, they are more significant for full-time fishers, for whom they represent on average 16 percent of total income. The average part-time fisher works for wages 15.2 weeks a year, fishes for 11.8 weeks, and collects unemployment insurance for 18 weeks (Task Force on Atlantic Fisheries, 1982:61). Wage labour, however, makes a larger contribution to household income than unemployment insurance, and only 52 percent of part-time fishers receive any unemployment insurance at all. Nonetheless, the income received from Unemployment Insurance not only keeps many independent production units viable but it supports market prices for the product. This is well understood both by fishers in the United States who produce for the same competitive markets, and by the MacDonald Commissioners in their recognition that in addition to low-income families the biggest losers in the continental free-trade regime which they recommend (and which the Mulroney-led government is pushing as a "historic effort to end unemployment and poverty in the regions") would be "workers in peripheral regions or peripheral jobs."

In writing of "peripheral jobs" the MacDonald Commission had in mind the seasonal or occasional producers and workers in fishing, farming, fish processing plants and pulp and paper mills, who now outnumber those who harvest the product. These are precisely the industries on which the Gordon Commission in 1957 pinned any hopes for the region's future—its capacity for growth and development—and they involve the region's leading manufacturing industries. In the fishing sector, processing plants constitute the largest source of non-fishing employment for members of the fisher households, affording as many jobs (47,000) as fishing itself (Canada, Task Force on Atlantic Fisheries, 1982:18, Table 4). About one-half of the region's 1,339 small fishing communities have a single-sector economy, with fishing and processing plant employment occupying 30 percent or more of the labour force (1982:70,72). About 20 percent of all fisher households in 1981 had one or more members working in processing plants, most of which were small or medium size in terms of the labour and capital employed (on this more generally see Barrett and Apostle, 1985). A typical employment pattern in these communities is for the male member(s) of the household to be engaged in the harvesting sector, either as an independent producer or a worker in the offshore, and for the women, most often wives, to work in the local fish processing plants. The hourly wage rates in fish plants are significantly lower than those in the other manufacturing industries in the region.

In the other productive sectors of the regional economy, especially forestry and agriculture, similar conditions exist. The MacDonald Commission, and the government, envisaged their being replaced, through outmigration on the one hand, and capitalist rationalisation and centralization on the other, by a "purer" and more productive regional capitalist economy. The question is, however, whether the regional political forces mobilized by the previous processes of regional capitalist development, are compatible with this project or point rather in some quite different direction.

3. The logic of regional capitalist development

The capitalist mode of production is based on the conversion of the means of production into capital and the transformation of direct producers into a population compelled to exchange labour power for a living wage. Once production is organized on this basis, and using the production methods of modern industry, the system becomes subject to a twofold tendency towards, on the one hand, the concentration and centralization of capital and, on the other, the growth of the wage labour force together with its reserve armies of surplus labour. This process is well advanced in Canada, capital having fully penetrated and to varying degrees directly subsumed the labour of the direct producers in all branches of production across the country. The peripheral regions of the country, although they are generally more heavily dependent on branches of production such as agriculture and fishing, which for largely structural reasons have been able to resist capitalist development to a significant degree, are by no means immune to this process.

The central dynamic of this process is the substitution of capital for labour, reflected in the tendency towards a rise in the organic composition of capital and, thus, under normal conditions (of class struggle) that militate against an equivalent rise in the rate of surplus value, towards a falling rate of average profit.[7] The conditions of this dynamic (the transformation of variable into constant capital) are not automatically generated nor easily come by. They require a periodic if not a constant restructuring and devaluation of capital. As capital is periodically restructured under crisis conditions (of either over-capitalization or over-production) it expands or moves into certain branches of production and withdraws from others, converting a part of the working class into a relative surplus population.

Most of the conditions for capital accumulation are normally secured by political action at the national level, but there is invariably a regional dimension to the process, particularly as it relates to the concentration and centralization of capital, as well as the formation of a relative surplus population. It is in this connection that Ernest Mandel, among others, argues that "unevenness of development between different parts of a single country is an essential precondition for capital accumulation" (1968:373). From this perspective "regional problems" are actually among the preconditions for accelerated accumulation and, as a consequence, rapid growth in areas where accumulation is concentrated. In periods of recession and crisis, such as 1981-83, in order to offset a system-wide fall in average profits, and to reconstitute a reserve army of labour, *new* regional problems are generated through the "devalorisation" of capital (the elimination of old productive capacity) that is required for renewed accumulation to occur. The devalorisation of capital in some regions, increasing regional unemployment, helps to create the conditions whereby the national rate of profit can begin to rise again. It is in this context that one should view the long-term and continuing trend towards lower per capita income and high unemployment rates in the Atlantic region (now hovering at around 14 percent for the region as a whole, and still rising, while falling in the rest of the country), as well as the specific forms and conditions of proletarianization and semi-proletarianization that we find in the Atlantic region. The positions taken by the Economic Council of Canada over the years (see, for example, 1980) and the recent Forget Commission can be viewed in a similar light, as can the recommendation of the MacDonald Commission that unemployment insurance should be abolished and replaced with a guaranteed minimum income set at 35 percent below the presently recognized poverty line.

In the face of declining profits it is vital that the conditions of profitability be recreated. Capital that is not reproduced at or above the average rate of profit ends up being wholly or partially destroyed; and, as the MacDonald Commission itself recognized, it is in "peripheral regions" that this tends to occur most.

During periods of crisis, as in the early 1980s, accumulation becomes more difficult and the rate of profit falls, more precipitously in some sectors than others. This is why, even with wage rates considerably below the national average, the MacDonald Commission can write of workers in depressed regions "pricing themselves out of the (national) labour market," and as needing to accept a lower living standard—or migrate.

The tendency to transform variable into constant capital—to replace workers by machines—is a law of capitalist development. The stages of this process stand out clearly in the region's history and can be traced in various phases of accumulation of capital in agriculture, the fisheries, and other sectors of the economy, and in the corresponding displacement of labour from these branches of production and the generation of a relative surplus population. Elsewhere (Veltmeyer, 1979) I have delineated some of the conditions of existence and growth of this surplus population in Atlantic Canada, which has the practical effect of intensifying the competition for employment as well as disciplining labour by maintaining a steady downward pressure on wages. This process has been studied extensively in the context of various developing societies; but it also applies to advanced capitalist countries, particularly with respect to peripheral regions such as Atlantic Canada (Veltmeyer, 1979, 1983). Indeed, the way in which a relative surplus population is (necessarily) created may very well explain the long-term tendency towards low per capita income and the high rates of unemployment and outmigration in certain regions, as well as the persistence of independent commodity and subsistence production and the persistence of small-scale capitals in the productive sectors of the regional economy (see Barrett and Apostle, 1985).

In the theory advanced by Marx, Lenin and others in the same tradition, the development of capitalism will destroy the capital of existing, small-scale (independent and capitalist) producers who cannot compete with the production methods of modern industry; the latter methods invariably become "the generally, socially predominant form of production" (Marx, 1967:478,586-7). As noted, this process is quite advanced in Canada, particularly in the manufacturing sector wherein capitalist production has become heavily concentrated and centralized, having extinguished all other forms of production. However, in primary resource activities such as farming, fishing, and logging, which in the 1981 Census employed over 40 percent of the Atlantic region's labour force in the goods-producing sector, as well as providing the inputs for the region's leading manufacturing industries (which employ a further 25 percent of the goods-producing labour force), the situation is quite different. Despite the dramatic expansion of capital in these sectors since 1946, and a correspondingly dramatic exit of independent producers and a decline in units of production, the vast majority of producers still rely on their own labour and, in the case of farming, that of their families or households. On the basis of available statistics it is difficult to gauge accurately the size of the wage labour force in the harvesting sector of these industries, but it is still small relative to the number of independent and small capitalist producers who in 1981 totalled 82,905 out of a labour force of 941,110. In the processing sectors of these industries, moreover, there is a proliferation of small and medium capitals as well as a cluster of strongly positioned, large capitals that rely on wage labour.[8]

Because of their scale of operation and market position, these large corporate or co-operative forms of capital account for a disproportionately large share of total production. However, the majority of producers (loggers, fishers and farmers) are still independent, small- and medium-scale operators of their own means of production. They are not homogeneous in terms of their production relations. In terms of the labour they employ, the capital assets they control, and the fact that they tend to valorize factors of production, including their own labour, in terms of market prices, a small but significant number of farm operators and fishers have become capitalists (9.5 percent in one estimate).[9] Then there is the petty bourgeois segment of independent producers (8.4 percent of the total by the same estimate) who with direct access to a valuable resource or efficient technology, and with effective market organizations, are able to realize the full value of ground rent.[10] But the largest number of producers are small operators who both exploit themselves, valorize their labour in wage-equivalent terms, and are proletarianized to various degrees through pre-harvest contractual arrangements or sale of their labour part-year or part-time. We have noted the reliance of fishers on wage labour. Among farmers the situation is similar. Well over 50 percent of all farm households and 36.3 percent of all farm operators were involved in off-farm labour as an alternative to abandoning their property. As in the fisheries, this propensity towards off-farm labour increases the lower the sales or output of the farm (Gillis, 1985:114-119).

In effect, we can identify here a sizeable semi-proletariat, individuals who manage to retain control of their means of production and manage to secure the conditions of their existence as independent commodity producers by resorting to wage labour (Sacouman, 1980). A semi-proletariat in this form is a characteristic feature of the transition towards capitalist development, but in the context of Atlantic Canada and in peripheral regions more generally, it is clearly more than a transitory phenomenon. Even though it is clear for many direct producers that off-farm or off-boat labour may be the first step towards the final loss of the farm (or boat and gear), partial proletarianization has been a fact of life for generations of small-producers and their families (Sacouman, 1980).

Under prevailing economic conditions, commodity producers in agriculture, fisheries, and logging are thus subsumed to various degrees under the logic of capital. Not only are the conditions of their production capitalized to an increasing degree (and thus subject to the forces of concentration, centralization and scale economies) and a propensity towards crisis, but independent commodity producers generally occupy a vulnerable position *vis a vis* the complex of capitalist institutions that supply finance and inputs of capital goods (machinery, gear, fertilizers, boats, etc.) and that dominate their markets. The apparent reason why capital has not directly subsumed the labour of so many "independent" producers is the considerable capacity of these producers for self-exploitation—their readiness to yield up absolute surplus value out of their own and their families' labour as well as rent in their property. Under the conditions of their dependence on financial, commercial and industrial forms of capital, simple commodity producers are effectively dispossessed of surplus value without losing their means of production, and without the real subsumption of their labour under capital (i.e. without a technical transformation of the work they do). The family farm and the inshore seasonal fishery have survived and have resisted the real subsumption of labour because of the willingness of their operators, as a condition for retaining at least their nominal independence, to accept a lower economic reward than their capital could earn elsewhere.

An examination of their recent history shows that many of these small-scale producers constitute an important ever larger part of what Marx termed a *latent* (or potential) surplus population. Every area of the regional economy—agriculture, industry, services, etc.—contains a similar mass of people liable to be forced out of work by the continued concentration and centralization of capital. The recent closure of fish processing plants in Newfoundland under conditions of crisis is a clear case in point. And, as the Economic Council of Canada observes, with respect to Newfoundland, if fish plant wages were to "go too high, a massive introduction of fish sorting and fish filleting machines [would] enable [and lead to] the wholesale layoff of some 5,000 to 10,000 workers, many of whom ... [are] with no alternative [sources of] employment" (1980:17).

When the tendency to expel workers is accompanied by a countervailing tendency to attract and absorb them (though for many this means migration), we have a second form of relative overpopulation—a *floating* surplus population. This part of the industrial reserve army (commonly designated the "technologically," "seasonally" or "functionally" unemployed) includes those most disposed to seek a reconnection to capital through migration. Movements of this floating surplus population are difficult to trace but they are reflected in the observed shifts in the pattern of outmigration from the Atlantic provinces to Ontario, where accumulations of manufacturing capital are most heavily concentrated. When these capitals expand, as in the early to mid-1970s, they attract large numbers of Maritimers and Newfoundlanders in search of productive employment. However, when these capitals contract, as in the 1981-3 crisis, the pattern of migration is reversed, with the Atlantic region not only retaining its existing surplus population but having to absorb large numbers of returning migrants (Economic Council of Canada, 1980; 1981).

A third so-called *stagnant* form of relative surplus population includes all variants of sub- and semi-employed workers—those sectors of the working class that endure the worst labour conditions, often on the basis of archaic production methods. While many of these workers work very long hours, wages in this category are always below average. This is the poorest stratum of the active work force in whatever sphere of production.

The rural petty bourgeoisie, as a class, may be regarded as furnishing part of both the latent and the stagnant surplus population. The constant process of attraction and repulsion of workers by capital permits and even encourages the persistence of pre-capitalist or non-capitalist production. In the long run, however, members of this class are increasingly subjected to wage labour and drawn into the reserve army of labour for capitalist production. At the same time the prevailing conditions of work (minimal earnings, unstable employment, etc.) make a large part of this group part of the stagnant surplus population.

This "stagnant" surplus population is also "latent" because of the low organic composition of capital in the sectors in which it is employed. They are destined, in the long run, to be eliminated or move on to higher levels of technological organization. They represent what the MacDonald Commission has labelled "peripheral jobs and peripheral workers." The only long-run mechanism for their survival must be the movement of capital to these reserves of low-cost, non-unionized labour, or the attraction of such reserves (as in much of Atlantic Canada's history) to concentrations of capital. At the same time, frequent withdrawals or recombinations of this kind of capital regularly throws workers from this sector into the "floating" reserve.

Within the floating reserve population, however, the dominant tendency is towards expulsion, not attraction, creating a reserve of unemployed whose prospect of being absorbed by any future expansion of capital is increasingly remote, *even* by means of migration. Writers in different contexts have referred to this surplus as a marginal mass, a growing mass of unemployed that augurs a deep crisis (Quijano, 1974; Sunkel, 1973; Nun, 1969). This marginal mass, having "no place in the productive structure or lack[ing] the capacity to become adapted to it," can no longer function as a labour reserve, having lost "in a permanent and not a transitory way the possibility of being absorbed into the hegemonic levels of production" (Quijano, 1974:148). It is these workers that are largely buried in the regional statistics on chronic unemployment and underemployment, as well as cycles of rural poverty.

To resolve these problems, it is not possible to generate conditions of economic growth in the region by providing incentives to capital. Nor will they be resolved through income transfer or maintenance programs, or further state expenditures, which already account for an astonishing 80 percent of the GDP in the Atlantic region. Even less will the problem of regional disparities in the conditions of employment and income be resolved through the neo-classical policies proposed by the MacDonald Commission and pursued by the Mulroney government in Ottawa. A solution to the regional problem can only come from a clear understanding of the forces of uneven capitalist development, and from actions in support of various struggles to break with the capitalist system and pursue a socialist path.

4. Responses to the Crisis

The conditions of the crisis in the region are deeply rooted in the economic, social and cultural structures of dependent and peripheral capitalist development. Workers and primary producers in the region, especially in Newfoundland and Nova Scotia, have over the years engaged in a number of struggles against these conditions, most notably in the 1920s and 1930s when the contradictions of the capitalist system spawned a movement of producers and workers that was oriented towards a radical break with capitalism. But although this struggle did force concessions from the state, softening the effects of capitalist development, the workers, independent producers and other social forces mobilized in the struggle against capital were ultimately defeated. In the wake of this defeat, and with a growing subordination of workers and producers in the region to capital, the mobilization of various potential forces for change has become more difficult.

Under crisis conditions, with staggering rates of unemployment and a mounting threat of further proletarianization, producers have been effectively demobilized. If and when they organize for collective action capital decamps, or threatens to, as in the case of Michelin in Nova Scotia in 1986. Whenever producers in the region have attempted to bargain over the prices of their fish, farm produce, or wood products, capital either turns for assistance to normally compliant provincial governments, or plays off producers against each other.

In spite of the odds, producers have won significant local victories over the years. But if they are to achieve radical structural change, workers and producers in the region have to build a more powerful and cohesive movement with an overtly political agenda. As we have noted, existing state policies and programs clearly do not address these structural forces that underlie the conditions of regional dependency and underdevelopment; nor can they change conditions that are widespread under capitalism but most acutely experienced as a "regional problem." Short of continued outmigration and a massive dislocation, the only solution is a mobilization that unites workers, producers and other groups subject to the vicissitudes of capitalist development as it affects the Atlantic region. Unless such a movement is formed, and available forces for structural change can be mobilized, the region is doomed to relive its past under even worse conditions.

Notes

1. Barrett (1980), Clow (1984a; 1984b) and Cannon (1984) provide brief summaries of these debates in both the radical (Marxist) and liberal (orthodox) traditions of Maritime Political Economy. For an extended review of the latter tradition see Mansell and Copithorne (1984).

2. The 1920s witnessed a resurgence of working-class organization and struggle, and represented the high water mark in the history of radical politics in the Maritimes. Canadian historians generally have ignored or downplayed the significance of this radical politics, and indeed very few studies on it

have been published even today. Reilly (1980), Frank (1976), and Morton (1986) provide systematic studies of particular struggles in this period while Burrill (1985) provides a glimpse into some of the debates.

3. In line with the Gordon Commission's recommendations the federal government in the 1960s enacted legislation, such as the Agricultural and Rural Development Act (1968), and instituted programs to develop natural resource industries other than farming, with the specific aim of absorbing surplus farm labour. In the case of Newfoundland, the federal and provincial governments introduced various programs designed to rationalize labour in the fisheries and to promote the outmigration towards the expanding sectors of the national economy in the central provinces. From 1966 to 1970 alone over 2,500 persons were relocated from outport fishing communities in various urban centres in Newfoundland and elsewhere (Copes, 1972:185).

4. Because so many family farms today to all intents involve a capitalist form of production (see Friedmann, 1980; Hedley, 1981; Chevalier, 1982; and Murphy, 1983 and this volume), their operators generally are led to allocate scarce factors of production, both goods and labour, according to market values and to calculate the "opportunity costs" of labour in the same form. Accordingly, depending in part on the degree and form of reliance on wage labour (see Barrett, 1983), the direct producers are converted either into capitalists, petty bourgeois proprietor-operators, or a distinct class of petty commodity producers subject to proletarianization and, in a number of respects, constituting a particular form of proletariat (see Note 9 below).

5. This calculation is based on Statistics Canada accounting for "Government Final Demand Expenditures," which includes government expenditures on goods and services plus government fixed capital formation (Canada, Statistics Canada, 1986). According to these Provincial Economic Accounts data, in 1982 federal government spending on a flow-through basis accounted for the following percentage shares of the gross provincial product in the Atlantic provinces: 80.9 percent in Newfoundland, 80.7 percent in Nova Scotia, 71.9 percent in New Brunswick and 89.2 percent in Prince Edward Island. For Canada as a whole federal government spending on a flow-through basis accounted for 45.6 percent of the Gross National Product (Canada, Statistics Canada, Provincial Economic Accounts, 1983).

6. In this analysis (Howland, 1957:156-71), lower rates of participation in the labour force accounted for 29 percent of the income disparity, while regional differences in relative intensity in the use of labour-power (measured by weeks worked per annum of part-time workers) accounted for another 10 percent. This second factor reflected the region's relatively greater dependence on industries that have significant seasonal variations in production-time. Regional differences in occupational and industrial structures (27.5 percent of the labour force in Atlantic Canada was engaged or employed in the

resource-extraction sector versus 12 percent in Ontario) accounted for another 12 percent of the disparity, while regional differences in rates of earnings (wage rates in Atlantic Canada averaged 63 percent of those in Ontario) accounted for the remaining 49 percent.

7. On the various conditions of these dynamic tendencies see Marx, 1967 (Vol. I):772-81; (Vol. III):211-231.

8. The Task Force on Atlantic Fisheries (1982:14-15) calculated that in the Atlantic fisheries there were 8,300 vessels operating in the small-boat "inshore" accounting for 15 percent of the catch (landed value); 5,300 medium-sized vessels in the "near-shore," with 35 percent of the catch; and fewer than 150 large vessels with wage-labour crews in the offshore, almost exclusively owned by the "Big Five" corporations in the industry, and accounting for 45 percent of the catch. Similar levels of concentration can be found in virtually all sectors of agriculture, with the top 25 percent of all farmers accounting for 91 percent of gross sales in Nova Scotia, 87 percent in New Brunswick, and 78 percent in Prince Edward Island, as opposed to 74 percent for Canada as a whole. Farms in the Maritimes also exhibit considerably greater levels of concentration (and skewed distribution of sales) than farms in the rest of Canada (Ehrensaft and Bollman, 1983:13-15).

9. Ehrensaft and Bollman (1983:26) have constructed a six- category typology of paid labour utilization, based on number of persons hired on-farm yearly, that can be used as a rough measure of identifiable differences in production relations and thus the existence of different "classes" of producers. On the basis of this classification, with very rough assumptions, the clearly capitalist farmers (category one) are those who operate on a large-scale and employ 5 person-years of labour or more. Producers who employ between 2 and 5 person-years of labour tend to be in an intermediate class situation where they are still involved in direct production as well as management and supervision and able to realize fully ground rent from their property. The next three categories of producers—those who employ from one to two workers (the third category), those who work the farm with only family labour (the fourth category), and those who have no employees and work fewer than 97 days a year off-farm (the fifth category)— constitute the dominant class of petty commodity producers. The sixth category, those without employees who work for over 97 days a year, can be conceived of as a semi-proletariat.

10. For an extended analysis of ground rent as the structural basis of independent commodity production in the fisheries see Barrett (1983).

Chapter Five

Crisis and Response: Underdevelopment in the Fishery and the Evolution of the Maritime Fishermen's Union

Rick Williams with Gilles Theriault

WHEREAS it is understood that the inshore fishermen are being exploited and are being eliminated by the bourgeoisie.

WHEREAS it is understood that the fishermen's interests are opposed to those of the bourgeoisie (capitalists and their state).

WHEREAS it is understood that any collaboration with our exploiters is in complete opposition with our interest.

WHEREAS it is understood that the only gains we made with our exploiters were the result of long hard fought battles.

IT IS THEREFORE MOVED that we reject any collaboration with the capitalists and their State and that we develop a fighting spirit in our dealings with them.

(Il est proposé que l'on rejette toute forme de collaboration avec les capitalistes et leur état et qu'une attitude de lutte nous serve de ligne de conduite dans nos rapports avec les capitalistes, leur état et leurs représentants.)

— *A resolution passed at the second annual convention of the Maritime Fishermen's Union*

1. Introduction

This chapter examines the development of the Maritime Fishermen's Union (MFU) in relation to the changing conditions in the fishing industry in Atlantic Canada.[1] In terms of their expressed ideological positions, the leadership of the MFU in its early stages in the mid-1970s saw the organization as a militant class struggle union. They intended it to serve the interests of inshore fishers through mass mobilization, militant action, and direct confrontation with both the government and the fish companies.

No close observer could argue that the MFU has since abandoned mass mobilization and militant action. However, the union has in recent years involved itself in activities which were not anticipated at the outset and which do not always fit comfortably with the class-struggle rhetoric. "Orderly" collective bargaining of fish prices, direct involvement in marketing activities, partnership with the co-operative movement, and participation in government policy making resource management processes are key examples.

These changes in the policies and practices of the union make sense only in terms of the shifting ground of the struggle for basic survival in which inshore fishers are engaged. We need, therefore, to examine the internal and external forces which generate the many specific issues that the union grapples with on a day to day basis.

2. The shifting ground

The post-war period saw the gradual decline of the inshore fishery as population generally shifted away from rural areas and from primary industries. For those remaining in the industry, the longstanding problems of inadequate prices and unstable markets were compounded in the late 1960s by the expansion of the Canadian corporate offshore fleet (MacDonald, 1984:33-34). These large stern trawlers joined with the foreign fleets in the largely uncontrolled over-exploitation of the groundfish stocks (25-27).

The infrastructure for effective resource management by government was only beginning to be put in place in this period. Fisheries policy was heavily weighted towards development of the offshore fleets and large scale processing units (Barrett, 1984). The theory was that the development of the Atlantic Canadian fishing industry was being held back by the overabundance of small producers and processors. As a result, the returns to the industry were insufficient to capitalize the modernization that was needed for it to be able to participate on a competitive footing in the international marketplace (Canada, 1976).

The late 1960s and early 1970s saw the rapid expansion of a few large, integrated fish companies in the Maritimes. Numerous small processors were bought out or swallowed up, and everywhere small plants were closing as production was shifted to new plants in a few central locations.[2] Two dominant companies emerged from this process— H.B. Nickersons Ltd. and the much larger National Sea Products Ltd. (Barrett, 1977). In 1977, with the backing of the banks, Nickersons gained control over National Sea to create one vertically integrated fishing empire (Barss-Donham, 1981).

Much of this expansion was financed by government grants and loan arrangements.[3] Quotas and licenses were provided to the new offshore fleets without much regard for conservation or for negative impact on the inshore industry. Government policies generally reflected the views of mainstream economists that the inshore fishery was obsolete and should be closed down (Copes, 1978). This was the period when Premier Smallwood in Newfoundland allegedly told fishers to burn their boats and move to urban centres in search of stable industrial jobs (Matthews, 1983:Ch. 6).

These, then, were the problems inshore fishers found themselves confronting in the early 1970s. The offshore groundfish draggers and the herring seiners were flooding the markets with low-priced fish, while at the same time over-fishing the stocks on which the inshore fishery depended. The closure of many small, local fish plants reduced local markets, making fishers more dependent on a few large processing companies (Williams, 1978). Growing monopoly control added to the downward pressure on fish prices. New fisheries management systems being put in place by government generally favoured the centralized, corporate, offshore fishery (Barrett, 1984). These systems did not, however, impose any rational order on the very serious overfishing of the stocks that was being perpetrated by both the domestic and the foreign offshore fleets.

Beginning in Canso in 1969, a new generation of fishers' organizations began to emerge in response to the deepening crisis in the inshore fishery. It quickly became clear that many fishers and their families were prepared to fight hard and long to maintain their communities and their way of life. What they needed, however, was a form of organization which was capable of taking on the powerful forces arrayed against them. As will be shown below, this was achieved in the late 1970s with the emergence of the MFU.

Later in the decade another important shift took place. Romeo LeBlanc became the federal minister for fisheries, and with him came a greater openness to the pressures from fishers' organizations and from within his department for more effective resource management and planning measures (MacDonald, 1984:34- 36). The 200-Mile Fisheries Protective Zone declared by Canada in 1977 provided the means to establish such control over the stocks.

It is still difficult to determine the extent to which fisheries policies in the LeBlanc period were shaped by the personality and outlook of the Minister himself. There is no question that there were senior bureaucrats and scientists in the Department of Fisheries and Oceans (DFO) who supported more "progressive" policy directions in response to the havoc wreaked upon both the resource base and the social base of the fishery by unrestrained corporate sector expansion. But, perhaps because of his roots in Acadian New Brunswick, LeBlanc seemed atypical in the extent of his awareness of the social dimensions of fisheries policy. Some commentators have gone so far as to label him a "powerful ally" for the fishers (Lamson and Hanson, 1984:7). He strongly advocated the organization of inshore fishers (although his attitude towards the]MFU was initially hostile),[4] and during his tenure there was an opening up of opportunities for fishers to participate in policy and management processes. The bias of fisheries policy shifted away from the sole preoccupation with expansion of the corporate sector,[5] and there was greater emphasis on community stabilization, effective conservation, and a more balanced distribution of quotas among the offshore, near-shore and inshore fleets (MacDonald, 1984:34-36).

The high point in this brief era of co-management or tri- partite politics was reached perhaps during the deliberations of the Task Force on Atlantic Fisheries, chaired by Michael Kirby. In 1981, the federal government opted to respond to the insolvency of the five major fish companies in the Atlantic Region not with massive price subsidies as it had done in the mid-1970s (MacDonald, 1984:53), but with a task force set up to find ways to stabilize and "restructure" the industry without such subsidies. Fishers' organizations in the region participated extensively in the deliberations of the Task Force.

The final report of the Task Force did not deal with the issue of restructuring of the companies, and placed its greatest emphasis for future development on improvements in productivity and fish quality (Canada, 1983:Chs. 14,16). It was inconclusive on many important conflicts between fishers and corporate interests, but it did come out firmly for collective bargaining rights for inshore fishers (Williams, 1983). The MFU clearly benefited from the process in terms of the establishment of its identity as the most effective representative of inshore fishers in the Maritimes. The most positive result of the participation of the MFU, the Newfoundland fishery union, and other fishers' organizations was perhaps that the Task Force report was not more explicitly hostile to the rights and demands of inshore fishers and to the "social fishery" in general.[6]

However, in the financial restructuring of the bankrupt fish companies in 1983, yet another major shift became apparent. While it appeared that Kirby, by then Deputy Minister for the DFO, was aiming at the establishment of a crown corporation to take over the large processor operations in both Newfoundland and Nova Scotia, the dominant financial interests in Halifax were not prepared to tolerate this *de facto* nationalization of the "commanding heights" of the fishing industry. Rather, they sought, and achieved, the consolidation of the viable elements of H.B. Nickerson in the Maritimes with National Sea Products under a new ownership structure which combined the Jodrey and Sobey financial empires. A new management dedicated to "leaner and meaner" operations was quickly established (MacDonald and Connelly, Ch. 5 below). The federal government contributed the $100 million subsidy it had initially set out to avoid, this time in the form of a giveaway to the new company and received only a minority share of its equity in return (Williams, 1984).

The subsequent change of government in Ottawa in 1984 brought into power a regime even more committed to de-regulation and "market-driven" economic development. At the end of 1986 it was too early to know the full implications of these shifts. It was clear, however, that the existing infrastructure for resource management and planning through co-management processes was seriously threatened.

This brief review of the major developments in the fishing industry over the past two decades provides the context for an examination of the evolving policies and practices of the Maritime Fishermen's Union. The MFU was very quick to adapt to these shifting conditions in its efforts to survive and to continue to win concrete gains for inshore fishers. Whether these adaptations strengthened or compromised the integrity of the union over the longer haul is, of course, a key issue.

3. The origins of the Maritime Fishermen's Union

In early January of 1977, a meeting took place at the Université de Moncton, New Brunswick, between New Brunswick and Nova Scotia fishers' associations.[7] Two New Brunswick groups had already been working on a constitution for a new Maritime organization to represent inshore fishers. Nova Scotia fishers had been invited to participate, and had finally agreed to discuss the proposal at quite a late stage in the process. Their new association was represented there by two former Company of Young Canadians (CYC) volunteers who had worked in fishing communities, and a few individual fishers who were willing to come along.

The New Brunswick fishers at the meeting were the elected executives of inshore fishers' associations in the Northeast and Southeast regions of the province. Revitalization and expansion of these associations had been supported over the previous few years by staff members of Le Conseil Regional d'Amnagement du Sud-est (CRAS), and Le Conseil Regional d'Amnagement du Nord-est (CRAN). These were regional development councils which had been set up by the federal and provincial governments in response to rising nationalistic feelings among the Acadian population and to growing demands for action on their very serious social and economic problems (Allain and Coté, 1984).

Among the staff of CRAN and CRAS were militant young Acadians who had participated in protests on language and cultural issues while students at the Université de Moncton, and who had later joined in the popular struggle against the expropriations for the Kouchibouquac national park. Gilles Theriault was one of these. By the mid-1970s the cultural nationalism of the 1960s had matured into a highly politicized effort to mobilize workers and primary producers to defend the economic base of Acadian New Brunswick against the powerful forces of regional underdevelopment.

By 1977 the staff and leadership of these New Brunswick fishers' associations had come to agree on two strategic imperatives which were to profoundly shift the focus of their activities. The first was the recognition that the association form of organization would never by itself give inshore fishers the collective strength to deal effectively with their problems. They opted instead for the trade-union model. They saw it as the only means to have any real impact on fish prices in light of the emerging monopoly power of a few large fish companies. They also concluded that a strong, fisher-controlled organization required an independent financial base, and the union system of dues collection through a check-off was the only way to provide this on a long term basis.

This key strategic and ideological change did not take place without struggle. In 1974 the staff and fisher leaders of the two associations decided to study the union option and to put it before the membership. They exhaustively researched the alternative ways of setting up a union and carrying out collective bargaining in the fishing industry. They went to Newfoundland and to British Columbia to study how inshore fishers participated in unions there. Following this, they held information meetings in every fishing community from the Quebec to the Nova Scotia borders.

Initially the fishers were very resistant to the idea of a union. They were particularly concerned about large international unions, fearing that they would be controlled by the larger numbers of members from other vocations who had no knowledge of or interest in the fishery. The issues were thoroughly discussed, over and over again, until, in 1976, the leaders felt that a decision was possible.

It was decided to put the matter to a vote of all the fishers. Again there were meetings in every community, and those fishers who did not attend were counted as voting against the formation of a union.

Some 55 percent of the licensed fishers from the Northeast and Southeast regions of New Brunswick participated in the meetings, and of these close to 90 percent voted in favour of a union.

This three years of painstaking work not only secured a mandate for setting up the union; it also laid a solid base for the organization. The necessity to begin with an independent, fisher-controlled union was clearly established. Local community leadership was identified, and wharf level committees were set up which are still operating today. The capacity of the union to mobilize a large membership dispersed in scores of small villages was developed in this early stage. Perhaps most important was what is called in French, literally translated, the "formation" of the fishers, i.e. the basic education and orientation of the rank and file with regard to union principles and collective decision-making processes.

The second major strategic departure was the recognition of the necessity for a regional inshore fishers' organization. The two New Brunswick associations represented fishers along the Gulf of St. Lawrence from Quebec to Nova Scotia. They shared the fishing ground with fishers from Prince Edward Island and from the Northumberland Strait area of Nova Scotia who were increasingly dealing with the same fish companies and the same government bureaucracy. Fishers throughout the three Maritime provinces shared the lobster grounds and the same migrating stocks of groundfish, herring and mackerel, and had a common cause in the fight to protect these stocks against the depredations of the large company fleets.

While perhaps not the first to think of the idea, the Acadian fishers' associations in New Brunswick were the first in the current era to take concrete action to bring together inshore fishers on a regional basis. The cultural and political significance of this move was considerable, given that most of the early staff and leadership of these organizations had only a very limited command of English, and all shared a strong, emotional commitment to Acadian language rights and cultural autonomy. It was, in fact, a major achievement to unite fishers from the Northeast and Southeast, let alone to link up with anglophone fishers from Nova Scotia and Prince Edward Island.

In stark contrast, the Nova Scotia Fishermen's Association was an organization in name only at the time of the meeting in Moncton in January, 1977. The inshore fishery in Nova Scotia was still highly fragmented, with many local associations representing fishers on single issues of local concern. While the fishers along the Gulf shore in New Brunswick shared much the same conditions in terms of seasons, fish stocks, markets, etc., fishers in different areas of Nova Scotia participated in many different fishing activities under widely varying conditions. Their organizational activities clearly reflected this diversity of conditions and issues. Along the Northumberland Strait inshore fishers, like those in New Brunswick, had a five- or six-month season because of ice conditions, and depended primarily on lobster for their livelihoods. In Cape Breton and the Eastern Shore inshore fishers participated heavily in the groundfish fishery (as well as lobster and herring) and were particularly threatened by overfishing by foreign and domestic offshore fleets. In Southwestern Nova Scotia, the most developed inshore fishery in the region, fishers enjoyed a ten- to twelve-month season, exploited rich groundfish and lobster stocks, and had direct access to the Boston market.

Inshore fishers in Nova Scotia had formed regional associations, unions and co-operatives at various times before the First World War and during the 1930s and 1940s (Barrett, 1979). But when the long period of decline in their industry entered a crisis phase in the 1960s, little remained of these previous efforts. The United Food and Allied Workers' Union from British Columbia recruited inshore fishers throughout the province in the period leading up to a bitter strike in Canso and Petit de Grat in 1970. But when the UFAWU local was raided, and the strike was settled with only the offshore crew-members making any gains, the inshore fishers' organization quickly melted away (Clement, 1986a: Ch. 7).

In 1975 and 1976 the two former CYC volunteers mobilized a campaign around the province to limit the activities of the offshore fleet on traditional inshore fishing grounds. Known as the "50-Mile Limit Campaign," this effort was successful in identifying and linking together a new group of fisher leaders from different areas who saw the need for strong fishers' organization. When demands for the 50-mile limit on offshore vessels were rebuffed by the government despite a very high level of support from fishers in all parts of the province, efforts shifted to building a province-wide association (Williams, 1977).

In the spring of 1976, a meeting was held in Tatamagouche to discuss the setting up of the Nova Scotia Fishermen's Association. It was attended by leaders of local associations in Northumberland (Pictou and Antigonish counties), Cape Breton, Guysborough, the Eastern Shore and Southwest Nova Scotia. The participants quickly found broad agreement on the need for a new organization and on many fisheries policy issues.

The only controversy at the meeting was about the relative merits of the association and union forms of organization. This debate was stimulated by presentations by Bill Short from the Newfoundland fishery union and Gilles Theriault from New Brunswick, on the necessity for the union approach. Most of the Nova Scotia delegates agreed with the idea of a union, but felt that fishers in general were not ready for it. Like the New Brunswick fishers they also insisted that any new organization be exclusively one of inshore fishers, and expressed opposition to joining a big international union.

The meeting concluded with the election of an executive committee which was given a mandate to meet with the provincial government to ask for start-up funding. While endorsing the plan of eventually forming a union type of organization, the participants agreed to call themselves an association and to keep the union idea quiet until they had got funding and were better organized. No plans were made to link to either Newfoundland or New Brunswick.

Within a few months the executive of the new association held two meetings with the provincial Minister of Fisheries to present the proposal for funding. On both occasions they were put off, and eventually the government announced that it would fund another organization based in Southwest Nova Scotia and dominated by mid-shore fishers. Without funding and clear direction the Nova Scotia inshore fishers' group quickly lost its impetus.

By the time of the Moncton meeting in early 1977, no significant leadership was being provided either by fishers or supporting groups. While the New Brunswick fishers had developed a comprehensive strategy including a detailed constitution for a fishers' union, the Nova Scotia group entered the discussion with no clear plan, no mandate and no organized base of support. They therefore backed away from any commitment to joining the New Brunswick effort, and the meeting ended inconclusively.

The New Brunswick fishers decided to proceed with their plan independently. In February, 1977, the founding convention of the Maritime Fishermen's Union was held in Baie Sainte Anne with some 100 fisher delegates, none from outside the province. The MFU's constitution was ratified and an all-fisher executive was elected. The priority to be given to regional organization was endorsed by the members present, as was affiliation with the Canadian Labour Congress and with the New Brunswick Federation of Labour. The one issue to generate any real controversy was whether the union would be able to bargain collectively with the co-operative fish buyers and processors.

Close to half the New Brunswick Gulf coast fishers belonged to co-operatives. However the co-operatives were widely perceived to have lost contact with their members, and many of these co-operative fishers wanted collective bargaining precisely in order to regain a say over them. It was not clear at the time of the founding convention whether a union could bargain with an organization which in principle was owned by union members. Many MFU delegates were convinced that the union would fail in their areas if it did not have power to bargain with the co-operatives. A resolution was passed calling upon the provincial government to pass legislation to give collective bargaining rights to inshore fishers and to treat the co-operatives the same as all other fish buyers or processors.

Later in 1977 the former CYC organizers in Nova Scotia were hired by the MFU to set up locals there, and the Guysborough and Northumberland associations affiliated with the union. By the time of its second convention in 1978, the union was able to constitute a Maritime Executive with representatives from Nova Scotia and Prince Edward Island. At this stage the union had some 600 dues-paying members in New Brunswick. The initial organizing efforts in Nova Scotia and P.E.I. brought in only a small number of members, although these tended to be among the more active leaders in their local areas. However, the base of the union was clearly in the Northeast and Southeast regions of New Brunswick, and this unevenness of organizational strength has continued to be a serious problem for the MFU up to the present.

4. The evolution of the MFU

From the outset the MFU was burdened with certain weaknesses and constraints. It sought to mobilize and represent a population of primary producers who had no widely shared experience of disciplined collective action. Inshore fishers in the Maritimes were dispersed over a wide geographical area, were involved in many different kinds of fishing enterprises, and were also differentiated by language and other cultural factors. Given the economic conditions in their industry, they could give only limited financial support to their own organization. In the early stages government was indifferent to the union's existence and refused to grant collective bargaining rights for independent boat owners, while the larger fish companies ignored the union's demand to be recognized.

It cannot be claimed today that the union solved many of these problems, or that it brought about major changes in the industry to reduce the constraints. Yet the MFU survived, and, more than that, it continued to expand its membership base and to win significant victories for inshore fishers. Under the circumstances, these clearly have been major accomplishments. How were they achieved?

One key factor that perhaps underpins all the others is that the MFU began with a core of exceptional fisher leaders and this core has generally been maintained and expanded. Paralleling this has been the continuity and ongoing development of the staff. Of six full-time organizers working for the union in 1986, two were original organizers and two others had been involved with the MFU or worked with other primary producer organizations in the region since the mid-1970s. Through the long struggle to survive, and through many battles with government and the companies, both fisher leaders and staff acquired the organizational skills, political acumen, and comprehensive knowledge of the fishery that were required for the union to keep growing and improving. With this capacity for making good strategic decisions and for implementing them, the MFU was able to recover from its mistakes and to expand in a number of directions as conditions required. This can be shown through an examination of seven basic aspects of MFU activity.

New organization

The MFU has continually expanded its membership base through new organizing efforts. The most important of these was in Southwest Nova Scotia, the most developed sector of the inshore industry in the region, where anti-union attitudes have traditionally been very strong among inshore fishers (Clement, 1986a:157). Mobilization began with the Acadian fishers along the coast of Nova Scotia from Yarmouth to Digby and focused on the specific problems of herring conservation and markets. In 1984 and 1985 the union led a successful battle to reduce seiner quotas on the spawning grounds, and then organized an over-the-side sale for inshore gill-net herring.[8] Success with these projects led to involvement in other issues, notably lobster regulations and groundfish quotas. The union became a strong force in the area with well over a hundred members paying dues on a voluntary basis in 1986.

Mobilization and militant action

In its first few years the union had to depend almost entirely on militant actions to win specific gains for the membership. Fish companies refused to recognize the union, and fisher participation on the few existing government committees was only token. In 1977 union members occupied the Associated Fisheries Plant in Shippegan, New Brunswick, to pressure the company to bargain over fish prices. In 1978 a long and bitter campaign was launched to rid the Gulf of St. Lawrence of herring seiners. In 1979 the police used tear gas to disperse a demonstration against the seiners by fishers and their families in Caraquet, New Brunswick, and union leaders were arrested. This struggle continues to the present although, as a direct result of the MFU pressure, only a few seiners now operate in the Gulf with a greatly restricted quota.

Union members in all three Maritime provinces held large demonstrations to pressure for collective bargaining legislation, and these actions were instrumental in achieving bargaining rights in New Brunswick in 1982. More recently there were demonstrations and occupations by fishers in all three provinces aimed at securing herring quotas and markets for the inshore. In August, 1984, the P.E.I. ferry was blocked by inshore boats in Pictou, Nova Scotia, and shortly afterwards the regional fisheries offices were occupied by New Brunswick MFU members. In September of 1985 the whole community in Caraquet, New Brunswick, was mobilized by the union to support fishers who were arrested for refusing to obey an overly restrictive quota. In September, 1986, MFU members again were arrested for collectively overfishing herring quotas as a form of protest, this time in Antigonish County, Nova Scotia. These actions led directly to concessions by the federal Department of Fisheries and Oceans on the reorganization of the herring fishery.

Another very significant event was the demonstration in February, 1986, at the Department of Fisheries and Oceans office in Yarmouth, Nova Scotia. Members of the new MFU local there put on a very strong show of unity on the issue of groundfish quotas for inshore fishers. There had been violent incidents in the area on lobster issues the year before, and many fishers were reluctant to get involved in direct action. The MFU's success in mobilizing their groundfish protest led to concessions from the government while strengthening the union's credibility in the area.

Collective Bargaining

The union bargained over fish prices from its inception through voluntary recognition arrangements with small local companies. Legislation granting bargaining rights was passed in New Brunswick in 1982 and on the certification vote the union won massive support to become the bargaining agent for fishers of some eight different species in the two New Brunswick locals.

As of December, 1986, two major collective agreements had been signed, one for lobster and another for herring, both in Northeast New Brunswick. Through two previous years of bargaining the union had refused to sign a contract without the Rand Formula, i.e. without a check-off system whereby the companies would deduct dues for all fishers covered by the agreement, whether union members or not, and pay them to the union. The larger companies had demanded fixed prices rather than floor or minimum prices in order to reduce the competition with small buyers for supply.[9] The agreements that were finally achieved involved a trade-off—the Rand formula for the fixed price.

It generally was felt that the achievement of contracts and the establishment of orderly collective bargaining in New Brunswick would break the log jam in the other provinces. Fishers and processors alike were waiting to see how it would work. If it proved successful, there would be much greater pressure on the other two provincial governments to fall in line. The financial stability of the union depended on the outcome.

In spite of the progress made in winning contracts, however, the actual experience with collective bargaining led MFU leaders to be more aware of the limitations of this approach. The problem is leverage. Effective bargaining depends upon the strike weapon, and inshore fishers have been hesitant to tie up their boats to win company concessions.[10] The weakness of market demand for many inshore species also limits their bargaining power.

These constraints also reflect the underlying structure of the fisher/ fish company relationship in the current conjuncture in the Maritimes. In both Newfoundland and British Columbia plantworkers and offshore crews are in the same union with inshore fishers, and they confront together a few dominant fish companies which control all aspects of the industry. Such consolidation has not yet occurred in the Maritimes, either on the corporate or the union side, and so the MFU is not able to generate the same kinds of leverage.[11] Based on the MFU's experience to date, it is questionable whether inshore fishers will be able to effectively utilize the collective bargaining weapon as long as the industry is as fragmented and unevenly developed as it currently is.

Until basic conditions change, collective bargaining will continue to be only one of several methods that must be used by inshore fishers to defend and develop their industry. In and of itself it may often be ineffectual, but when combined with other tactical weapons it may prove to be more workable.[12]

Relations with government
When the MFU was established, inshore fishers had virtually no access to fisheries policy and management processes. The leadership of the union saw this as a direct expression of capitalist dominance through the mechanism of the capitalist state.

Militant action forced recognition and concessions because politicians and state bureaucrats tend to come to terms with organizations which are able to mobilize real political power. Both because fishers demanded it, and because the exigencies of planning and managing a very complex fishery required it, the Department of Fisheries and Oceans began in the late 1970s to put in place a system of consultation which offered real opportunities for input by fishermen.

Among the gains made by the MFU through participation in this system (backed, of course, by continuing militant action), were those already mentioned above—cutbacks in the herring seiner fleet and reorganization of the herring quota system. Other significant policy gains in which the MFU played a central role were the banning of groundfish draggers from the Gulf, the establishment of over-the-side sales, the adoption of a new licensing system which resolved the issue of part-time fishers by phasing out their licenses over time, and the implementation of many reforms in the management and regulation of the lobster fishery. Such concrete achievements have become key elements of the union's identity for inshore fishers, and have contributed significantly to the union's expansion in recent years.

Marketing projects

As mentioned above, the union has increasingly involved itself in direct efforts to find markets for under-utilized inshore catches. Traditionally fishers worked through their associations to find new markets for their products. This usually involved bringing in new buyers to force a dominant local buyer to pay more competitive prices. In recent years, however, fishers have faced increasing difficulties in finding any buyers at all for their herring, mackerel, gaspereau (alewives), hake or even cod. In some cases the problem was that the fish were landed in great quantities over short periods of time and the buyers and processors could not handle the glut. In other cases, such as catches of hake or gaspereau, there could simply be no buyers.

Experiments with direct, so-called "over-the-side," sales to foreign buyers have had mixed results. A mackerel direct sale run by the union in the Gulf in 1979 failed because the migratory schools did not arrive and the Russian boat had to leave virtually empty. Direct sales of herring in the Bay of Fundy were more successful because the union negotiated a deal to have the seiners participate in order to guarantee adequate supply to the foreign boats.

In Cape Breton the union set up its own fish handling depot in 1985 in order to attract new buyers to break the control of a local processor. This resulted in higher prices generally but also in improved market demand for local fish. In New Brunswick in 1985 the union helped set up a new mobile fish handling system in order to relieve the glut in herring landings and to process all the fish that is caught. In 1986 the union was negotiating a deal to sell large quantities of hake to Third World countries through the co-operatives.

In all of these areas the union gained experience and expertise at finding ways to do what the private companies were not able to do for the fishers. Marketing projects have proven to be an excellent organizing tool in areas where direct conflict with companies was not the main concern. The projects also generated economic surpluses which were used to support the union infrastructure.

Co-operating with the co-operatives

From the outset there were serious tensions between the MFU and the co-operative movement. The setting up of the union was resisted by many co-operatives, and red-baiting tactics were widely used to discourage participation in the union by co-op members. After the certification vote in New Brunswick, the co-operatives went to court to argue against their inclusion under the collective bargaining legislation. When they lost their court battle, they went directly to the government and succeeded in getting the act changed so that they were not required to bargain collectively. This appeared at first to be a very serious blow to the union's efforts to get first contracts, since a major player in the industry would no longer be at the table or bound by the agreements negotiated by the private companies. In fact the situation did not turn out to be as disadvantageous to the union as it initially appeared.

In the early 1980s a new senior management team was put in place in the main co-operative central, the United Maritime Fishermen's Co-operative (UMF). As part of a general modernization and development effort, they undertook to rebuild relations with the union and with the co-op membership base. Following the legislative changes to exclude the co-ops from bargaining, the UMF made a commitment not to undermine the bargaining process and to be governed by the shore price negotiated with the companies.[13] This commitment has been maintained through 1986. Senior management of the UMF subsequently negotiated an agreement with the MFU which would eventually give the union the equivalent of the Rand Formula for co-operative members, in return for which the union agreed to represent co-operative fishers in dealings with government. In effect the UMF recognized the MFU as both bargaining agent and representative on policy and management issues for co-op members. The union also agreed to assist the UMF in the setting up of new co-operative units in new areas. In return the UMF agreed to make its services available wherever possible to assist with union marketing projects.

MFU leaders were uncertain about the longer term implications of this quite dramatic change in their relations with the co-operatives. The MFU had always seen the labour movement as its primary source of external support and solidarity. The shift towards linkage with the co-operatives implied ideological and strategic changes as well. Would fishers as "workers" or petty commodity producers make the greatest gains by directly confronting the owners of capital, or should they work to become collective owners of capital in rejuvenated democratic organizations?

New services to fishers

In the past few years the union has become increasingly involved in the provision of new services to inshore fishers. The most important example of this was the insurance program initiated in 1986. Fishers now have access through the union to a low cost plan offering family medical and dental coverage, life insurance, and long term disability benefits. Research carried out by the union revealed that only a minority of fishers had life or disability coverage, and very few had medical coverage for their families (MFU, 1985). The fishers reception of the new plan, developed in co-operation with the UMF, was very positive. The union also committed itself to lobbying the provincial governments for coverage for inshore fishers under workers' compensation programs.

As a direct follow-up to the insurance project, the union undertook a research and education project on accidental deaths and injuries on inshore fishing vessels. There has been a relatively high rate of fatalities among inshore fishers, and safety programs and search and rescue services were clearly inadequate, so MFU involvement in this area held great potential benefits for fishers (MFU, 1986).

5. Revising the analysis

In the early days of the MFU the union's analysis of the situation of inshore fishers could be summed up as follows: a few large fish companies were establishing monopoly control over the entire industry with the complete support of the capitalist state. The resulting closure of many small fish plants, the depression of prices and the expanded efforts of the Canadian corporate offshore fleet were pushing many inshore fishers out and undermining the economic base of their communities. Co-operatives, small companies and independent buyers were fighting a losing battle for survival, and so inshore fishers could only protect themselves through the creation of a militant, class-struggle union.

Looking back over the past decade, we can recognize that this analysis was incorrect on many key points. Among the developments which were not anticipated by that analysis, and by the practical strategies that flowed from it, were the following:

❑ virtually all the "monopoly" companies in the region went bankrupt in the 1981 recession, largely as a result of over-expansion and generally poor management;

❑ the supposedly obsolete small and medium-sized independent companies survived, and some proved to be the most profitable elements in the industry (Apostle, et al., 1985);

❑ the co-operatives survived, and have recently undergone something of a renaissance with improved profits and the establishment of new co-operatives. MFU members originally wanted a union to fight their own co-operatives. More recently, however, they have demonstrated a deep loyalty to and a continuing economic dependence upon their local co-operatives (Clement, 1986a:Ch. 10);

❑ collective bargaining did not prove to be a panacea for the economic problems of inshore fishers. Many of the smaller, locally based companies could not pay better prices unless markets improved considerably. Where there were gains to be made, most fishers were unwilling to use the strike instrument because of the potential costs;

❑ government's role in the fishing industry has proven to be more contradictory than originally expected. In the 1977 to 1984 period a sphere of pluralist politics evolved within a developing system of consultation and co-management mechanisms. In the period 1981 to 1986 the MFU made greater gains for its members through various forms of participation in policy and management processes, backed up of course by militant action (or the threat of such action), than it did through collective bargaining or other forms of direct confrontation with private companies.

These unanticipated developments give rise to two theoretical tasks. The original analysis should be revised to take better account of realities revealed through experience, and new strategies for future action should be elaborated.

The weakness of the monopoly sector and the resilience of the small companies and co-operatives point to one general theoretical problem. Two somewhat conflicting streams of thought ran through the analysis of the fishing industry by the union and its sympathizers on the left. One focused on the confrontation between capital and the increasingly proletarianized, or semi- proletarianized, producers, and anticipated a class struggle for control over surplus value. The other was based on the underdevelopment problematic, and focused on issues of unequal exchange within the industry, between the industry and other sectors of the economy (e.g. the banks), and between dominant and dependent regions (Brym and Sacouman, 1979; Williams, 1979).

This conflict needs to be resolved. It is the view of this writer that the underdevelopment approach has often generated the more useful understandings for dealing in practical terms with such a complex reality. The strength of the co-operatives, for example, makes more sense when we realize that many fishers live and work in geographically and culturally isolated situations and have had very limited access to monopoly sector companies to sell their fish. In such situations the co-operatives have often provided the only economic infrastructure for participation in the industry.

Even where competitive private companies were operating, inshore fishers have understood that the co-operatives were an essential balance and a means of retaining economic surpluses for investment back into the community. In contrast to its earlier analysis, the MFU has come to understand that, while fishers are often critical of the co-operatives themselves, the co-operative ideology remains strong because it directly addresses their need for greater control over marketing and capital accumulation processes.

The survival and business success of many of the small and medium-sized companies also is more understandable when we recognize how well-adapted they are to the underdeveloped economic environment of the rural fishing communities (Apostle et al., 1985). They have tended not to acquire heavy debt loads because they have been able to depend upon readily available, low-wage, often mainly female labour rather than expensive capital equipment (Connelly and MacDonald, 1983; 1986). They have secured markets through their ability to adjust their production costs to fit market conditions, i.e. through their capacity to hand on losses to workers and fishers. These companies both benefit from and perpetuate the underdevelopment of the industry and of the rural economy in general. If fishers and/or workers began to seriously challenge these companies, their equilibrium would be easily jeopardized. Strong demands for better prices or wages would be met with threats from the companies either of closure or of investment in labour saving technologies.

Under these circumstances again, fishers and workers who have wanted a better life in the fishery have been forced to envision new ways of developing their industry rather than just pushing for a better price for their labour or their products. While always dealing with class oppression, they have had to face the challenge of directly transforming the fishery and of creating new structures if their needs are to be met over the longer term.

Finally, the underdevelopment approach provides an important basis for understanding the unique role of the state in the fishing industry in the Atlantic Region. Despite its dramatic expansion in the 1960s and 1970s, the monopoly sector failed to consolidate the overarching planning and coordinating function typical of large corporations in more developed regions. This failure by the corporate sector to bring about the overall rationalization of the industry and to impose their own regime of resource management created a vacuum which drew the state into these roles. When it became apparent that the companies were seriously damaging the resource base and destabilizing the social base of the fishery in order to support their gross over- expansion and subsequent cash-flow problems, the state had little choice but to come into direct conflict with them.

The general crisis of underdevelopment in all sectors of the region has further reinforced the state's role as planner, co-ordinator and enforcer of order. The massive costs to the state of the social breakdown associated with the decline of the inshore fishery and of the industry in general, linked to the failure of the regional economy to generate alternative sources of employment, led to government investment in the "social fishery" as an alternative to explicit welfare and other forms of social control or "legitimation" expenditure.

In a more developed industry (in conventional terms), fishers could expect to make the greatest gains by pressing claims for a "fairer" share of the economic surpluses accumulated by the monopoly sector of the industry. In the absence of such successful capitalist accumulation, government became the main, if not the only, game in town. Fishers' organizations focused their efforts on government because they knew who was making real decisions, and who had money to spend. Government had to deal with these pressures in a political manner, i.e. they had to negotiate and compromise, because the working out of all these sectoral conflicts was clearly a planning task rather than a market process.

As a consequence, fisheries policy over the past decade evolved quite differently than it would have had a viable monopoly sector been in place, and had the state been able to play a more secondary role. Fishers won concessions they would not have won, and shaped their industry in ways they would not have been able to do had the corporate sector been firmly in control. If that had been the case, fishers might still have won victories and concessions, but it would have been by quite different tactics and for very different goals.

Another element which deserves a more central role in our analysis is culture. A concept of struggle based purely on social class fails to take into account the "overdetermining" influences of other social relations, notably gender, language and ethnicity, and community. Much of the strength of the MFU came from its emergence as a key leadership structure in the Acadian community of New Brunswick. This provided the political leverage necessary to win major concessions.

At the same time, the reality of community, i.e. organic relations among people with conflicting class interests, often blunted the sharpness of the class issue in the struggle for concrete gains for inshore fishers. In the case of the co-operatives, for example, co-operative managers exercised strong social as well as economic control over the fishers. Among inshore fishers themselves it was often the most economically successful individuals with distinct interests arising from their larger investments in their fishing operations who became the key spokespersons for all the fishers.

The divisions between association and union fishers often reflected just such economic differences, and the survival of the associations despite the union's comparative successes speaks to the resilience of these relations. In P.E.I., Southeast New Brunswick, Cape Breton, and the Eastern Shore and Southwest areas of Nova Scotia, fishers are still split between association and union forms of organization, largely because of strong leadership from high income-earning fishers who dominate local associations and claim, with some success, to speak for all fishers.[14]

The role of women in the development of the union has not been emphasized here because it has remained so much in the background of union activities and decision making. While it is true that the inshore fishery is fundamentally constituted by family units in both economic and social terms (Connelly and MacDonald, 1983; 1986), until very recently women for the most part have appeared to occupy subordinate positions both in the fishing operations themselves and in normal union activities. However such appearances, as always, obscure more complex realities. During the periods when the union was involved in continuous militant action, for example, the active involvement and support of spouses and other family members was very evident and was crucial for success. But under the union's constitution, as of this writing, spouses cannot be members of the union unless they themselves hold fishing licences.

There have recently been important signs of change. More and more women are getting fishing licences both to work on their partners' boats or to operate their own boats. In 1985 there were an estimated 200 women who operated their own boats in the Maritimes (Squires, 1985). These women had not become very active as members of the union, but this could be expected to evolve over time. A large number of wives, several of whom were official delegates, attended the 1986 Convention and participated very actively in the sessions. Resolutions have been passed several times at the union's executive level to develop programs to bring women more actively into the union, but to date the issue has not been given high priority for action. It probably will not be until the women themselves begin to pressure more effectively for this change.

6. Conclusion

At the time of writing in late 1986 the Maritimes fishing industry appeared to be on the verge of another major transition. Federal government policies emphasized devolution of planning and coordinating functions to the private sector, and what Claus Offe (1984:119-129) terms the "recommodification" of the "decommodified" economic and political processes engaged in by the liberal welfare state. In the period 1977-1984 the financial weakness and irresponsible behaviour of the large fish companies, and the resulting social breakdown and destruction of the resource base, forced the state to intervene heavily in pursuit of a variety of objectives beyond and often in conflict with capital accumulation. Given the fiscal crisis and the predominance of neo-conservatism within the ruling class, these policies have increasingly come under attack since 1984 for ideological as much as for economic reasons. If capital proves able to organize and discipline itself around a core of monopoly or oligopoly units, and there is some evidence that this has been happening, the particular kinds of gains that have been made by workers' and fishers' organizations over recent years will be jeopardized.

Our brief review of the history of the Maritime Fishermen's Union points to the uniqueness of that organization compared to many other fishers' groups. Most fisher organizations in the region have been localistic, have mobilized primarily around single issues, and have had difficulty building and sustaining active membership bases. The MFU is the one example in Eastern Canada of an exclusively inshore organization, set up on a regional basis, which represents fishers on everything from price negotiations to dealings with government to resolution of conflicts among fishers over gear types, quotas, etc. The fact that it has survived and expanded since 1977 is evidence of the awareness among inshore fishers of their need for such an organization, as well as of the high levels of skill and commitment of the union's leadership and staff. However the failure of the MFU to establish a secure and independent financial base is equally clear evidence of the difficulties involved in organizing inshore fishers, given the marginal economic conditions under which they operate.

In its early years the MFU attracted a lot of attention because of its militancy and radicalism. As it became more established and gained recognition from government and fish companies, its image changed along with its methods of winning concrete gains for inshore fishers. With the current resurgence of the monopoly sector and the shift in government policies in favour of the corporate fishery, the MFU will be presented with new challenges requiring mobilization and militant action. Its ability to respond will depend on its success in resolving its serious financial problems and perhaps in generating new leadership.

This author among others has previously commented on the socialist direction of the MFU, and on the socialist implications of the survival struggles of inshore fishers within which the union has played such a key part (Williams, 1979). Several more years of experience force us to recognize the limitations on what a single organization of small producers can achieve in this respect, regardless of its ideological orientation. In a period of crisis in the fishing industry culminating in the virtual collapse of the corporate sector, the MFU exercised remarkable political influence and won important victories for inshore fishers. At no time in this period, however, was the strength of the union great enough or the crisis so severe that capitalist hegemony was really at issue. In the absence of a generalized crisis of capitalism attended by a clearly delineated class struggle for actual control of the means of production, the MFU's radicalism was significant and often heroic, but ultimately anomalous.

The union's future role in wider struggles for political, economic and social transformation is at this point in time a matter of conjecture because of the financial and other issues with which the organization is currently grappling. One thing, however, can be said with certainty: the MFU has provided very clear evidence of the leadership and organizational strength that inshore fishers can potentially contribute to a socialist movement. This is a lesson that must not be lost on all who hope to build such a movement in this region.

Notes

1. An earlier version of this paper was presented to the International Working Seminar, "Social Research and Public Policy Formation in the Fisheries: Norwegian and Atlantic Canadian Experiences", University of Tromso, Norway, June 1986.

2. According to a New Democratic Party research paper, "in 1978 Statistics Canada data shows that the four largest processors in Atlantic Canada accounted for 53.6 percent of processing activity and the largest eight controlled 63.5 percent.... The degree of concentration in the offshore industry relative to the inshore fishery is evident when we note that 98.2 percent of all offshore fish is in the hands of the four largest processors, compared to 26.1 percent of inshore fish.... The large processors do not have to compete in the open market for the bulk of their raw fish supply as about 75 percent of their fish comes from their own vessels" (Pollock and Miller, 1982).

3. Wrobel (1981) reports that the Nickerson/National Sea group of companies received "considerable sums of Federal Government monies." These included grants of some $15 million from the Department of Regional Economic Expansion and $6 million from the Department of Environment. At the time of the restructuring of the two companies in 1984 the Nova Scotia government forgave a debt of $50 million owed it by National Sea (Williams, 1984). For a more detailed analysis of this history, see Barrett (1984).

4. LeBlanc was not initially receptive to the MFU and clearly perceived it to be too radical. He had better relations with Richard Cashin and the Newfoundland fishery union. In a move which was probably designed to offset the growing influence of the MFU in the Maritimes, in 1979 he provided an allotment of offshore fish worth approximately $1,000,000 to finance the setting up of the Eastern Fishermen's Federation (EFF), an umbrella group of fishermens' associations opposed to collective bargaining (Clement, 1986a:152-156).

5. LeBlanc took several steps which antagonized the large fish companies. He banned the large draggers from the Gulf of St. Lawrence, and froze licences for steel draggers over sixty-five feet, blocking the early introduction of freezer trawlers. On several occasions he spoke publicly about the need for a law to prevent fish processors from also owning fishing vessels, although he never actually brought forward such legislation. One issue on which he was slow to move, despite many militant protests in his home area, was to ban or reduce the herring seiner fleet in the Gulf.

6. The term "social fishery" was widely used during the Kirby Task Force proceedings and before to describe policies and practices aimed at maintaining fishing enterprises and communities which were not viable in strict market terms. Unemployment insurance for inshore fishermen and subsidies to keep certain fish plants operating in rural Newfoundland communities were seen by supporters and critics alike as efforts to maintain the fishery for "social" rather than purely economic reasons. The Kirby Task Force Report waffled on this issue, proposing economic viability as a primary policy goal, but rejecting the "pure free enterprise school of thought" as a means of resolving the social and political problems associated with rationalization of the industry (Canada, Task Force on Atlantic Fisheries, 1982:8).

7. Since so little of the following information about the development of the MFU has been documented, the main source is the personal recollections of the author and of Gilles Theriault.

8. "Over-the-side sales" or "direct sales" are contractual marketing arrangements whereby foreign buyers purchase fish directly from the fishers, usually right out on the fishing grounds, rather than going through shore-based processors and fish markets. Such sales are set up through negotiations at the inter-governmental level, although fish brokers are also often involved. The main purpose has been to provide markets for under-utilized species such as gaspereau, mackerel or herring.

9. This refers primarily to lobster. The largest buyers of lobster are the processors such as National Sea Products Ltd. They establish a "shore price," i.e. a base price in the area, which primarily reflects conditions in the Boston

market, and they buy the greatest proportion of the landings. They also supply the fishers with bait and other supplies and sometimes with credit, as well as buying other fish from the fishers throughout the year. However small buyers come in just for certain quantities of lobster for specialized markets (e.g. local restaurants, a small broker in Montreal, etc.) and pay an automatic 5 or 10 cents over the shore price. The large processors may then have to meet that price to guarantee supply. In 1985 the price for canner lobster in New Brunswick became inflated relative to actual market demand in this manner, and many buyers, large and small, lost money. This sparked renewed interest among the more established buyers in getting a collective agreement with a fixed price.

10. Most inshore fishers in the Maritimes earn a half or more of their annual fishing incomes in the first few weeks of lobster season, and a tie-up at this time, while putting very heavy pressure on the buyers, would be too costly for most fishers to bear. They might also lose their best unemployment insurance stamps, jeopardizing their incomes over the winter. In spite of these constraints, there have occasionally been such tie-ups—e.g. for lobster in the Pictou area in 1975 and for groundfish in Souris, P.E.I., a few years later. Such actions are usually spontaneous and target one particular buyer upon whom all the fishers in the area depend.

11. This point has often been expressed by Richard Cashin, President and co-founder of the Newfoundland fishery union, in meetings with the MFU, and perhaps explains his reluctance to date to get involved in organizing inshore fishermen in the Maritimes. The social base of the Newfoundland union is clearly in the proletarianized sectors of the industry, and it is not clear that inshore fishermen are effectively organized there or that they participate fully in the life of the union. The fact that the Newfoundland fishery union bargains on their behalf, with the larger companies at least, ties Newfoundland inshore fishers to the organization but does not make it their own vehicle for struggle. Recently, in fact, a new inshore fishermen's organization has appeared on the west coast of Newfoundland to deal with resource management questions. The MFU is clearly and unquestionably an inshore fishermen's organization, and, while this may limit its efficacy for collective bargaining, it is a source of great strength in dealing with other political or resource management issues.

12. General questions have been raised by Bryant Fairley and others regarding similarities between the MFU and the Newfoundland fishery union in terms of their common focus on the price (exchange value) of fish rather than on the exploitation of labour, and the developmental (class) implications of the former focus. MFU leaders have always thought of collective bargaining in rather complex terms. They have wanted to improve prices, but they have also emphasized simply knowing the price prior to the season in order to be better able to assess the prospects of making or losing money.

There has also been a clear sense that check- off of dues from all fishermen serviced by the union (i.e. the Rand Formula) would be a primary benefit of having collective agreements. Despite some recent success with bargaining, it seems clear that MFU members do not see negotiating fish prices *per se* to be the *raison d'être* of the organization. Perhaps to a greater extent than the Newfoundland Union, although the latter is far from being a typical trade union in this regard, the MFU involves itself in a multi-faceted struggle to defend the position of inshore fishermen relative to the management and development the fishing industry as a totality. Efforts to improve fish prices are clearly seen as one, and only one, element of this larger process.

13. The UMF is an umbrella organization that provides marketing services to local co-ops. It also owns some of its own processing facilities. While the UMF is very influential, it does not control the local co-op units. For example the Lameque Co-operative in Northeast New Brunswick played the dominant role in the fight to exclude the co-ops from collective bargaining, and its management has generally been more hostile to the MFU than that of most of the other co-ops.

14. The Eastern Fishermens Federation (EFF) operates as a kind of network of these local fisher associations. It is effectively dominated by a few relatively prosperous inshore and near-shore fishers who make little effort to consult or democratically represent inshore fishers in general in advocating policies which are often very much in their own particular interests (Munroe and Stewart, 1981; Clement, 1986a:152-155).

Chapter Six

A Leaner Meaner Industry: A Case Study of "Restructuring" in the Nova Scotia Fishery

Martha MacDonald and Patricia Connelly

The media and the politicians called it "restructuring" the industry, a term that conveys a sense of major or radical change in the fishery.[1] But an examination of the recent changes in the fishery in Nova Scotia in fact shows that the term "restructuring" was used to gloss over a "business as usual" approach (Williams, 1984). Prior to the "restructuring" the largest fish company, National Sea Products, was controlled by private interests, H.B. Nickerson, with money from the Bank of Nova Scotia and with support from the government. After "restructuring" only the number of plants, the names, and the amounts of support had changed. The industry was still controlled by the private sector with bank and government support. The need to make these organizational changes, however, resulted from real structural problems. These problems can only be understood by an historical examination of the cause and effects of the concentration and centralization of capital in the fishing industry (Barrett and Davis, 1984). This in turn must be done in the context of regional underdevelopment. As Rick Williams (1984) observes, the Atlantic fishery is an underdeveloped industry in an underdeveloped region.[2]

The current situation in the fisheries is complex, as always. There are many important issues, both of a theoretical and an empirical nature. The political "restructuring" was a *bailout*. However there has been real restructuring in the world economy, with a new international division of labour and an international economic crisis. The way in which this has affected the fishing industry needs to be understood. Has there been a real structural change in the fishing industry or simply a crisis within the present structure? Certainly the continued crisis has been understood as an expression of the contradiction between the forces and relations of production, in that the concentration of capital in the industry has gone beyond the limits of economic efficiency or rationality. The large capital-intensive companies, with their need for steady production and their resultant dependence on an offshore fleet, are seen as unsuited to the nature of the resource or the markets (Williams, 1984).

An important question is whether these underlying contradictions are actually manifesting themselves now in a restructuring of power relations between big and small capital. Has the bailout temporarily propped up an unviable industry, or is the power of the big companies essentially unchallenged—as evidenced by the bailout? Certainly there has been an increase in the number of "independent" fishers/packers, bypassing the big companies, and there is increased survival and relative success among the small processors (Apostle and Barrett, 1985). Is this a temporary phenomenon, while the big companies regroup, or is it a reflection of permanently changed market conditions and economic relations?

Another question concerns changing class relations and class structure, particularly the class position of the primary producers. Is the class position of the successful midshore boat owner different from that of the marginal inshore fisher conjured up in earlier analyses (Sacouman, 1980; Barrett, 1980)? What are the class membership implications for owners, crew, and plant workers? Conditions have altered for each of these groups in recent years. Finally, we must consider the function of households in relation to class position and structure. Do we have semi-proletarianized families these days, or has there been a change in the allocation of labour and its relation to the means of production within the household?

The current challenge is to try to understand all these interrelated layers of restructuring so as to see if anything fundamental has changed. Then we can better understand the potential for organization and struggle in the industry by fishers and plant workers and communities. In this paper we address these issues through a case study of one fishing community. It is an examination of historical changes in one industry, concentrating on changes in the present period of crisis and restructuring. Particular attention is paid to household work and income patterns related to changes in the industry.

Our analysis is informed by the theoretical literature on underdevelopment, including women and development. In this paper, we focus on the way in which the subsistence or household sphere relates to the production sphere (Deere, 1976; Saffioti, 1977; Connelly, 1984; Humphries and Rubery, 1984).[3] People respond to changing conditions not just as individuals or groups of workers but as members of households. We are interested in how households rearrange and reallocate wage and nonwage labour as economic changes occur, that is, how the flexibility of the household economy, and specifically women's work, contribute to the survival of the rural economy.[4] This allows us to see that households and domestic labour are a necessary part of the capitalist mode of production and significantly contribute to the way in which different modes of production articulate to one another. For example, in Maritime fishing communities independent commodity production is maintained through the wage labour and subsistence activities of household members (Sacouman, 1979). This facilitates capitalist development (and underdevelopment) in the industry and region.

Underdevelopment and the fishing industry in the Atlantic region have been continuously affected by the internationalization of capital, and in recent years most notably by the new international division of labour (NIDL). Whereas the traditional international division of labour was based on drawing raw resources and labour from underdeveloped areas, the NIDL involves the movement of production to the cheap labour and raw materials of the Third World.[5] This has different effects on different industries. The fishing industry is not subject to the same kind of direct pressures as textiles and electronics since the resource is already here and is not moveable.] However, the NIDL has had an effect on the fishing industry in several indirect ways. Industries that might have come to the Atlantic region for its raw resources, government subsidies and cheaper labour force can often now move more profitably to the Third World. The Atlantic region has always provided a reserve labour supply to the rest of Canada (Veltmeyer, 1979), but with a decrease in the need for such labour more people remain in or return to the rural communities. This in turn puts more pressure on industries like fishing to provide incomes for more people, while also increasing the reserve labour supply available to those industries.

At the international level there have also been new sources of competition for the fishing industry, with other countries getting into the fishery for the first time. And there have been new innovations and important changes in the labour process in the U.S. poultry market which make fish substitutes like chicken less expensive (Fairley, 1985b). The fishing industry is also seriously affected by the pressures for both free trade and protectionism, which are themselves responses to the changes in the world capitalist system. Finally the microelectronic revolution is having a direct impact on the fishing industry, particularly on the processing sector.

Regional underdevelopment, then, is broadly structured by national and international conditions, but the way in which members of local areas or communities relate to these broader structures differs according to their own specific political and economic conditions and struggles

(Johnson, 1983; Chilcote, 1983). To understand the complexities of the fishery it is necessary not only to place it in the broader context of structural changes in the international, national and regional setting, but also to understand how real people experience and respond to these changes as individuals and as household members. This is the context within which we place our case study of a fishing community in Nova Scotia.

Fieldwork for our study was conducted in the summer of 1984 and involved key informant interviews, oral histories and a survey of employers, supplemented by archival and secondary data sources. As part of our case study we also interviewed a 10 percent random sample of thirty-two households in the town of "Bridgeport." Complete work histories were collected for all family members as well as information on unpaid subsistence activities, the household division of labour, and current jobs. The sample was grouped into young (born since 1950), middle (born 1930-1949) and older (born before 1930) households. These groups were used to investigate the changing patterns of husband/wife work histories as major changes occurred in the industry. We were particularly interested in the combinations of wage work and self-employment and the relation between fishing and plant work.

The community has a long history as a major fishing port in Nova Scotia. As such, it has been affected by all the developments in the fishery for more than one hundred years. It provides an excellent case study of the processes at work—the changing structure of the industry and the changing household strategies of survival. It is typical of a handful of ports which have also been centres of trading, offshore fishing, and fish-processing activities throughout the development of the fishery. It is not representative of the many small communities scattered along the coast which are mainly dependent on the inshore fishery alone.

1. Periods in the development of the fishery

The nineteenth century—merchant capital and salt fish.
"Bridgeport" was founded in the mid-eighteenth century and its economy has always been based on fishing. Throughout the nineteenth century it grew as a centre of the West Indies trade, dominated by a handful of key merchants. The town reached its peak of prosperity in the 1880s and 1890s during this period of merchant dominance. It had shipyards, blacksmith forges, cooperages, a tannery and a boot and shoe factory, and was the business centre for the district. The town had a clear class hierarchy from early on.

During the period of the West Indies trade, most of the fishing in the area could be characterized as offshore. The merchants outfitted and sometimes owned the large schooners, and most fishers made their main living as crew. There were also some small boats which were involved in catching lobster, bait for schooners and some groundfish. It seems that the typical pattern was for men to crew on the schooners and then to do small boat fishing as part of a package of subsistence activities. This pattern seems to have followed both seasonal and cyclical lines with men doing a combination of inshore and offshore fishing over a period of years, including going away to fish. While the men were away fishing, the women kept their large households running. They kept gardens, sewed, preserved food and salted fish, but they needed to buy staples such as flour, sugar and molasses. Very little cash changed hands at this time; most purchasing was done through a credit/debt system at the merchant's store. It is questionable whether these fishers and their families could be characterized as independent commodity producers even at this early stage.

The early twentieth century—industrial capital and fresh/frozen fish.
The early twentieth century brought a major structural change with the gradual shift from the old merchant capital to industrial capital with an exclusive involvement in the fishery and a focus on processing (Barrett, 1984). Most of the big merchant families who dominated the town in the late nineteenth century had left the fishing industry by World War One. A related and overlapping development which began at this time was the gradual switch from salt fish to fresh fish.

In "Bridgeport" the two fish companies which have dominated the town down to the present were both established between 1900 and 1910 by people from outside the community. One stayed in family hands throughout the period, while the second, which eventually became National Sea Products after World War II, was sold to Halifax interests very early on. Thus, from the beginning there was considerable concentration in the buying/processing sector of the industry in the area.

These two companies began in salt fish but turned increasingly to the fresh fish market, with the advent of cold storage facilities. Salt and fresh fish overlapped through the 1920s and 1930s, but by World War II salt fish was finished. Offshore fishing on company-owned schooners continued through this period and overlapped with the introduction of trawlers and draggers, which were also company-owned. Conditions on the boats were deplorable, and incomes were low. During this period the companies also dealt with fishers who owned their own small boats, and directly employed increasing numbers of men in processing. Women were not employed in the plants until the war years when there were not enough men to do the jobs. Work for women was available in tourism, which was an important part of the economy of the town in the 1920s and 1930s.

The incomes and social standing of the fishers (inshore and offshore) and the plant workers seem to have been equally low and men moved between these two types of work. Even in this period very little cash changed hands, as workers got credit at local grocery stores on the basis of forthcoming pay cheques. It is noteworthy that plant workers and fishers were involved in organizing for better working conditions and higher wages throughout this period. This alliance is evidence of the class solidarity between these two groups.

Post World War II—modernization and concentration.
The period from 1945 to the early 1970s was another period of structural change in the industry. Barrett (1984) characterizes it as a modernization phase, with government policy promoting the industrialization and centralization of the fishing industry, leading to the increasing dominance of the National Sea Products company. There was also a change in the inshore fishery with the rise of a "nearshore" longliner fleet, beginning in the 1950s, and a continual decrease in the total number of fishers. The offshore fishery changed from schooners to offshore draggers and trawlers, whose ownership and home base became more and more centralized. Plant work also changed, becoming increasingly mechanized and employing more and more women. Overall, the numbers of people supported by the fishery decreased and outmigration was high.

These general trends were played out in "Bridgeport." One plant went from 150 employees in 1945 to 240 in 1974. In 1950 there were six or seven women in the plant, while by 1974 two-thirds of the employees were women. Plants also became less seasonal, operating, if sporadically, throughout the winter months. In the 1950s there was a shift from work in offshore boats to work in (or ownership of) the new longliners. Both companies and individuals owned them, though the trend was increasingly toward individual ownership of four- or five-person boats, with help from the company for the downpayment. The number of small boats (under 30 feet) declined. During 1972, National Sea consolidated its fleet in another community, eliminating much of the offshore crew option for "Bridgeport" men. There was some movement back and forth between small boat, longliner and trawler crew, depending on a man's experience and age.

Analysis of our household sample helps clarify the family work patterns. We found that in the older group (born before 1930) 80 percent of the fishers began working on the schooners and then had their own inshore boats after World War II. In the schooner days some crewed on company boats in the winter and fished inshore in the summer, and occasionally did other wage work such as road construction. Once they got their own boats they were mostly exclusively self-employed, though a few ended their working lives with a stint in the plant. Many of the wives of these older fishers (40 percent) worked for long periods in the plant after the war. By our calculation, only 20 percent of the fishing families in the older group survived solely on income from "independent" inshore fishing.

In the middle group—who reached working age in the post World War II period—again only a minority of the fishers were totally self-employed, though in this group the wage work of wives seemed less important (perhaps because fishing incomes improved during their prime working years).

Of the older group of men, 36 percent were mainly fishers (with their own boats for much of their worklives) while 29 percent were mainly plant workers. Seventy-five percent of the wives of the older male plant workers worked for long periods outside the home, though none at the plant. Female plant workers in the older group were more likely to be married to fishers. In the middle group this same general pattern was found, though with a small increase in the importance of plant work for the wives of male fish plant workers.

The later part of this period (the 1960s) saw the beginning of a crisis in the industry which was understood as a crisis of overfishing—related to the combination of the domestic and foreign offshore fleets. The crisis turned out to be as much about overexpansion as about overfishing.

The contemporary period—crisis and restructuring.
By the early 1970s many fish plants and fishers were in trouble, and a new period of change began in the industry. This period—from 1973 or 1974 to the present—is characterized by Barrett (1984) as the period of "regulation." This categorization is also used by people in the industry, from fishers to plant workers. There is a policy dimension to the change, and there is also a more real economic dimension. The period from 1974 to the present is often conceived of as two periods of crisis and recovery (1974-77 and 1981-84) with two concomitant policy thrusts (the 200-mile limit and licensing, followed by the Kirby Report (Canada, 1982) and "restructuring"). However, it is probably best understood as one steady process of crisis and adjustment in the industry (Williams, 1984).

"Bridgeport" provides an example of the developments in this period: increased consolidation of processing through bankruptcies and mergers in the early 1970s; growth of a more profitable midshore fleet in the wake of the 200-mile limit; increasing attempts by fishers to bypass/escape the control of the big buyers/processors; crisis in the large companies and "restructuring" since 1982; and technological change/modernization in the processing sector.

In "Bridgeport," the mid-seventies saw the bankruptcy of the large local company. It claimed it could have survived if the government had supported its attempt to switch back to the improved salt fish market. However, it was allowed to go into receivership, as were many other independent fish plants around the province. National Sea was also in trouble, but was supported by the government (and the bank) through the crisis. The bankrupt plant was bought by another local processor who had previously been processing lobsters. The reopened plant did not resume groundfish processing, but rather concentrated on processing scallops (caught out of another port), buying and shipping lobsters, and acting as a middleman by buying groundfish and selling it to the National Sea plant for processing. The number of jobs in the plant fell from over two hundred to fifty-five.

This is a good example of the concentration occurring in the industry at this time. The effect on communities was that there was less competition for plant workers. There was also less opportunity for fishers, and a worsening bargaining position for those plant workers and fishers left in the industry. Furthermore, the community was more dependent on the remaining company. The power of National Sea is illustrated by the response of government when its "Bridgeport" plant burned in 1980. This coincided with the end of the 200-mile limit "honeymoon" and the beginning of the crisis of the big companies in the industry, and as well with one of several fires in the industry during the period. After considerable lobbying by the community, the union, and the company, the plant was rebuilt at a cost of $14 million, much of which was government money. Furthermore, the town financially supported the new plant by tax relief concessions. An earlier attempt by National Sea to modernize with land concessions from the town had been blocked by the local fish company. Only after the 1980 fire did National Sea get the support it needed to build its modern plant. The community is now totally dominated by National Sea. It was in this way that National Sea got its most modern, capital-intensive plant. Its opening in 1982 coincided with the extreme financial crisis of the company, followed by the ownership change called "restructuring." As will be seen later, these changes have had a major impact on employment conditions in the "Bridgeport" plant.

2. The impact of the crisis and restructuring

We focus now on three dimensions of the changes: harvesters and processors and their relationship; processors and plant workers and their relationship; and the household and its relation to the industry in terms of patterns of labour allocation. In these sections we are particularly interested in the extent and nature of any fundamental changes in conditions and relations in the industry.

Harvesters and processors

In the harvesting sector, the last decade has been one of change. The changes in numbers of boats and numbers of fishers are quite small, but there are significant changes in conditions in the sector, in the species caught, and in relationships among fishers and processors. There are now about five locally owned longliners over 65-feet, and an equal number in the 45-foot to 65-foot range. There are also three vessels of over 100 feet, owned by the local plant or by individuals, and about thirty inshore boats in the area (145 in the whole district). Most of the bigger boats are 20 years old, and there was little overexpansion here with the introduction of the 200-mile limit, as there was in many ports. One owner of a 60-foot boat said he never saw good enough fishing to warrant buying newer, more expensive boats, even in the "good" years. In total, there are probably sixty local men fishing inshore and another sixty fishing on midshore boats. Perhaps twenty-five of these are from the town itself.[7]

There has been some change in the species caught. A crab fishery was started in 1983, with one 40-foot boat and one 90- foot boat, one of which is owned by the remaining local company and one by a fisher. Another new species is offshore lobster, and in 1984 one local fisher had a licence for this, using a 60- foot boat. The larger longliners also fish halibut and swordfish for part of the season, but the bread-and-butter is still groundfish and lobster.

One of the most striking changes in the harvesting sector in this area is the changing relationship between the fishers and the companies. The inshore fishers remain tied to the companies, but some of the midshore longliner fishers have attempted to become independent. National Sea now deals with about twenty small boats and six midshore boats, though 70 percent of their supply comes from their own offshore boats located in another community. The companies' hold over the fishers is formidable in terms of providing freezer facilities, storing bait, and supplying gear to the fishers—paid for out of their sales of fish to the company. The companies also help with repairs and loans for boats. In return, for these services the fishers sell their catch to the company. If they tried to sell their lobster elsewhere, for example, the company might refuse to buy their groundfish. In this atmosphere, it is significant that some fishers have managed to go "independent." There are four fishers (or partnerships) who have gone on their own. They all have at least two large (midshore) longliners, and they ship their fish directly to the U.S. or sell to the highest local bidder.[8]

The rise of the independent fishers/shippers began in the late 1970s when the industry was temporarily booming. There have been attempts by the companies to crush the independents, but in 1985 three of the four in the area were holding on. Methods of interference by the companies have included dumping fish (taking a loss on price), and refusing to buy any fish from the independents if they had trouble selling elsewhere. It seems also that the independents still have a harder time getting government help to build their facilities (such as freezers and bait sheds) than the large companies do, despite some official changes in government policy to aid the smaller companies. The independent fishers have in fact had to become small packers/processors/shippers in order to circumvent the control of the large companies. The modest success enjoyed by these "independents" raises questions about whether the balance of power in the industry is changing. Are the large companies temporarily too weak to resist them? Will they be tolerated within limits, but then be restricted, or will they in fact be able to grow and challenge the big companies? The independents feel that the companies still have immense power and still enjoy state support. They feel vulnerable and uncertain about their ability to survive. Yet, the real economic conditions in the industry at the moment seem to favour more small-scale development, and provide market openings that the smaller companies and independent fishers can respond to more easily than can the big companies, who are locked into the frozen fish market and their offshore fishing technology. Opinion among academics seems divided on the meaning of these changes.

Processors and plant workers

One of the most dramatic changes in this period involves the conditions of work in the new modern National Sea plant. While all of the National Sea plants are trying to increase productivity there is some feeling that this plant is a test case because they are the most technologically advanced. The new plant is larger and more capital intensive and has doubled the volume of fish processed. This is part of the continuing National Sea strategy of centralization. The plant is also designed to facilitate increased product diversification and higher quality packs. There is an overall drive to increase productivity through a combination of higher volume, improved technology and new management methods. In terms of technological change, the plant has a cutting/filleting machine, new skinning machines, a computerized refrigeration system, different table designs and computerized scales. The number and type of workers have changed as a result. A total of 235 worked in the old plant, two-thirds of whom were men. In the new plant there are about 320 regular workers plus eighty on a second shift. The ratio of men to women is now about 50/50. There has been an increase in the number of packers and trimmers, while the number of cutters (male) has decreased with the new technology and the number in maintenance and engineering (male) has stayed the same. The new technology has thus directly increased the productivity of the male workers, whereas the female workers are working with much the same capital as before. As we shall see, any increase in their productivity has essentially been due to a speed-up. The technological change also involves some organizational changes, in that there is a relative increase in the proportion of service people on the floor—such as weighers and icers. There is also an increase in "control" people and office personnel to monitor performance and quality. This has been facilitated by the computerization of scales and office records. If the workforce were broken down by skill, the net result of the changes has been a decrease in the proportion of highly skilled (cutters) and highly qualified workers. The net increase in productivity has been quite small, considering the massive capital expenditures.

The former plant was a much smaller, and quite old, wooden structure with outdated equipment. The scales, for example, did not always work and the building was draughty and often cold. Yet the workers describe it as having a relaxed family atmosphere. The work force came from the nearby area and everyone knew everyone else. There was little turnover and people saw it as their plant. Since it was a small plant it did not work steadily year round. This was especially important to the women, most of whom were married with children. While they worked long hours at the height of the season, they also had long periods to spend time with their children, get their housework under control and rest.

When the new plant opened most of the original workers were rehired and the old management remained.[9] The company's strategy, however, was to drastically reorganize and "Taylorize" the labour process. They brought in time management people, used the new computers to measure individual performance, and strictly enforced individual performance levels. Previously, individual performance levels were more difficult to measure for both quality and quantity and were only loosely enforced. Average production levels and average bonuses for the line were emphasized. In the new plant there was more emphasis on getting the individual women line workers to perform. Conditions were somewhat better for men, since they did the jobs that were not only better paid but also allowed for some freedom of movement and a more varied workload.

The performance level is an index based on the amount of fish processed in a given time period, and the quality of the product obtained. While each worker has to meet a performance level, the complexity of measurement differs by job. Cutters know approximately how many pounds they must cut and packers know approximately how many packs they must do. The greatest change has been for the trimmers. In the old plant the trimmers only boned and wormed the fish while someone else graded them. Now trimmers are expected to do all three at the same time and still make the required performance level. The different quality or grades of fish are packed in colour-coded packs which are assigned different values. The number and values of the packs are calculated each day to determine whether the performance level was met. Since the quality varies significantly so does the combination of types of packs and amounts of fish needed to meet the performance level. Only the most experienced trimmers know at the end of the day whether they have made it or not. Management, however, keeps everyone informed and if they do not make it they are "let go."

These changes can be interpreted as a move from simple to technical managerial control (Edwards, 1978). With the new technology women who do the line work can be monitored individually. The jobs become more demanding but the workers are more easily replaced, since control depends not on the loyalty and stability of the workers and their relationship to management, as in simple control, but on the specific measurement of individual performance levels by computers. Technical control involves less direct supervision, essentially deskills the workforce, and creates the possibility of speed-ups.

One reason why the workers object to the increased pressure on their performance is that they are expected to create a quality product out of fourteen-day old fish. This points to the vicious circle that the company finds itself in. In order to keep a large scale capital-intensive plant operating it must have a constant supply of fish. To keep the volume up they depend on large, capital-intensive draggers which are very expensive to operate. To make them pay they stay at sea for up to fourteen days. As the market pressure increases for quality fish the only immediate response open to the company is to change the processing end, which in turn further increases dependence on the large draggers. Each step the company takes further escalates the problem.

Another important change is that the new, larger plant and the dredging of the harbour made it possible for larger boats to land fish for processing year round. At the height of the season there is a considerable amount of work and the union contract requires people to work two nights per week overtime (with overtime wages). After two nights overtime in one week people can refuse to work more. There is a different reaction to overtime by the women and men in the plant. The women, who are still responsible for the children and work in the home, find it difficult and nearly impossible to work eleven-hour days, still make their performance levels and keep up their household responsibilities. This is compounded by the fact that, except for a few slack months in winter when they do not work full weeks, the plant operates all year. This leaves them little time to catch up on domestic work and recuperate from the exhausting plant work. This, together with the increased pressure for performance levels, has led to high turnover rates among the women, even though for most the alternative is unemployment (cf. Balderson, 1984). As a result, less than half the women from the old plant remain.

Today the workforce is drawn from a much wider area, and fewer people from the town and surrounding area work in the plant. A different labour reserve is being drawn on. Emphasis is now on hiring young people who can consistently make the performance level. People do not know each other, and with the turnover rate, will not get to know each other well. The workers say the atmosphere is poor and working conditions are high- pressured and stressful—"people work like robots." Some say the company keeps turnover high so it can pay the lower probationary wages. The management view of these changes is that turnover is voluntary, and is not a problem, since they can easily recruit and train more people, given the high unemployment and underemployment in the area. Management's view of the replacement of the workforce is consistent with the change from simple to technical control. Management also claims that women do not want to work year round, which is true, given their burden of domestic responsibilities.

The union has been trying to respond to the restructuring of the labour process, but is in a very weak position. The union leadership indicate that there are more problems now and that there are five times as many grievances. At the time of our research they had been without a contract for eighteen months and their last wage increase was in 1982. The main outstanding issue was wages. The company had said that after restructuring they would be in a better position to negotiate, but that apparently was not the case. According to the union, management's position is that wage increases must come out of profits. Since there have been no profits there have been no wage increases. The union, on the other hand, felt that if enormous amounts of money could be found to buy out the former owners and pay off debts, some should also have been found to pay the workers.[10]

Five National Sea plants are under the same union contract. With restructuring National Sea closed one plant and workers in the other plants worry about which will be closed next. People in very old plants have more to fear than those in the new plants and this difference affects their bargaining position. Everyone admits that the company has real problems, but the union feels that they are carrying the heaviest share of these, both as wage earners and as tax payers. However, the union has little bargaining power since the plant is the only major employer in the area and there are large labour reserves to be drawn on. Unions face extreme difficulties in this context.

Household and industry

To this point we have mainly examined the relationship of individuals in the industry to the means of production—fishers and processors, plant workers and processors. It was noted that the numbers, working conditions, power and status of each group of workers have changed as restructuring has occurred on various levels. However, as emphasized earlier, a full understanding of the industry dynamic, the articulation of the modes of production and the process of underdevelopment, requires an integration into the analysis of the household as an economic unit. How have the patterns and strategies of household labour allocation altered as conditions have changed? What has this meant, not only for the well-being of families but for class relations in the industry, the sources of profit for the companies, and the direction of development?

In the middle- and older-age groups, as noted earlier, men had sometimes moved between fishing and plant work, and had generally moved from fishing on company boats to owning their own boats or to crewing for someone else. The wives of fishers in these groups frequently worked as well. They were the career plant workers who were displaced by the restructuring in the new plant.

In the young group in our sample, the fishers are now and always have been midshore crew. Furthermore, male plant workers in this age group have never fished. Thus, for men fishing and plant work have become increasingly separated. The wives of the young mid-shore crew have worked some, though less than in the young age group generally. The trend over the years, then, has been for fishers to become less self-employed and for both them and their wives to be more fully proletarianized. Fishers who are crew have become totally proletarianized while a smaller number have become more or less exclusively self-employed—though perhaps still tied to the company.

The development of the fishing industry, then, has reduced the relative numbers of inshore fishers and increased the numbers of midshore crew and male plant jobs.[11] In the young group, 57 percent of the men are plant workers while 28 percent are fishers, all of whom crew on midshore boats. Thus increasingly the men are primarily wage workers. With regard to wages, plant employment now pays considerably less than fishing. Average income for young fishers in our sample was $16,333 compared to $11,250 for young plant workers; for middle-aged fishers and plant workers it was $25 thousand and $16,875 respectively.

How do the trends in household labour allocation and incomes relate to questions raised in the literature about the semi-proletarianization of fishers and their families, and whether capitalist underdevelopment was facilitated by semi-independent commodity production (characterized by low wage labour of many household members and low prices to primary producers)? Fairley (1985a) argues that, in fact, capitalist development is occurring with the straightforward proletarianization of most people, while some formerly marginal independent commodity producers become small scale capitalists in their own right. We suggest that a more useful way of understanding these changes is that the family and community pattern of exploitation has altered, though the end result is essentially the same from the company's point of view and in terms of development. To see this, we must examine the changing family patterns in relation to plant work.

We have identified the increased importance of plant work for men, as well as the very low incomes earned by male plant workers. Not surprisingly, this usually necessitates a two-earner family. In the older groups it was the wives of fishers who mainly worked in the plants—the old example of the double exploitation of the family through low prices to fishers and low wages for plant work. In the younger group all the male plant workers' wives have worked in the plant within the past two years and 80 percent of the husbands of female plant workers work in the plant. Thus, increasingly the trend has been toward husband/wife teams in the fish plant and for female plant workers to be married to plant workers rather than fishers. The combined income of a two-earner fish plant family is typically less than $20 thousand barely above the 1984 low-income floor of $16,544 for a family of four in a small centre (National Council of Welfare, 1985).

Certainly, the response of the company to changing conditions can be argued to have substituted one form of household super exploitation for another. A "family wage" is not being paid to anyone in the plant and, as argued in the previous section, the brunt of the pressure caused by financial crisis has been felt at the processing end, through largely vain attempts at productivity increases. This is simply a continuation of the distorted capitalist development that occurs in an underdeveloped region.

As for the fishers, certainly there has been an increase in incomes—but this has come via real productivity increases, due to capital investment, improved stocks (at least temporarily) and decreased inshore competition. The increase has not come from prices paid by the companies for fish. These prices have been falling due to the international factors discussed earlier. In the face of depressed prices, increased volume is the only way to make a living, which of course further depresses prices. In the "Bridgeport" area, probably the greatest increase in income has come from pursuing new markets, and high value species such as offshore lobster, crab and halibut. At least for now, family wages are being earned by the men on these boats, but this could change and if it does the household would once again have to rearrange and reallocate their resources.

In the context of underdevelopment the company can and does pay less than subsistence wages and prices to some of the people they deal with. While this takes different forms at different times, it is still the household that absorbs the major impact of the industry's crisis.

3. Conclusion

The analysis of the present crisis made by fishers, plant workers and the union in Bridgeport is as follows. There is a vicious circle, whereby the big companies have overexpanded, with the help of government subsidies. Their large plants need a steady supply of fish, which is met by an increase in the offshore dragger fleet. The draggers have to stay out until they are full, so poor quality, fourteen-day old fish results. The draggers always fish at a loss—the investment can never be recouped— so the companies try to squeeze their profit from the processing end, at the expense of the workers. A more profitable size boat would be in the order of 60-feet but this would not meet the big plants' need for steady, controlled, supply. One result is overcapacity at both the plant and dragger level, and a combination of poor quality and high volume which depresses the price of fish. The large companies are totally inflexible and unable to manoeuvre through the ups and downs of a volatile market. When they get into financial trouble, the government bails them out, repeating the vicious circle. The alternatives to this require such far reaching changes, that they are neither politically acceptable, nor feasible, given the political power of the big companies. To this local analysis must be added the impact of changing external conditions in the world market.

Meanwhile, the high quality fish caught by the small- and mid-size boats are shipped directly or sold to the smaller processors who are more flexible and can respond to the changing demands of the fresh fish market more easily (cf. Apostle and Barrett, 1985). For these fishers, at this time, markets are good and incomes are reasonable. Though these independent fishers have had some success at circumventing the direct hold of the big companies, they had little sense that the overall power of the companies had diminished. They see their attempts to grow being thwarted by economically irrational government regulations, and constantly threatened by the big companies.

The National Sea plant workers, on the other hand, are supposed to turn poor quality, fourteen-day old fish into high quality packs, in addition to processing fish blocks for a declining market. To accomplish their production goals the new capital-intensive year-round National Sea plant has changed from simple to technical managerial control. This has meant high-pressured, stressful working conditions with a high rate of turnover of the labour force. The high percentage of female plant workers find these conditions particularly problematic since most of them combine their wage work with domestic work in the household.

Fishers' wives do not work in the plant as they once did. The fishers are now making more money than plant workers. The income level, the pattern of fishers being away for long periods of time with women entirely responsible for the household in their absence, and the more industrial conditions of work in the plant, all combine to account for fewer fishers' wives working in the plant. Whereas there was once considerable movement between plant work and fishing we now find a clear division between these two types of work for men. And while fishers' wives do not work in the plant, plant workers' wives do. The pattern of household labour allocation has changed but from the company's point of view the results are the same. They still pay below subsistence wages and prices to the plant workers and the fishers.

We have tried to understand something of the nature of the real structural changes occurring in the industry as well as the impact of the political restructuring. Our community provides an excellent example of the changing conditions of plant work and the changing relationship between large companies and the more successful nearshore/midshore independent fishers. We can, however, say little overall about the state of more marginal inshore fishing or prospects in the independent processing sector. Our small part of the picture needs to be combined with the observations of other researchers and observers of the Atlantic fishing industry. Only then can a complete analysis of the extent and meaning of restructuring be undertaken.

Notes

1. We would like to thank the people in the community we studied and the members of our research team, Kathy Moggridge, Joyce Conrad, Suzan Ilcan and Daphne Tucker for their contributions. This research was supported by an Social Science and Humanities Research Council (SSHRC) Women and Work Strategic Grant. All papers out of this joint research are co-authored, with alternating order of names.

2. In recent years, the underdevelopment of Atlantic Canada has been the subject of considerable theoretical and empirical analysis (Veltmeyer, 1979; Sacouman, 1980; Bickerton, 1982; Clow, 1984a; Matthews, 1980, 1983). And in the past few years there has been an increasing amount written on regional underdevelopment and the fishing industry. There is now a considerable body of research on Newfoundland (Wadel, 1969; Anderson

and Wadel, 1972; Matthews, 1976; Brox, 1972; Fairley, 1983, 1985a; Sinclair, 1985c; Porter, 1983a, 1985a, 1985b; Antler, 1981; Neis, 1981). Conditions in the Nova Scotia fishery are somewhat different, however, so that generalizations from the Newfoundland case must be done with caution. Recent political economy work on the Maritime fishery has included a useful community case study focusing on the labour process in a plant (McFarland, 1980), as well as one which examines the relationship between domestic and wage labour (Connelly and MacDonald, 1983). Tony Davis (1975, 1983) has done anthropological work on one fishing area in Nova Scotia, focusing on primary producers. Historical work on unionism in the Nova Scotia fishing industry has been done by Gene Barrett (1976), while Jim Sacouman (1979) has analyzed the history of the co-operative movement in the industry. Class relations in the fishing industry have been examined by Rick Williams (1979) and recently by Wally Clement (1983; 1986a). These studies focus on the contradictory class location of the fishers, due to the partial transformation of independent commodity production, so that they are neither truly independent nor truly wage labourers. Current research is also underway at the Gorsebrook Institute at Saint Mary's University on many aspects of the fishery in Nova Scotia.

3. There is a growing body of literature on women and development which takes this position. See, for example, Aguiar, 1983; Beneria, 1979; Beneria and Sen, 1981; Cross, 1981; Deere and de Leal, 1981; de Leal and Deere, 1979; Kelly, 1981; Nash and Kelly, 1983; Nash and Safa, 1980; Safa, 1981; Sen, 1980; Young, 1978.

4. For research on the role of women's work at the aggregate level of the Canadian economy see Armstrong, 1984; Armstrong and Armstrong, 1983a; 1984; Connelly, 1978; MacDonald, 1979.

5. According to Frobel, Hienrichs and Kreye (1980) this trend towards the new international division of labour is the result of: a) the existence in developing countries of a practically inexhaustible reserve army of labour which is cheap and will work long hours, can with short periods of training reach levels of productivity comparable to those in developed countries, can be chosen according to age, sex, skill and discipline and when used up can be replaced easily; b) the existence of an advanced division and subdivision of the production process which means that the fragmented process can be learned in a short time and carried out with minimal skill levels; c) the existence of transportation and communication techniques which make it possible to transfer the complete or partial production process to any site in the world at reasonable costs. This new set of conditions "has brought into existence a world market for labour and a real world industrial reserve army of workers, together with a world market for production rates" (Frobel, Heinrichs, Kreye, 1980).

6. This does not mean, however, that the fishery is excluded from the possibility of direct affects of the NIDL. For example, if the multinationals are supported by government policy in their efforts to get freezer trawlers these could be, at least in the first instance, on contract from other countries and might use cheap labour from the developing world.

7. In the fishing district, there are 244 registered fishers, 90 percent of whom are officially full-time. There are eighty lobster licences in the area and about 160 groundfish licences. Half of those with groundfish licences would also have lobster licences. There was a buy back program in lobster licences in the early 1980s, and many older fishers sold them back. The fisheries officer noted a definite decline in the number of lobster fishers.

8. For example, someone fishing halibut could bid it or ship directly. If it was bid, whoever got the halibut would also take their groundfish. However, if the halibut is shipped directly, then the groundfish must be also. If it is not shipped then it must be sold to little buyers in the area, since the big companies would boycott this groundfish.

9. When the old plant burned down many workers found other jobs, usually at lower wages. Some travelled a fair distance to other fish plants, some worked in a local nursing home, and some as store clerks or waitresses. At least three retired and some remained unemployed.

10. They now have a new four-year contract in which "they got a lot less than what they asked for." The union feels that the company has even more power now that the contract is signed.

11. Of the current male labour force, over half work in the plant (53 percent) and less than one-third are fishers (29 percent), with most of the fishers being crew on midshore boats. For women in the households, the labour force participation rate is 47 percent, close to the provincial average. Forty percent of the female labour force are plant workers and unemployment among women is high (27 percent), mostly related to conditions in the plant. Two-thirds of the young working women mainly work in the plant, compared with one-third of the middle-age group. The pattern has also changed, from a core of steady workers to many women passing through the plant.

Chapter Seven

Class and Gender in Nova Scotia Fishing Communities

Martha MacDonald and Patricia Connelly

This paper[1] explores the complexity of class relations in Nova Scotia fishing communities, using a conception of class which takes into account gender and household relations. The purpose of any class analysis is to better understand the conditions under which people live and work, and the way they act in their lives. Workers often behave in ways that surprise and frustrate Marxist theorists—being passive where they should act, and rising up and resisting in the most unlikely circumstances. It is our view that an understanding of gender and household dynamics as they relate to class would help make sense of such behaviour. There is always a danger, however, that attempts to clarify class positions degenerate into static exercises in labelling and filling boxes.[2] Our purpose in this paper is to show that a more complex, gendered class analysis can illuminate otherwise anomalous characteristics of the pattern of labour relations and capital accumulation in an industry.[3] We use a specific case study of the fishing industry to illustrate our general point.

Our concerns with the literature on class, both theoretical work and applied work on the fishing industry, are its focus on the individual, ignoring household dynamics and gender, and its static focus on an individual's work at a single point in time. In traditional analyses, class position is determined solely by an individual's own direct relationship to the means of production,[4] or for dependent individuals by the class of the (male) head of household (Goldthorpe, 1983). When the mode of production is understood to include relations of reproduction as well as production, then the conceptualization of class must change. Household and gender relations must be taken into account. Both life cycle work patterns and spousal work patterns will affect a person's current class identification. This is crucial for understanding class struggle.

After some theoretical discussion of these issues, including attempts in the feminist literature to come to terms with class, we illustrate from our research in Nova Scotia fishing communities how an expanded interpretation of class provides a better guide to understanding relations in the industry. We focus on the behaviour of family household members in relation to each other, exploring the use of the family household as a crucial unit in class analysis. The actual dynamics of the formation of family class consciousness and decision making are not directly analyzed, though this is a crucial part of the overall feminist project of reevaluating the traditional concept of class.

Class Revisited

In recent years a considerable effort has been put into a reevaluation of orthodox Marxist class categories, primarily to understand the position of the expanding "middle class" (such as managers and professionals). Attempts to locate these predominantly white collar workers have led to debates over the key defining elements of Marxian class positions and the notion of contradictory class location. A number of schemas for revised class categories have been proposed.[5] In this literature renewed attention has been paid to the category of petty bourgeois (Poulantzas, 1973; Hill, 1975). However, petty bourgeois is itself a problematic category in the literature.[6]

Issues of the petty bourgeoisie and contradictory class positions have been at the heart of the literature on class structure and struggle in the fishing industry of Atlantic Canada, which has motivated and informed our research. The main problem in this literature is the position of fishers, for processing workers are seen as clearly working class, and owners of fish plants with employees as capitalists.[7] There is general agreement in the literature that offshore crew are essentially working class, though in terms of ideology they may identify as petty bourgeois, holding onto the notion of the "independent" fisher. Crew on inshore and nearshore boats are argued by the unions and most analysts to be also working class, though through kinship ties many can also be considered to be members of family businesses. Furthermore, many aspire to becoming boat owners themselves, which affects their class identification.

The main debate in the literature and in organizational efforts in the fishery has to do with the status of fishers who own their own boats. Are they small scale capitalists, or petty bourgeois, or in a contradictory class location? Williams (1979) and Sacouman (1980) were early writers on this issue. More recently, Clement (1986b) identifies five patterns among fishers: subsistence production (no exchange); capitalist commodity production (both company owners and owners of longliners with four or more crew would be considered capitalist); independent commodity production (the fisher has formal and economic ownership of the means of production, has non-exploitative labour relations, and faces prices determined by supply and demand, therefore he is part of the traditional petty bourgeoisie); dependent commodity production (the fisher is tied to buyers in a relationship of unequal exchange, having formal but not economic ownership); and co-operative commodity production (where the boat owner is either capitalist or petty bourgeois). Williams (1982) has a similar scheme but includes an additional category of semi-proletarian, or semi-proletarian dependent commodity production, where fishers engage in wage labour to help make ends meet. He also recognizes that this wage labour may be sequential, not seasonal, and that the wage labour of other family members may also be involved. We elaborate this point further in this paper.

The class position of dependent commodity producers is considered to be either contradictory (Williams, 1979) or inherently unstable or transitory (Fairley, 1985a). The debates on this are part of the larger debate about underdevelopment and the future of independent commodity production within capitalism. Sacouman (1980) and Williams (1979) argue that part of the process of underdevelopment is the distorted maintenance of this mode of production, while Fairley (1985a) argues that straightforward capitalist development is occurring in the industry, with some fishers becoming small scale capitalists. One concern in this debate is the implications for class struggle, and the potential for fishers' organizations to be progressive.[8]

This literature on the Atlantic fishery is very rich, and is grounded in concern for political struggle rather than academic classification. However, it is our view that important implications for understanding class struggle are missed by inadequate attention to gender and household in most analyses.[9]

As Marxist feminists have reiterated over and over, mostly to nodding heads but deaf ears, there are problems with Marx's analysis based on the individual's relationship to the means of production. They have tried to sort out the interrelationships of class and gender, arguing for a gendered analysis of class and a class analysis of gender (Armstrong and Armstrong, 1986). The process of developing an integrated, comprehensive theory of gendered class struggle is long and difficult, with work proceeding on the level of grand theory and through empirical studies.

Feminists have strongly criticized Marxist theory for the fact that its concepts don't apply to the household, which is the traditional area of women's work. Among feminists, there has been more unanimity in the critiques than in the proposed revisions to received theory. Much intellectual effort has been expended in trying to integrate women's work in the home into the Marxist class framework through the "domestic labour debate" (Fox, 1980). Radical feminists have argued that the "domestic mode of production" has its own mechanisms of exploitation, creating sex classes which coexist with the classes of the capitalist mode of production (Delphy, 1977, 1984). Walby (1987) argues that gender interests operate independently and often in contradiction to class interests, and that gender subordination is independently created in the workplace as well as in the home. Others disagree with this "two systems" approach, arguing that the concept of mode of production should be expanded to include both the reproductive and productive spheres, with relations of reproduction and production seen as interactive and dialectically related. There is continuing debate over the extent of autonomy of the spheres of social reproduction and production (Humphries and Rubery, 1984).

Others have posed the problem in terms of women's relationship to the wage in capitalism, focusing on the contradiction between women's roles as wage labour and domestic labour. This dual relationship to the class structure, it is argued, has important implications for consciousness and forms of resistance (Coulson, Magas, Wainwright, 1975). Along these same lines, it has also been argued that the working class should be defined not as those with a particular relationship to the means of production but as all those who are dependent upon the sale of labour power - directly and indirectly. As wage earners women have a direct relationship to the wage but as domestic workers they have an indirect relationship to the wage experience through their husbands' wage labour (Gardiner, 1977; Acker, 1988). In this approach women's relationship to the class structure is, at least partially, mediated by the family household, domestic labour and dependence on men. Even when women are themselves wage workers, the integration of gender and class relations gives a distinct meaning to their experience of class in the workplace (Pollert, 1983). In the feminist literature, therefore, as in the Marxist literature discussed above, there is an emphasis on contradictory aspects of class position. The contradictory forces identified by feminists analyzing the class positions of women (i.e. both direct and indirect relations to the means of production) must also be applied in a revised class analysis of men.

Recent feminist work has focused on showing theoretically and empirically the centrality of women's household labour and the relations of reproduction to any analysis of the economic system. This is especially true in the literature on gender and development, which shows that women's work, gender relations and household forms are integrally related to the accumulation process. In a variety of ways they both affect and are affected by the specific form accumulation takes in particular countries and regions (Leacock and Safa, 1986).

The literature on gender and development reminds all political economists of the need for an "analysis of the interconnections between capital accumulation, class formation, and gender relations" (Beneria and Sen, 1981). Part of the feminist agenda is to show that gender analysis is not something to be done separately, but is something that profoundly affects the "main business" of Marxist analysis (Smith, 1987). Ignoring issues of gender and household may quite simply lead to a wrong understanding of the world. "Gendered class analysis" does not mean class analysis of women; it means a new approach to all class analysis.

How can we begin to revise the standard class analysis to take into account these concerns? Feminists have strongly criticized the sociological approach of defining women's class position as that of their husbands (Acker, 1973; Delphy, 1984; Stanworth, 1984; Porter, 1983b). The class position of women must take account of their direct and indirect relation to the means of production—their own productive and reproductive labour as well as that of their husbands. By implication, the class position of husbands must take account of the work of their wives.[10] An excellent attempt to analyze the joint determination of the class positions of family members is the work of Beneria and Roldan (1987), which analyzes the class trajectories of wives and husbands and their interactions, in Mexico city. They show that advances in the class positions of the males are facilitated by downward mobility of their spouses, and they relate this to the general process of capital accumulation.

There have been attempts to assign class locations to households by taking account of the work of both husbands and wives, such as that by Britten and Heath (1983) using aggregate data for the United Kingdom. There are many conceptual and empirical challenges in such undertakings. It is our view that such revisions are better explored at the level of local data, with particular issues of class struggle and economic change in mind. In the next section we outline some of the elements involved in this expanded class analysis, and suggest why it should make a difference to the analysis of the fishing industry. Later sections use specific examples from our research to explore how such an analysis could be used.

The Fishing Industry Revisited

As mentioned above, most of the class analysis of the fishery has focused on individuals at one point in time, ignoring their work histories and family work patterns. But people's class identification is affected by both, as well as by their gender. Rick Williams (1979) pays attention to the work history aspect in his sketch of a "typical" inshore fisher. He describes a person who began by fishing with his father and who then decided he wanted to be a fisher. Later he spent five years crewing in B.C. (working class) to raise capital to buy a boat. Now he owns a boat, is a "highliner," sells competitively and employs no labour (petty bourgeois, or independent commodity production). However, if the fishing is bad he occasionally still goes to Prince Rupert to crew for a season. His experience on the West coast gave him a belief in unions, and he is active in the Maritime Fishermen's Union, though his concerns reflect a mixture of working-class and independent business ideology.

One can imagine another equally "typical" fisher who inherited his father's boat and never had the wage-labour experience, or one who worked on offshore boats for awhile, or one who drove a cab in the city for years. Each of these would have a different identification and orientation towards the struggles in the inshore fishery. Understanding the patterns that operate should enable us to better understand class behaviour at a given point in time.[11] Furthermore, work patterns may differ by community, or may be changing over time, which will help us understand the changing class dynamic across communities.

Women's work histories also affect their current work behaviour.[12] Women may move between formal wage labour and informal activities such as babysitting, selling handmade goods, taking in boarders and so on. The class position of these informal sector activities is seldom examined. For women there is also the ever-present work of reproduction, the class position of which has been subject to scrutiny in the domestic labour debate (Fox, 1980). The combination of production and reproduction work undertaken by most women adds complexity to their class position and class consciousness.[13] In fishing communities there is another kind of work activity of women that is often ignored, and that is the work that wives of fishers do for the family enterprise, generally without pay. There are certainly implications for class analysis of women who are not only fish plant workers but are also working for their husbands' fishing operations. Most of the research on the fishery has ignored the implications of the complex work histories and pluralistic work patterns of the individuals involved in the industry.

For the most part, household/spousal work patterns have also been ignored in analyses of class relations in the industry. One of the questions that motivated our own research was "who works in the fish plant?". It seemed to us that it made a great deal of difference whether it was wives of fishers, wives of fish plant workers, single people, people whose spouses were unemployed, or whose spouses worked in unrelated industries. The employees class identification and the terms of struggle in the plant (and in the fishery) should be profoundly influenced by the answer to this question. For example, analyzing the relation between fishers and plant owners, and separately analyzing the relationship between plant owners and processing workers makes little sense if the fishers are married to the plant workers. Their interests are intertwined. Higher prices for fishers may mean lower wages for plant workers. This may be acceptable to the wives of fishers, given unequal gender relations; it may not be acceptable to women plant workers whose husbands work outside the fishing industry, or alongside them in the plant.

There are many examples which illustrate that spousal work patterns should be an essential part of the analysis. For instance, Clement (1986b) tries to explain the internal dynamics of co-operatives (co-ops) in the fishing industry by analyzing the complex class relations within the co-ops. He points out that co-ops contain within them all the classes of capitalism, creating internal class struggle. He emphasizes that the member fishers may be independent commodity producers in their own fishing enterprises, but that in their role as co-op members they function as capitalists in relation to the processing workers. This helps explain why co-ops have a very bad record as employers, in terms of wages. However, gender relations are ignored, even though most fishers are men and many processing workers are women. Nowhere, furthermore, does Clement take into account the household relations between co-op plant workers and member fishers, or between crew and boat owners for that matter. How this complicates the class struggle within the co-ops, and their potential for progressive action, is illustrated in the final section of this paper.

Spousal work patterns and gender relations also need to be more closely addressed in the analysis of semi-proletarianization of fishers (dependent commodity production). We expect it makes a difference whether it is fishers who take wage jobs, or their wives, or even their children. If it is the fisher himself, it may give him a contradictory sense of his class, and may incline him more to a working-class analysis of his situation, with implications for the kind of political action in which he will engage. If it is his wife, given asymmetrical gender relations in the household, her proletarianization may facilitate his acquiring a purely bourgeois class identification, which of course may also limit his wife's political action. We would expect differences in the struggles over time and by area, depending on the form this so-called semi-proletarianization of the fishing household takes.

A final general point about the importance of household and gender relations to a class analysis is that the terms of struggle are both shaped by, and in turn shape these household relations. How do household strategies for survival, individual strategies regarding work, and strategies of capital interact over time? Does capital encourage (or benefit from) a particular spousal work pattern over another? Do households choose a pattern of labour allocation as a conscious part of class struggle (Humphries, 1977)? If so, what are the gender implications of this choice? We can look for evidence that capital has consciously tried to manipulate family work patterns, through hiring practices, for example, to strengthen its hand. The state has of course also played a role in altering the work patterns and this has changed the class and gender relations in the fishing industry (Connelly and MacDonald, 1987).

In other words, an expanded class analysis enables us to take a fresh look at the processes of struggle and economic change in the industry and in the communities. In the remainder of this paper we use two types of data from our research to examine some of these issues. Firstly, we document the family work patterns, exploring the combinations of individual class positions and the question of a family household class position. Secondly, we examine changes in industrial relations in two communities, showing that using the household as a unit of analysis helps clarify our understanding of the struggles.

Household and Lifecycle Work Patterns and the Complexity of Class

In this section we examine household survey data from a sample of six Nova Scotia fishing communities.[14] We are interested in individual work history patterns and spousal work patterns.[15] The purpose is to show the complexity of the work patterns and therefore of class positions. We suggest implications for class relations in the industry, which are more fully explored in the next section. The six communities include two larger fishing centres, dominated by National Sea plants, three medium size communities with independently-owned fish plants, and one small community with a co-op buying station but no processing plant. With these data we are able to examine overall trends and differences in patterns by age group and by community.[16] First we look at the individual work histories, then we examine combined work patterns of wives and husbands.[17]

Approximately 30 percent of the male spouses had fished, 30 percent had worked in the plant, and 15 percent had done both. We are interested in movements among boat owning (petty bourgeois), crew, and wage labour (particularly in the fish plant). We found that 70 percent of men who had owned their own boat at some time had also worked in a crew position and three-quarters of them had other wage work experience, with 17 percent having worked in the fish plant. Typically those who owned their own boat had spent only 60 percent of their working lives self-employed and a pattern of multiple job holding throughout the year also characterized about 40 percent of them at least some of the time. Of men who had ever worked in the fish plant (45 percent of our sample), 40 percent had also fished at some time and a quarter of those had moved between plant and fishing more than once. The most common direction of move was to go from the plant to crew, however 15 percent had owned boats before going into the fish plant, and 10 percent left the plant to buy their own boats. For these men, it is likely that the experience or aspiration to be a boat owner coloured their consciousness while they were in a working class position.

In general, then, there is considerable evidence for complex individual class positions of male fishing industry participants over the course of their lives. Therefore, interpreting male fish plant workers as strictly working class, or boat owners as petty bourgeois will have limited ability to explain their behaviour.[18] We found considerable variation in the patterns by community. For example, in the largest port all of the boat owners had wage work experience, whereas in the smallest, most traditional community, only 25 percent had done anything other than fish. The pattern of multiple job holding during the year was particularly common in the Eastern part of the province, where the fishing is poorer. We also found differences by age group, with the younger cohort less likely to hold multiple jobs, or move from one class position to another.

Turning now to the work patterns for women in the communities, we found them to be equally complex. Approximately three-quarters of women have done wage work at some time since marriage, typically for about a third of their married lives. Much of this wage work experience was outside the fishing industry, primarily in the service sector; however 40 percent have worked in the fish plant at some time. Women have also been active in various forms of self-employment, such as babysitting, selling crafts, or selling Avon products. In addition to doing most of the domestic labour for their households (wives of fishers do essentially all the household work), women engaged in subsistence production of various sorts, including keeping gardens, making clothes and preserving food. These activities, which are often associated with independent commodity production, have declined rapidly in recent years, with the younger cohort more likely to substitute wage work for subsistence activities. We also found that subsistence activities remain more common in the Eastern part of the province where, as mentioned above, the fishing is poorer. Women whose husbands have been boat owners have also engaged in a variety of work (generally unpaid) that supports the fishing enterprise. This adds another dimension to the class fabric of their work histories.

As emphasized above, in our view it is critical to class analysis to link up the work experiences of household members, and in this paper we focus on the spousal work combinations. In examining spousal work patterns, we are particularly concerned with combinations of work which are relevant to understanding class relations in the fishing industry, in both the harvesting and processing sectors. Therefore we focus on the work of wives of fishers (owners and crew), wives of male plant workers, and husbands of female plant workers.

We found that almost half of the wives of boat owners worked for wages during at least part of the time their husbands owned the boat. In fact, one-quarter of the wives of boat owners worked at the plant at some time while their husbands owned boats. We found this to differ by community and by age group. In the larger fishing ports the recent trend has been away from wives of fishers (both crew and owners) working outside the home. This implies more consistent family class positions emerging. In smaller communities it is still common to have wives of fishers working in the plants, which affects the struggles of both fishers and plant workers against the plant owners.

We also collected data on the extent to which wives of boat owners contributed labour directly to the fishing enterprise. We found that the amount and kind of work contributed by wives has changed over the years. Since World War II they have become more involved in the bookkeeping tasks and less involved in production of supplies or processing of the catch.[19] Among the wives of the current boat owners, the most common involvement was in bookkeeping work (50-60 percent do books and bills) and running errands (50 percent). One quarter of the wives also arranged sales. Only 25 percent of wives now prepare meals for the men or ever fish with their husbands. Interestingly, in our sample we found no differences in the extent of involvement in the fishing enterprise between those wives who also held paid jobs and those who did not. From interviews with key informants in the communities we know that many of the larger independent fishers have their wives working as partners (often unpaid), running the business side of things. These households fit the traditional model of petty bourgeois, though of course the class position of these wives is still problematic.

When we examined the spousal work patterns for men who have been fish plant workers, we found that their wives were more likely to have a history of work outside the home than the wives of fishers. Almost three-quarters of the wives worked outside the home during the time the men were in the plant and almost 40 percent worked in the plant at the same time as their husbands. The class position of most of these households thus appears to be working class, although as mentioned above many of the men would have also fished and some would have been boat owners, affecting their class identification.

It is also crucial to know the work patterns of the husbands of female plant workers. In our sample, 40 percent of the wives had worked in the fish plant at some time. There was great variation in the pattern of their husbands' work by community. In the larger ports (dominated by National Sea), the more common pattern was for husbands of female plant workers to be in the fish plant or other wage work, whereas in the smaller ports the husbands were more likely to be fishers. We also found variation by age, with the younger generation more likely to have both husband and wife working in the fish plant.[20] This is particularly significant for class struggle in the processing sector, which we examine in the last section of the paper.

When we examined the current family work patterns in our sample[21], we found that none of the wives of current boat owners were in the plant, though 63 percent were doing wage work.[22] This differed by area, with the wives of owners on the more prosperous South Shore more likely to be at home. We found that 18 percent of the wives of crew and 21 percent of the wives of male plant workers were in the plant,[23] again with differences by community.

Looking at the husbands of female plant workers, 46 percent were also in the plant, none were owners, 23 percent were crew, and 8 percent were unemployed or retired. In one medium size inshore port none of the female plant workers' husbands worked in the plant, and 75 percent were crew, whereas in the large National Sea dominated ports 67 percent and 80 percent of the husbands were also plant workers and none were crew. These differences by community should help explain observed differences in industrial relations.

In conclusion, our data illustrate the complexity of household class positions in the fishing industry. We find differences by community, which seem to be related to the nature of the fishery in each area (inshore/offshore, prosperous/marginal, corporate/independent). These differences also reflect the stage of capital accumulation, since the ports studied represent the spectrum from traditional small scale fishing to monopoly capital. We find some evidence that male work patterns have become more stable, with less movement between fishing, plant work and other work, at least in the more corporate communities. The evidence also suggests that clearer family class positions are emerging in the more corporate sectors of the industry. This means that the class interests of family members are compatible; for example, both are wage workers, or both are dependent on one income, whether it be from wage work or self-employment. Contradictory household class positions characterize the more marginal sectors of the industry, with the class interests of family members potentially conflicting. In such cases, the class identification of either spouse can deviate from what one might predict by observing only their individual relationship to the means of production. Unequal gender relations in the household and the workplace will affect what the dominant class interest in the family household will be and what the household strategy will be regarding the allocation of labour.

Analysis of Particular Struggles

In this section we use particular examples from our community case studies to demonstrate that an expanded class analysis helps clarify the state of industry relations. In our first community, a medium size port, the fishers co-op built a processing plant in 1950. Fishers earned low incomes and their wives worked in the plant at low wages. The benefit of the co-op was that the people felt they were working for themselves and they were keeping some surplus in the community. Since the fishers owned the co-op and their wives worked in the plant there was a perception of it as a family affair; men caught the fish, women processed them. Therefore, despite the fact that women were doing working-class jobs and earning low wages under poor conditions, the petty-bourgeois class consciousness of the husbands prevailed and there was no talk of unionization in the plant. Women essentially saw themselves as family help (processing the catch) in a petty-bourgeois enterprise.

In the early 1970s, as a result of expanding at the wrong time and a refusal of the Nova Scotia government to provide support, the co-op was sold to private interests. This was a period of crisis in the fishery. Many fishers sold their boats and more women entered wage labour. Conditions in the plant worsened, if anything, under private management. But fishers needed to sell their fish to the plant and their wives, along with other women, needed the wage, so unionization was still not on the agenda. A fight for higher wages could have negatively affected the price of fish and even the sale of fish to the plant. Once again the family household work patterns affected the potential for working-class consciousness and militancy of women wage workers.

When fishing improved and fishers' incomes rose in the late 1970s, it no longer made economic sense for wives of fishers to work for low wages in the plant. Rather than raise wages to keep the labour force, the employer found a more marginal female labour supply in a nearby community (with the help of a government-supported ferry). These women were married to men who had low paid, often seasonal jobs outside the fishery, such as cutting pulp or working on the roads. At first there was no sense of class consciousness among these women and no sign of resistance. They were grateful to have the work. The fishers' wives, as part of their household strategy, withdrew from the labour force even though some said they would have preferred to stay. In this case, the household strategy and gender relations within the household took precedence over women's wishes and employers' needs.

In the 1980s the plant ceased buying fresh fish from local fishers and began to process northern cod to supply a fast food chain in the United States. A new manager was hired to double productivity and increase the quality of fish, with no corresponding increase in pay for the workers. Women on the line bore the brunt of these changes. Most of the women from the nearby community were the most stable, if not the main, breadwinners in their households. They were unprepared to continue working under deteriorating conditions and they sent for a union organizer. The employer's response was to threaten to close the plant. The women called the employer on his threat and after a lengthy struggle the union was certified.

When we first interviewed these women several years ago they showed no signs of militancy of any sort. In this case, however, the women's class position was not only the dominant one in their households but also their husband's position in no way conflicted with theirs. As a result, their household strategy reflected a working-class consciousness and led to working-class struggle.

We next illustrate the implications of this approach for clarifying class relations in the industry with a brief case study of another community, a larger fishing port which has been an industry centre for over a hundred years. It has had two large processing plants since the early 1900s, one of which is a National Sea plant, recently modernized. The plants have been the largest employers for the town and surrounding area. It had an offshore fleet until the early 1970s when National Sea consolidated its fleet in other ports. Recent years have seen the rise of a few successful midshore boats, owned by independents.

Up until World War II, no women were employed in the fish plants, though they worked in the service/trade sectors. Most married women did not work outside the home. The early pattern for men, when processing was minimal, was to crew on the schooners and then to do small boat fishing as part of a package of subsistence activities. This pattern seemed to follow both seasonal and cyclical lines, with men doing a combination of inshore and offshore fishing over a period of years, including going away to fish. In the period between the two World Wars, the men were increasingly involved in processing (wage work), and there was also an increase in small boat fishing as well as a continuance of company-owned offshore boats. The incomes and social standing of the fishers (inshore and offshore) and the fish-handlers seems to have been equally low, and men moved between these two types of work. In this context, it is not surprising that in the organizing efforts of the 1930s, fishhandlers and fishers (offshore) formed one union and waged a strong, lengthy struggle for recognition. These men had a shared class consciousness. Furthermore, they were strongly supported in their fight by their wives.

After their bitter defeat, and World War II, relations changed in the industry. More men turned to inshore fishing, moving between crew and owner status. Increasingly, once they got their own boats they were mostly exclusively self-employed, though a few ended their working lives in the plant. At the same time, the companies began hiring women in the plants, a change variously explained by the labour shortage of the war and by technological changes in processing. It is our opinion that the change had also to do with the bitter labour struggles which had just occurred and the companies' desire to continue to pursue a cheap (docile) labour policy.

The ensuing period saw much more passive labour relations in the community. Many wives of the fishers who sold to the companies now worked in the fish plant. These fishers were in dependent commodity production (Clement, 1986b; Williams, 1982), tied to the companies who had monopsony power as buyers. They were further tied by their wives' wage work in the plants, and often by the work of their children.[24] The companies had considerable leverage over these families. In terms of consciousness, it seems that these inshore fishers developed more of a bourgeois consciousness of "independence," facilitated by their wives' proletarianization. The combination was not conducive to political action on either front—in the plants or on the boats.

When we look at changes in the community in the last twenty years, we find that gradually fewer of the wives of fishers worked at the plant. This is partly due to higher incomes for fishers in the area. More and more the male labour force is being divided between boat owners, crew and plant workers, with less movement among these positions. A further trend is for the number of boat owners to decrease, so that more and more men are in a working-class position in terms of their own relation to the means of production. The men who remain as boat owners have been able to achieve more independence from the companies, due to the rise of the fresh fish market and independent buyers. They are less tied to the companies as families, too, for increasingly their wives do not work in the plants.

Most male plant workers' wives worked outside the home throughout the post-War period; however, only in recent years have they tended to work in the plant. Increasingly the trend has been towards husband/ wife teams in the plant, and for the female plant workers to be married to plant workers rather than to fishers.[25] There are also many female plant workers who come from outside the community and who are typically married to men not involved in the fishing industry (working at low-wage jobs), or are single parents. In terms of the family class orientation of the plant workforce, then, it has become more clearly working class in recent years.

How has this affected relations in the plant? Relations between workers and management have been very bad in recent years. The successful paternalism that the company employed in the past is no longer used or workable. The withdrawal of fishers' wives from the plant probably contributed to this, as it did in the community discussed above. The corporate strategy as described by both the company and the workers is much like any capitalist labour strategy. Class struggle in the plant has become more pronounced, the lines more sharply drawn. The company's strategies include technological change, speed-ups and dividing the labour force by its recruitment strategy. During one of our visits, this seemed to be working in capital's favour, for the workforce was demoralized and frightened for their jobs. However, a later visit reassured us that class struggle was alive and well, and there was more sign of resistance by the workers who, as analyzed above, have a fairly clear class position.[26] Resistance has mainly taken the form of turnover and individualized responses to the bad conditions. The company is feeling the effects.[27] These workers have a great deal of potential power, although as usual in an underdeveloped region this is offset by the pressure of a reserve labour force. Management is looking for a more desperate workforce (single parents, women whose husbands are unemployed). They also have the ever-present option of closing the plant. At the time of writing, subsequent to our fieldwork, there is a strike in this plant, confirming our expectation that clearer household class positions should facilitate increased worker resistance.

Conclusion

The theoretical debates about class and the literature on class structure and struggle in the fishing industry focus on the individual at a point in time and ignore both women's unpaid and paid work, the family household and gender relations. Feminist research, on the other hand, has shown the importance of these issues to class analysis. In this paper, we have argued that women's work, gender relations and household strategies are necessary to understanding class relations and class struggle in the fishery.

Using data from our study of fishing communities we have explored ways of modifying class analysis using the family household as a unit of analysis. Class is a dynamic and complex relationship affecting, in the majority of cases, women and men who live together in unequal gender relations within households. By looking at women and men's work histories (domestic and wage labour) and their family work patterns and strategies we are better able to understand their class position and their class consciousness. Using the household as the unit of analysis, it appears that class conditions gender relations and gender conditions class relations. The challenge for political economy is to understand more fully these processes. Research is needed on the dynamics of family decision-making, the formation of class consciousness, and the interaction of class and gender interests at the level of the family.

In this paper we have illustrated in a preliminary way the implications for analysis of class positions and class struggles in the fishing industry. We have demonstrated that an expanded class analysis clarifies the state of relations in the industry. Insights are gained which go beyond those possible using the traditional, individually-based class framework of most Marxist analysis.

Notes

1. We would like to thank the people in the communities we studied and the members of our research team, Joyce Conrad, Beth McIsaac, Kathy Moggridge and Daphne Tucker for their contributions. This research was supported by a SSHRC Women and Work Strategic Grant and by the Donner Canada foundation. All papers out of this joint research are co-authored, with alternating order of names.

2. This accusation has been made of much of the debate over the proper class location of the "new middle class." It has also been made of the "domestic labour debate," for example in an article titled "Wiping the Floor With Theory" (Kaluzynska, 1980).

3. There are of course many class-related issues in the feminist literature which we do not address in this paper. For example, we focus more on struggles in the sphere of production than on intra-family relations and domestic labour.

4. We are referring particularly to the literature on a reevaluation of Marxian class categories (Wright, 1976, 1978; Poulantzas, 1973) and to attempts to enumerate the class composition of countries, such as Clement (1983) and Veltmeyer (1988) in Canada. The literature on class consciousness takes more account of formative factors such as father's occupation. For an interesting example of such work on the fishery, see Lummis (1984).

5. Veltmeyer (1986) summarizes the positions. One approach is to add all these workers to the traditional working class, since all are dependent on selling their labour power. However, it seems that the identification and interests of these workers is often more similar to the capitalist class than the working class. Some writers thus emphasize the ways that this group have similarities to capital, either in their real economic control (though not ownership) of the means of production, their ownership of significant "human" capital, or their control of their own or other people's labour. Depending on the factors emphasized, the group is then viewed as forming a new class. This may be either a professional-managerial class as argued by the Ehrenreichs (1978), or a new middle class as argued by Carachedi (1975), or occupying a contradictory class position (Wright, 1976, 1978), or being part of the petty bourgeoisie (Poulantzas, 1973; Hill, 1975). Veltmeyer (1986) and Clement (1983) essentially take the latter position, at the same acknowledging the contradictory aspects of their class position.

6. There are debates about the definition of petty bourgeois, for example whether they may purchase any labour power. There is some disagreement about their relation to the working class and whether they can be part of a progressive alliance for social change. There is also interest in the evolution of this class, whether it will whither away or stubbornly persist.

7. The problem of classifying fishers on the East Coast is reflected in the law, where until recently all fishers were excluded from trade union legislation and classified as co-adventurers (self-employed), based on the fact that crew are paid on a share basis rather than with a wage. Newfoundland was the first to change the law, so that all fishers (other than captains on big company trawlers) are now able to be members of the union. Nova Scotia changed the law in 1971 for crew on large trawlers.

8. Fairley (1985a) argues that the NFFAW is dominated by the larger boat owners and the union's agenda has become the development of capitalist production in the fishery. Most other Marxists argue that the contradictory class position of fishers means there is the potential for more progressive organization and struggle in the industry. Both Williams (1982) and Clement (1986b) emphasize the mixture of working-class and independent commodity producer ideology in fishers' attempts to organize and in the issues they pursue. Sinclair (1984) argues that for Newfoundland the direction of development seems to include both an increase in small capital (as emphasized by Fairley) and a growth of dependent commodity production (as emphasized by Sacouman and Williams).

9. A literature on women and fishing, including this research, is now emerging to redress this imbalance.

10. This continues to be resisted, and the traditional approach defended, by some leading class theorists (Goldthorpe, 1983). See Phillips (1987) for a discussion.

11. One relevant determinant of class consciousness is of course class of origin, routinely decided with reference to father's occupation. The influence of mothers on children's future class identification should equally be investigated.

12. This is sometimes recognized in the literature on unionization, for example. The point is often made that women are not interested in unions because of their short commitment to the job, or because the experience in household work gives them an ideology of "independence."

13. This has been explored in many case studies of women and the labour process. A good example is Anna Pollert's (1983) study of tobacco plant workers.

14. The data was collected from 1984 to 1986 and included a household survey which focused on family work patterns, including paid and unpaid work (n=150). In addition we conducted oral history interviews and interviews with key informants, including fish plant managers.

15. We focus on spousal work patterns both because of their theoretical importance in discussions of class and gender, and for empirical reasons. Our data is from a project focusing on women, and our universe for sampling purposes was all households with adult females. As it turned out, only one of our respondents was a single (never married) woman.

16. We divided our sample into three age cohorts, those born since 1950, those born between 1930 and 1949, and those born prior to 1930. Our interest in community in this paper is to document that there are community differences in work patterns which relate to community differences in observed class relations. Given the primary focus of this paper and limitations of space, we are not able to discuss the detailed differences among communities, or the theoretical role of community in class analysis.

17. Our sample was a random sample of households (with adult females) in each community, therefore not every household was necessarily involved in the fishing industry. However, of the male spouses in our sample, only 25 percent had no work involvement in the fishery.

18. Lummis (1984) in a study of East Anglia fishermen considers the boatowners to have a predominantly working-class consciousness.

19. Wives of men who owned boats prior to World War II mainly knit lobster heads (75 percent), cooked meals (75 percent), cleaned and salted fish (38 percent), and sometimes fished with their husbands (63 percent). In the

period from the War to 1970, 25 percent helped with bookkeeping, while running errands, knitting lobster heads and salting fish declined in importance. Preparing meals remained an important job (77 percent). Fewer women fished with their husbands in this period (31 percent). The pattern remained similar from 1970 to the present for wives whose husbands owned boats during that period.

20. Other papers based on this research examine the sexual division of labour in the plants. There are many differences in the way the husbands and wives experience the labour process, even if they work together in the same plant.

21. Of the men, 22 percent are in the plant, 22 percent are fishing, 29 percent are in other wage work, and 27 percent are retired or unemployed. Of the women, 10 percent are in the plant, 27 percent are in other wage work, and 62 percent are at home (including retired). There is considerable variation in the labour force participation rates of the women under age 65 by community, ranging from 25 percent to 60 percent.

22. Our sample of current boat owners is very small. Our key informant interviews in the community indicated that in the smaller communities many fishers' wives do still work in the plant.

23. There is wide variation by type of crew in whether wives of crew work outside the home. Wives of offshore crew, who earn good money and are away for extended periods, tend to stay home, whereas wives of inshore crew, particularly in the smaller ports, have a high labour force participation rate. There is also a life cycle effect, of course, with younger wives more likely to be home with small children.

24. It is our estimation that only 20 percent of the fishing families in our sample from this community who were born before 1930 and had their own boats after the War survived solely on the income from "independent" inshore fishing. There was often a seasonal pattern to the work of wives and children in the plants, with older children working in the summer while mothers stayed home to look after the younger children who were out of school at that time.

25. Today we see a situation where in our sample all the young male plant workers' wives have worked in the plant in the last two years; furthermore, two-thirds of the husbands of the female plant workers in our sample also worked in the plant.

26. There are still gender differences in the experience of class of the men and women, which affect the possibility of unified action. See, for example, Pollert (1983).

27. One manager gave an analysis of the power that two-earner families have. He said that neither one feels the responsibility of a primary earner—the women quit for periods of time and want their jobs back, and the men are increasingly slacking off in other ways, such as absenteeism.

Chapter Eight

The Crisis, the State and Class Formation in the Newfoundland Fishery

Bryant Fairley

1. Introduction

This chapter is about the impact of the crisis of the 1980s on class formation in the Newfoundland fishery, and the light which this throws on the nature and significance of the social movements which emerged in Newfoundland and the Maritimes in the 1960s and 1970s, and of the popular resistance to restructuring in the 1980s. Before turning to this, however, it is necessary to first clarify some theoretical and methodological points.

Previously (Fairley, 1883; 1984; 1985a) I criticized those who saw in some of the social movements of the 1970s, and especially the struggle of primary producers in the inshore fishery for higher fish prices, "not just a struggle for better returns but, at least structurally, an anti-capitalist, working class struggle," as Jim Sacouman put it in a 1980 article (Sacouman, 1980). Other examples of the same tendency were Williams' contention that the logic of the struggle of the Maritime Fishermen's Union "would place socialism squarely and inexorably in our path" (Williams, 1979), and the notion held by seemingly all the contributors to *Underdevelopment and Social Movements in Atlantic Canada* (Brym and Sacouman, 1979) that the central fact of the postwar period was the *de facto* (but not *de jure*) conversion of inshore fishers into the "proletarian" or "semi-proletarian" owners of fishing boats. Against this I argued that what was at least equally distinctive in the 1960s and 1970s was the emergence and growth of a class of capitalist fishers in the inshore fishery, and that, in light of this, the primary producer social movements were more realistically to be seen as populist struggles, against "big capitalism" perhaps, but *for* the capitalism of this new element of capital.

In advancing this interpretation of the political economy of inshore fishing in Newfoundland and (by extension) the Maritimes as well, I implicitly advanced what in retrospect were two very different approaches to class analysis. Developments in the 1980s, as well as lessons I have learned in the course of the debate which this book is about, and in my current research on North American agriculture,[1] require that these two approaches be made explicit, and one of them abandoned. One approach I took to the class analysis of the Newfoundland fishery was that which is usually seen to constitute an "orthodox Marxist" class analysis (although this "orthodoxy" in fact dates not from Marx, but from Karl Kautsky (1971) and other leading theorists of the Second International). Central to my initial contributions, especially, was the economic and structural identification of a class of people I variously referred as the "the *nouveaux riches*" (an unfortunate and inaccurate rhetorical flourish) or, better, the "new fishery bourgeoisie." In the Newfoundland fishery, in 1979, this was a group of perhaps 1,000 people who owned the largest inshore fishing boats—most of them so-called nearshore vessels or "longliners" of 35-65 feet in length and often worth $100,000 or more—and who employed some 3,500 workers paid according to the "co-adventurer" or "share system" (essentially a form of piece-wage whereby the employee receives a pre-determined percentage of the fish caught rather than a fixed wage). During the 1960s and 1970s the number and size of the enterprises owned by this new fishery bourgeoisie, and the number of workers they employed, had grown chiefly on the basis of an expanding market for many species of raw fish created by the establishment of fresh-frozen fish processing plants. Many of these owners, especially those owning enterprises using mobile gear or those solely engaged in the pursuit of crab or shrimp and groundfish, were making a lot of money. Furthermore, as Sinclair showed in his case study of longliner owners in the Port au Choix area (Sinclair, 1984c:42), these owners were "completing the circuit of capital" by re-investing earnings in their enterprises. By the end of the 1970s these small capitalist enterprises accounted for almost one-half of the annual output of the Newfoundland inshore fishery, and more than one-quarter of all fish landed in Newfoundland; similar developments were apparent in the Maritimes.

My subsequent economic, political and ideological analysis turned on the "objective" economic fact of the new fishery bourgeoisie so identified. *Given* this new bourgeoisie, I argued that the development of the Atlantic fishery was clearly an example not of "underdevelopment," but of a normal process of capitalist development. Capitalism was rapidly extending its sway not only in the form of large-scale fish-catching and processing firms (Fishery Products, National Sea Products, etc.), but also via the differentiation of small-scale inshore fishers into capitalists, on the one hand, and increasingly pauperized and then proletarianized petty bourgeois, on the other. *Given* the new bourgeoisie, "manifestations" of it becoming a "class-for-itself" could be found in the policy positions during the 1970s of the federal state and the main primary producer organizations, the Newfoundland Fishermen, Food and Allied Workers Union and the Maritime Fishermen's Union. Given the new bourgeoisie (and the ongoing development of capitalism), primary producer social movements, and "Maritime Marxism" itself, exemplified *narodnism* or populism—the typical response of the pauperized primary producers to the forces of developing capitalism—and were, objectively, unwitting supporters of the new bourgeoisie. Another example of this kind of class analysis of primary producer social movements and ideologies is Alain de Janvry's critique of Samir Amin, et al. in "Social Differentiation in Agriculture and the Ideology of Neopopulism" (in Buttel and Newby, 1980), which achieves levels of reductionism I would like to think I never reached.

This kind of class analysis of primary producer social movements in Newfoundland and the Maritimes (or in other areas of the First or Third Worlds) needs to be explicitly abandoned. In the first place, the analytic significance attributed to *actually existing* classes and class fractions in this approach spawns (as it did in the debates about the relative significance of the "new bourgeoisie" versus the "semi-proletariat" in social movements in Atlantic Canada) fruitless arguments about the "essential" character of these purportedly "objective" classes. How "really bourgeois" was the new bourgeoisie? How "really proletarian" were the semi-proletariat? How many fishers were capitalists and how many could be described as their employees? How high were the profits earned, how low were the wages paid? How "independent" were the new bourgeoisie from other fractions of capital? These kinds of questions left room for innumerable answers (witness Sacouman's comment in the next chapter that the importance I attached to the new bourgeoisie was "vastly over-stated empirical insight"). For they were not really so much empirical, as practical and political questions. More than this, given that any class or class fraction historically has to start somewhere, and is then bound to appear "small," "weak" or "dependent". The question is in fact only resolvable *ex post*, when the struggles which interested us in posing questions about classes are over and done with, with one outcome or another. In the second place, this kind of class analysis leads almost inevitably to political and ideological analysis and debate which is reductionist and sectarian. The issue is the degree to which the objective reality of the actually existing classes constitutes the subjective motivation of concrete actors, in this case the federal state and the Newfoundland or Maritime fishers' unions, not to mention the "Maritime Narodniks" and the "metropolitan Marxists."

The fundamental problem with this kind of class analysis is that it is ahistorical. Classes are treated as existing independently of the social, economic, political and ideological conditions under which they emerged and developed. This is only satisfactory so long as conditions remain the same. As Leys notes in his preceding chapter, what made Lenin's analysis so powerful was that he was "right," i.e. the conditions that underpinned social differentiation and capitalist development in Russia continued to be maintained through the 1890s and until World War I. But what happens to such class analysis when conditions change, and especially in an era of crisis, when the future of all classes and class fractions becomes ambiguous, and new social forces emerge, and contingency rules? Under such conditions the actually existing, "objective" classes of class analysis may prove very unreliable.

For these reasons, this kind of analysis needs to be supplanted by another conception of class analysis, such as that proposed by Adam Przeworski (1977). In this approach,

> we must think along the lines, also suggested by Marx, in which economic, political, and ideological conditions jointly structure the realm of struggles that *have as their effect* the organization, disorganization or reorganization of classes. Classes must thus be viewed as effects of struggles structured by objective conditions that are simultaneously economic, political and ideological (Przeworski, 1977:343).

A class analysis of this kind is, as Przeworski puts it, "a form of analysis that links social development to struggles among concrete historical actors" (343).

This is the kind of class analysis of social movements in the Atlantic fishery that I was groping toward in my 1985 article (Fairley, 1985a)— as was signified by its title, "The *Struggle* for Capitalism in the Newfoundland Fishery," not "The Development of Capitalism in the Newfoundland Fishery" (Fairley, 1983). From this perspective, the pivotal fact was not the *actually existing* "new bourgeoisie," but its ambiguous economic significance, on the one hand, and, on the other, the implications for resolving this ambiguity of the actual struggles and policy positions of existing actors (the federal Department of Fisheries and Oceans during the Romeo Leblanc era (1974-1981), the fishers' unions, the Maritime Marxists). The key question was the situation of the owners of the generally smaller and more numerous longliners which used hired labour and fixed gear (notably gillnets) to pursue groundfish. While many of these—50 percent according to one 1979 survey (Canada, Fisheries and Oceans, 1981:23-24)—were earning positive returns, at least 50 percent were not; in 1979 the average enterprise lost 3.3 percent of its total capital after interest and insurance payments. These relatively small *average* losses meant that the future development trajectory of the fishery was highly contingent. A full-blown process of differentiation and capitalist development on the basis of the inshore fishery (with the concomitant formation of a new bourgeoisie employing a new class of workers) was a distinct possibility which depended on the economic, political and ideological realities of the 1960s and 1970s.

In the first place, apart from the troughs of the normal capitalist trade cycle, through the 1960s and 1970s total North American consumption of various protein commodities made from fish (breaded or batter-coated sticks and portions, standard-quality frozen fillets) increased steadily, thereby validating ever-increasing investments in processing plants. The strong price performance of raw fish, specifically year-over-year increases in Newfoundland inshore prices of 12 percent in 1977, 23 percent in 1978, 13 percent in 1979 and 15 percent in 1980, also validated ever-increasing investment in catching capacity. And while in 1979 a 28 percent price increase would still have been required to receive an adequate return on the average investment in light of recent experience it was not unreasonable to assume that this might soon be realized.

Then there was that peculiar "force of production"—uncaught fish. "It appears paradoxical to assert, that uncaught fish ... are a means of production in the fishing industry. But hitherto no one has discovered the art of catching fish in waters that contain none" (Marx, 1967:181n1). After 1977, when Canada claimed a 200-mile economic zone, groundfish stocks (or more accurately, quotas) had increased substantially for the inshore sector, and catch rates seemed to be following suit. More than this, all the possible "shoulders" to the groundfishery developed chiefly by longliner owners—herring, mackerel, seals, caplin, crab, shrimp—were entirely positive, contributing 15 percent to 20 percent of the revenue of nearshore groundfish enterprises (Canada, Fisheries and Oceans, 1984:10). In other words, a real prospect of increasing catch rates and a longer operating period (through the pursuit or the discovery and development of alternative species), *without additional capital investment*, meant that the increase in the groundfish price actually required for the average enterprise to receive an adequate return was significantly less than the 28 percent suggested by the returns on the volume of fish caught in 1979.

Nonetheless, the necessity of achieving yet higher prices made the outcome of the fishers' political efforts pivotal; but the prospects offered by these for an emergent "new bourgeoisie" were also bright. In 1972 a joint, corporate economic institution, the Newfoundland Fishermen, Food and Allied Workers Union, had been successfully established. This organization merged the Northern Fishermen's Union, an organization of emerging longliner owners, with the most advanced segments of the working class in the fishery, the plant workers and workers on trawlers. These workers were being organized by the Canadian Food and Allied Workers Union, a branch of the U.S.-based Amalgamated Meat Cutters and Butcher Workmen (later the United Food and Commercial Workers Union UFCW]). Beginning with the purging of the conservative international trade-union representative in 1972, followed in 1987-1988 with the decision of the Newfoundland local to abandon the UFCW and join the new Canadian Auto Workers union led by Robert White, the union became a socially- and politically-active, autonomous, comprehensive fishery organization which was "more than just a union" (cf. Inglis, 1985). By 1980 it was a social movement of more than 20,000 members in which the concerns of inshore fishers were at least central (Inglis, 1985). Precisely which groups, if any, actually predominated, was and is open to debate, but by 1974-1975 it was certainly *as if* this Newfoundland fishery union (as it will be referred to hereafter) was the political organization of an emerging new bourgeoisie. The main policy positions taken (restrictive licensing, limitations on trawler operations, increased "inshore" fishing quotas and, most of all, improved fish prices for and improved *profitability* of "inshore" fishing enterprises) dealt precisely and directly with the central obstacles to the consolidation and growth of capitalist enterprise in the inshore fishery. Furthermore, it did so with an effectiveness only dreamed of by fishing organizations elsewhere in Atlantic Canada. As the union's Secretary-Treasurer put it,

> I would much prefer our system to the kind of splintering you see, for example, in Nova Scotia.... We've frequently had issues where there was pretty serious conflicts of interest between different groups of our members. In a great many of those we've been able to bring everybody together, close the doors, and try to work something out....
>
> I'll give you one example.... Back in the late 1970s there was a hell of a commotion for a couple of years about the deepsea trawlers fishing in inshore areas—fishing too close to the mouth of the bay, interfering with inshore fisher[s]....
>
> At the same time this was happening, in the Maritimes the fisher[s'] groups were taking a public position that there should be a 50-mile limit, and no trawlers within 50 miles off shore. Now that's nonsense in some areas.... But that was the public position

they took—hard and fast, rigid, 50 miles. No more likelihood of being accepted now than I have of jumping over the moon.... [A]nd the trawlers were saying: "The hell with you, we're going to fish wherever we want"....

What we did was call a meeting, then we had a small committee of trawlermen and a small committee of longliner skippers (because they were the one's most affected). We more or less said: "You sit down over here and you sit down over there; you remember he's got to make a living, and you remember he's got to make a living, because we're all in this together".... And we worked out ... a recommendation: ... a three mile zone from shore out was closed to trawlers, plus there were "windows" that could be opened or closed depending on the inshore activity. Since that time the issue has died down (McCurdy, 1985).

Thus the union in this as in other cases, through "bringing everybody together" for whatever subjective reasons, effectively compromised the hitherto *superior* position of trawler owners (and trawlermen *qua* trawlermen) in the Atlantic fishery in ways that further secured the prospects of longliner owners.[2]

The effects of the policies implemented by the federal state during the 1970s were at least as important for the formation of the new bourgeoisie as the policies fought for and won by the Newfoundland fishery union. In 1974 Romeo Leblanc was appointed, as he said, "minister of fishermen," and which ones he was thinking of is open to interpretation. Ralph Matthews, for example, cites this and other similar Leblanc statements as "making it difficult to accept that the federal state in Canada almost invariably acts in the interest of capital" (Matthews, 1983:209). But given that the fate of the full-blown formation and consolidation of a new fishery bourgeoisie hung on the thread of somewhat higher fish prices, it was *as if* the new bourgeoisie had developed a significant representation within the federal state during the 1970s (on this concept of representation see Mahon, 1977:170). Dating from 1974 (if not somewhat earlier), "the central themes of federal fisheries policy changed from those that encouraged large-scale industry in fish-catching to those which promoted and consolidated capitalist development from the small-scale inshore base," a change manifested in a variety of new policies (Fairley, 1985a:58ff.).

It is this kind of class analysis of the political economy of fishing in Newfoundland in the 1980s, in which class formation and social development are seen as *effects* of the struggles of concrete actors rather than as an immediately "given" reality, that I seek to take further in this chapter.

2. The economic crisis of the 1980s

When we turn to the Newfoundland fishery and the question of the "new bourgeoisie" in the 1980s, it is if as we were examining an entirely different world. Economic events in the 1980s made more and more improbable the achievement of price and/or productivity increases which would see the new bourgeoisie, and the continuing differentiation of inshore fishers into proletarians and bourgeois, consolidated as general phenomenon. First, after 1979, the real, after-inflation price of Canadian groundfish blocks and frozen fillets (the major products of the Newfoundland industry) seriously weakened in the United States, which was the market for 74 percent of Canadian groundfish in 1981, and for 77 percent of Newfoundland cod blocks (Newfoundland and Labrador, 1981). With few exceptions, cod and pollock block prices, and frozen cod fillet prices, dropped year after year, and the price of turbot blocks fluctuated.[3] This, in turn, was reflected in prices to fishers for raw groundfish which stagnated in 1980 and, in real terms, fell continuously for an unprecedented five successive years through 1984.

What made the situation yet more serious, however, were catch failures. To put it mildly, the expectation of increasing groundfish stocks and increasing catches—even in 1982 the Task Force on Atlantic Fisheries was predicting that the total Atlantic groundfish catch would increase by 77 percent between 1981 and 1987, and the northern cod stock by 75 percent (Canada, 1982:161-162)—was not realized. With the exception of 1982, the fish did not come into the inshore and nearshore fishing grounds on the east coast of Newfoundland, and ice and mucky water fouling gear and catch were continuing problems. These conditions meant that even in 1987, when sharply increasing U.S. consumption of fresh fish and frozen fillets sent all prices soaring to new heights (before dropping off again in 1988), low total returns were earned in Newfoundland. Indeed poor inshore catch levels in Newfoundland were one of the primary causes of the short-term high prices (*Financial Post*, July 27, 1987:7). Equally significant was the deterioration of all the shoulders to the longliner groundfishery. As Earle McCurdy of the fishery union described it in 1985:

There's been a really, almost unbelievable combination of misfortune.... Herring has gone to virtually nothing. Crab has had a dreadful decline in the last 18 months [1984-1985]. Seals are practically a thing of the past. Squid (though that wasn't so much a longliner fishery) somewhere down the line disappeared. Mackerel has declined. It's been a wipeout (1985).

Surveys by the Department of Fisheries and Oceans (DFO) of the costs and earnings of inshore and nearshore enterprises in the 1980s give some sense of the "wipeout." According to the 1982 data, at the height of the crisis the average Newfoundland longliner primarily pursuing groundfish with fixed gear had losses amounting to 6.4 percent of the total capital value of the enterprise, and after interest and insurance payments the loss was almost 11 percent. Similarly in 1983 the average enterprise lost a sum equivalent to 5.8 percent of its capital value, and 9.4 percent after interest and insurance payments (Canada, Fisheries and Oceans, 1984b,c).[4] Vessels pursuing groundfish with seines did even worse, the DFO data suggested. In 1982 the average seine-equipped longliner lost a sum equal to 7.6 percent of its capital value before insurance and interest payments (11.2 percent after), and in 1983 it lost 11.0 percent (14.6 percent after interest and insurance payments). Only the average longliner enterprise devoted entirely to the crab fishery earned positive returns in 1982 and 1983, according to the DFO data, and these were reversed by the drastic decline in crab catches in 1984 and 1985.[5]

From the point of view of class formation and the continuing differentiation of inshore fishers, the implications of these figures were enormous. In 1982 the average, fixed-gear, groundfish longliner would have had to receive no less than 8.6 cents per pound more, or a 53 percent increase in fish prices, to receive a 10 percent return on the total capital value of the enterprise. In 1983 the enterprise would have had to receive 7.4 cents per pound or 44 percent more per pound to realize an adequate return.[6] All this in a situation not of rising real prices (which was the case in most of the twenty years preceding 1980) and rising catch-rates (as in the years 1976 to 1980), but one of stagnant or falling real prices and catch rates.

The real economic problem here was not so much that negative returns occurred; enterprises, and especially fish-catching enterprises, are always having periodic bad years which can be made up from depreciation allowances. The problem was that prices and returns remained low year after year. The drop in fish prices was *not* one of those "cyclical variations ... which are not markedly different from those of other food products," as some catch rates in 1982 or some price rises in 1983 or 1987 suggested (Canada, 1982:91). It was, rather, the product of two entirely new developments. First it was a reflection of a value movement— a consequence of a change in the labour-time socially necessary to produce a unit of product—led most importantly by the North American, and especially the United States, *poultry industry* (Fairley, 1985b:13ff.). During the late 1970s the price advantage of fish forms of protein (breaded sticks, batter-coated portions and standard quality frozen fillets) over chicken as the cheapest forms of protein rapidly deteriorated—so much so that in 1981, for the first time, the retail price of a [*three*-pound broiler chicken was less than that of a fourteen-ounce package of fish sticks or portions, and equivalent to that of *one-pound* of frozen cod fillets (Calculated from U.S., Department of Commerce, 1968, 1978; U.S., Department of Agriculture, 1983). The result was stagnating and declining consumption of groundfish blocks (and probably of standard frozen fillets as well)[7] in the United States, and consequent oversupply and falling prices. These changes in the relative values of fish and other forms of protein were further reinforced by changes in the industry itself. Danish fish-block producers, driven from the U.S. market in the late 1970s and early 1980s by the cheaper Canadian product (and by falling chicken prices), came back with a vengeance in late 1983 with a top-quality block produced cheaply in new, expensive, "roboticized" fish factories (Shortall, 1985). These helped bring U.S. block prices to a new low in 1984, yet Danish blocks were reportedly still profitable under those conditions (Shortfall, 1985; Roche, 1985:58,60).

The implications of changes in protein markets for fish prices were made still more significant by a second new development: the rapid expansion in the 1980s, especially in the U.S., of the market for fish as fish, i.e. the market for high- quality, usually fresh, seafood. The rapid growth of this market could have positive spinoff effects for all fish market segments, as it did in 1987 when unfulfilled U.S. demand for fresh seafood ultimately drove all prices up, yielding the major integrated processing companies in Atlantic Canada their first significant profits since the end of the 1970s. But for the Newfoundland fishery, organized as it has been since its inception (both as a salt and a fresh-frozen fishing industry) to produce groundfish as a form of protein for the protein market, and distant from the fresh fish markets of Boston and New York, the changed consumption patterns meant a shift to new fish products that it was not as well situated to supply.

As for the catch failures in the 1980s, even these were not the purely "natural" fluctuations that many liked to believe, especially with regard to the 'shoulders' to the groundfishery. Instead, the continuing failure of the groundfish catches to recover to their pre-1968 levels, and the decline in crab, mackerel and herring catches, were also likely the products of previous capitalist development in the inshore fishery, and evidence of the limitations of a natural fishery under capitalism where the development of the productive powers of labour inevitably come to exceed those of Nature. This contradiction of capitalist development, the fact that "no fish can be caught in waters that contain none" regardless of the efficiency of the devices employed, was brought home to the capitalists who had invested in trawlers in the late 1960s and mid-1970s. In the 1980s it was brought home also to prospective capitalists who had invested in longliners using similar gear (trawls and seines), as well as gillnets and crab-pots, and it is doubtful if much reprieve is to be expected.[8]

The crisis in the fishery in the 1980s was therefore really an entirely new economic situation which interrupted the continuity of *both* lines of previous capitalist development (the integrated trawler-processors, and the longliners). The crisis thus posed the question whether the old "regime of accumulation" would be restored, whether a new regime would be discovered and implemented, or whether the fishing industry as it had been previously constituted would dissolve, and perhaps be reconstructed in an historically novel way. What was clear was that, so far as the longliner fishery and the new bourgeoisie were concerned, their demise as a general phenomenon was imminent if higher fish prices and/or catch levels were not restored.

> If this continues with nothing happening what we see as likely to remain of the fishing industry in 10 years time, or whenever, or maybe quicker than that, will essentially be a deepsea fishery, a good bit of which will be taken by foreigners, and there will always be, I suppose, some kind of a trapfishery, a small-boat fishery, artisanal, where nobody makes much money at it, so they kind of muck along. They have low overheads, so they'll survive and more-or-less be able to spend [on consumption] what little money they make selling fish, as opposed to having to plough it back into the operation [as longliner operators do]. And there might not be a great deal more than that (McCurdy, 1985).

3. Political crisis and the new bourgeoisie: the federal state

As in the 1970s, so also in the 1980s, the aim of the Newfoundland fishery union was to ensure that there would be a "great deal more" left than an artisanal (petty bourgeois) fishery and a large-scale, offshore fishery. While fulfilling the trade union needs of plant and trawler workers for better wages and working conditions (though less vigorously than a significant percentage of its membership might have liked),[9] the union continued to pursue the same "basic principle." As McCurdy explained this principle in 1985, it was "the same tune we've been flapping away at for ten years or more ... establishing fish prices which bear a relationship to the economics of operating a fishing boat," i.e.

prices which would at least effectively stabilize the longliner owners confronted by the necessities of capital accumulation (Fairley, 1985a).

> [What is needed is] a price which would allow a reasonably prudent operator to survive and get a modest return on his investment. You might disregard the bottom 10 percent or something—even if it was 20 percent—and say "forget about him, he's not up to mark, up to speed, probably never will be, so forget about him." Of those who are left determine what kind of landings in a particular boat type he can reasonably expect (in the final analysis you'd probably end up, if the system were ever adopted, with some kind of averaging thing). Then, what are their operating expenses in order to achieve those landings—what are their capital costs and so on—and what price do you need to make this a paying proposition (McCurdy, 1985).

The difference in the 1980s was that the struggles to see this basic policy position implemented were repeatedly unsuccessful, and increasingly more desperate and militant.

The fishery union conducted the struggle for the realization of its basic principle of higher fish prices by various means and with a variety of policy proposals. Among them were:

❑ a six week boycott in July and August 1980 by the union's inshore membership of the firms represented by the Fisheries Association of Newfoundland and Labrador (FANL). In retrospect, with this action, the power of the union seemed to peak. As well, the failure to achieve at that time permanent recognition of the "economic needs of fishers" obviously had enormous implications for the future formation and consolidation of the new bourgeoisie.

❑ repeated advocacy of a restructuring of the fishing industry along two lines: centralized groundfish marketing by a federal crown corporation in which fish-catching and processing enterprises were equally represented; and the establishment of a relationship between the "cost of catching fish and the price of fish" (*inter alia* Union Forum, October, 1981:14-15).

❑ a comprehensive statement on a suitable restructuring of the fishing industry made to the Task Force on Atlantic Fisheries in early 1982. It recommended (in order of presentation): (1) a "Fish Procurement Agency ... whose responsibility would be to handle the purchase of all species of fish from inshore fisher[s]" and pay prices which "would give the average, reasonably productive and prudent operator a return on investment.... Certain requirements as to effort and investment are implied...."; (2) a "price stabilization fund" which would collect surplus revenues from processing or harvesting sectors in good years, and pay it back in bad; (3) a change in the method of calculation of Unemployment Insurance benefits such that they would be based on the ten best, rather than ten last, weeks of fishing. "The present method acts as a disincentive to fisher[s]"; (4) a positive discrimination in state policies in favour of "full-time" fishers as opposed to "part-time" fishers, and "a meaningful restriction on the creation of new enterprises"; (5) the establishment of a marketing corporation for all species, operated by the government with processors and fishers' organizations represented on the board of directors; (6) first priority in the allocation of offshore stocks to existing year-round plants. "There is not enough fish to satisfy all of the seasonal plant operators who claim they can no longer operate based upon the conventional inshore fishery." (7) considering the option of "public ownership" of The Lake Group, with the federal government acquiring and modernizing the trawler fleet, and the provincial government acquiring the shore assets (*Union Forum*, June 1982:5-6).

❑ the resolution at the union's regular convention in December 1982 describing the crisis as one of "the longliner-gillnet skippers," and proposing a host of measures for both the "inshore" and the "offshore" sectors to ameliorate the situation (*Union Forum*, January 1983:7-8).

❑ support for a quality fish program providing it was accompanied by a productivity bonus scheme in the order of $0.06 per pound. "In [Michael] Kirby's [Task Force on Atlantic Fisheries] report one of the few things which in any way addressed or recognized that fisher[s] have economic needs and problems was the recommendation for the quality bonus system or production incentive...." (McCurdy, 1985; *Union Forum*, October 1981:13).[10]

❑ most significantly the "UNITY '84" campaign in 1984 and early 1985; the major instance of popular resistance to the kind of industrial restructuring ongoing; an attempt "to show the people of Atlantic Canada that fishers and fish plant workers had been left out of the [federal-provincial state's] restructuring plan" of 1983. Although during the period of this campaign the union was able to stop a further roll back of the trade-union rights of plant and trawler workers, and to achieve fish price rises keeping pace with inflation, the campaign did not achieve its stated goal of mobilizing public opinion around the fishery union's vision of a restructured fishery.

❑ Arguing that the price of raw fish was not the true "market" price, but a subsidy to an (inefficient) processing sector which put the cost of local processing employment on the backs of fishers, the union repeatedly called—for example in May 1985 to the provincial government—for an "Employment Credit" program. Under this proposal, the government would pay a credit on account at the Fishermen's Loan Board for every pound of fish landed at a provincial fish plant "in the same way that they give a tax write-off to a company that hires women or youth." This would either "go against the payments or accumulate to [the boat owners'] credit for the purposes of getting a down payment for a future vessel" (McCurdy, 1985).

As some of the union's activities reviewed above already suggest, however, the problem for the fishery union in the 1980s, and effectively for the future of the new bourgeoisie, was the federal state, on whose fishery policy the union had exerted so much influence, and whose policies had so much encouraged the emergence and expansion of the new bourgeoisie during the 1970s. A statement by the union's president Richard Cashin in late 1983 exemplified the problem:

In the late 1970s when things were better than they are now, the federal government paid inshore fisher[s] $0.02 per pound quality bonus; the provincial government paid $0.005 per pound to assist in the purchase of gear. Fisher[s'] loans were arranged through the Loan Board at lower interest rates. All of this before 1979.

A stranger coming to Newfoundland, knowing the plight of the fisher[s], would at least say: well, surely the governments improved what they were doing for you in 1978. No one could possibly believe that now these above-mentioned programs have all been cut out, cut out notwithstanding that the financial and economic situation of the inshore sector is worse today than it has been for many years (*Union Forum*, November 1983:5).

But the elimination of, or failure to introduce, programs for the inshore sector which had as their effect the furthering of the new bourgeoisie was more than a policy reversal. It was part of a profound political defeat of the Newfoundland fishery union and other fishers' organizations in the Maritimes with similar policy positions. This defeat included the isolation of the Department of Fisheries and Oceans (DFO) within the federal state, its subordination to central agencies and the purging of its personnel during the 1980s.

The isolation and defeat of the DFO and its policy positions—and not just the publication of another (faulty and hypocritical) report on behalf of "large capital and its state" (Barrett and Davis, 1984)—was the really significant accomplishment of M. Kirby, P. Nicholson and the whole "Task Force on Atlantic Fisheries" exercise of 1982-1984, as Diana Royce has shown in painful detail (Royce, 1985). Among the "moments" of this process, according to her, were:

❑   the appointment of the Task Force itself by the Privy Council Office in 1982, as a response to the DFO's proposal for the nationalization of the trawler fleets of the "Big Four," the lease of the vessels back to individual fishers, and federal control over export marketing as solutions to the growing crisis in the processing sector (Royce:38-41).

❑   the appointment of someone external to the DFO, in this case Michael Kirby, Deputy Clerk of the Privy Council, as chairman of the Task Force (42-45)

❑   the appointment of an outsider to the DFO, Donald Johnson, Minister of State for Economic and Regional Development, as chairman of the Cabinet subcommittee on the fisheries crisis to which Kirby would report (44)

❑   the cooptation by Kirby of the leadership of the fishery union, notably Richard Cashin, the union's president during the critical period of the establishment and inquiry of the Task Force in 1982 (113-114)

❑   the defeat of the DFO position on fish marketing which involved a direct buying and selling role for the federal government, DFO coordination of marketing and sales, and increased funding for the Fishery Prices Support Board (originally set up by the DFO under Leblanc to provide subsidies to fish-catching and processing enterprises in 1975-1978) (72-80).

- ❑ the tactical withdrawal of the DFO personnel from the offshore restructuring negotiations and implementation in 1983-1984, in an attempt to discredit these processes (85-88)—moves which obviously backfired.

- ❑ the defeat of "Option 4" (the complete nationalization of the "Big Four") and "Option 3" (the creation of two inter-provincial companies with varied resource bases and equivalent assets), the DFO's first and second options, by "Option 1" (two provincial companies based in Newfoundland and Nova Scotia) (88ff.).

- ❑ the co-optation by Kirby of Pierre Debané, Minister of Fisheries 1982-1984, and once the strongest advocate of "Option 4," and the severance of the relationship between Debané, and A. May, the Deputy Minister, and the rest of the DFO bureaucracy (103-104).

Perhaps the accomplishment of Kirby, Nicholson and the Task Force which had the greatest overall significance for the future of the new bourgeoisie was the successful ideological organization, or perhaps reorganization, of conflict over the fishery around a "social" vs. "economic" dichotomy. The latter referred to the processing sector generally, and the integrated sector particularly, and the former referred primarily to "inshore" fish-catching, and the positions of the DFO and the fishery union (see also Fairley, 1983:120-122; 1984:26 and Royce, 1985:120-121). Cashin certainly appreciated the significance of this ideological victory:

> They [the central agencies] didn't want to hear anything. They wanted to "strictly run it like a business" and then we'll have a "social safety net," whatever that means. Then … they'd say … "well Cashin is talking about the social fishery. We're talking about the economic fishery." Now how do you separate them? There are social and economic aspects of the fishery but these became buzz words to separate the smart guys, the bank guys, the National Sea guys and the central agency bureaucrats and dismiss the others as fringe people…. Somebody could come over and say "What's he talking about?" "Oh, it's just the social fishery." (Cashin, 1983:121-122)

Peter Nicholson, for example, quite consciously devoted himself to ideological restructuring. In a paper presented in Washington, D.C. in August 1984, he stated that the first element of the Task Force's "Negotiating Strategy" in pursuing a restructured Atlantic fishery was "Control the

Analytical Process," and the first lesson learned was "Control of Analytical Resources Confers Great Power, at Least Initially" (Nicholson, 1984).

It was this isolation and defeat of the DFO (and purges and staff replacements within it), rather than only the new economic situation and the iron rule of the law of value as such, that was critical for the continued formation of the new bourgeoisie. On a short term basis, it meant, in the name of an "economic" fishery, the denial of financial assistance, i.e. subsidies such as were provided in 1975-1978 to help carry enterprises through the cyclical low groundfish prices of 1974-1975. And all this, of course, while hundreds of millions of dollars were provided in 1983 and after to assist the restructuring of the "economic" (integrated processing and catching) sector and to bail out the banks.

More critical still for the long-term future of the new bourgeoisie were the implications of the defeat of the nationalized marketing recommendation, the quality production bonus scheme, and the complete nationalization of the "Big Four." First, these measures were an effective institutional basis for maximizing returns, on a per unit basis, to inshore fish-catching enterprises. This was the explicit purpose of the DFO and the fishery union in proposing them. Second, to the extent that the Newfoundland fishery is in any geographical position to exploit it, these proposals were a basis on which the new bourgeoisie might have moved their fish-catching enterprises into the production of fresh and high-quality frozen groundfish products for the only growing sector of the North American fish market. This line of development, which offered a real "economic" solution to the problems of the new bourgeoisie in Newfoundland (Fairley, 1985b:21), was closed off. Indeed, the situation was worse than that. The federal state—through the Department of Regional Industrial Expansion and a beaten and purged DFO—announced policies which actually aggravated the problem, such as strict quality standards on inshore fish-catching *without price compensation* to ensure that the processing sector would have maximum flexibility in choosing to produce either high-quality fish products, or protein products. For its part, the fishery union leadership said it would "do [its] damnedest to subvert" their imposition (McCurdy, 1985).[11]

4. Inshore vs. inshore?: the provincial state and the fishery union

The changed policies and structure of policy-making in the federal state were thus of crucial significance. What about the provincial state? In other parts of Canada (and, indeed, in the Newfoundland hog industry)[12] policies of provincial states have been integral to the promotion and consolidation of the development of capitalism in primary (agricultural) production—subsidizing producer prices, waiving provincial taxes on key inputs (such as fuel), restricting entry into the production of certain commodities (supply management), and authorizing single- desk selling agencies. These are precisely the policies which the fishery union had long pursued and which would underpin the continuing formation of the new bourgeoisie. Furthermore, except for direct control of the catching of fish (e.g. through licensing), the Newfoundland provincial state possesses the constitutional power to implement all these policies in the fishing industry.[13]

But precedent and constitutional capacity notwithstanding, neither the fishery union nor the formation of the new bourgeoisie were about to be furthered by the provincial state in the 1980s. To the contrary, and especially since Brian Peckford became Premier in 1979, the provincial state had effectively sacrificed the development of capitalism in inshore fish-*catching* to other policies which had as their effect the opening of so- called "inshore," "independent" fish-*processing* as another field of accumulation for members of the "new middle class" (Overton, 1979).[14] Exemplified by people such as Joe George (of Blue Ocean Products, Island Seafoods and, most recently, Harbour Grace Fishing Co.), Ches Blackwood (of Clarenville Ocean Products) and Phonse Best (of Port Enterprises), this field showed remarkable development in the 1970s as exemplified in the four-fold increase in the number of processing plants in Newfoundland, the growth in the number of independently-owned plants to more than 100, and the formation of the Newfoundland Independent Fish Producers Association (NIFPA).[15] And the obstacles in the fisheries to the formation and consolidation of this fraction of the class of capital were effectively dealt with time and again in provincial fishery policy. Furthermore these provincial interventions, by maximizing the supply of raw fish to processing plants, minimizing prices, and expanding "domestic" (non-capitalist) production, constituted yet more obstacles to accumulation among commercial inshore fishers.

It is not generally appreciated that the provincial state in Newfoundland effectively furthered the formation and consolidation of a capitalist class fraction very different from that fraction furthered by the policy positions of the fishery union. The onset of the crisis, the role of the press, and the work of many academic commentators generally created the impression that the provincial state and the fishery union shared a common desire to promote small-scale production, inshore fishing and rural Newfoundland. The impression of fundamental unanimity was also promoted by "real Newfoundlanders," such as Douglas House. According to him the Peckford Government's differences with the fishery union were only consequences of the incompetence of the provincial Department of Fisheries and partisan differences between Peckford

(Progressive Conservative) and Richard Cashin (Liberal), whereas in substance they shared many goals (House, 1982:27-28).

More often though the behavior of the provincial state is simply conceived ahistorically and apart from processes of class formation and disorganization, and its conflicts with the fishery union over the inshore fishery are seen as a natural but uncertain function of the complexity and overlap of the many interests involved. The union is viewed simply as an umbrella group of fishers and plant workers (D. MacDonald, 1980; Inglis, 1985), while the provincial state is simply categorized as provincialist (House, 1982) or populist (Johnstone, 1981), or a state of the "state elite" (Sinclair, 1985).

This inattention to the real significance of the provincial state's role in class formation in the fishery has a real basis. It reflects a convergence between the interests of the province's "new middle class" (Overton, 1979) and the immediate needs of many other groups in Newfoundland society. One such group was the small independent producers, the latent reserve army of labour, who were liable to proletarianization and pauperization. The formation and consolidation of the new middle class depends to a considerable degree on the preservation of "rural Newfoundland" as a basis for accumulation (notably in providing cheap fish for small processors), although, as even its proponents recognize, the successful consolidation of the new middle class itself will actually further the dissolution of rural Newfoundland in the long run (House, 1982:26).

The interests of the new middle class also neatly jibe with the immediate needs of the intelligentsia, as Overton showed (Overton, 1979:236-237). This is because its own expansion calls for some expansion of professional and state personnel, and these personnel share some of the sentiments of the small independent fish producer, who similarly stands in between capitalist and worker. Consequently, the defence of the proprietary producers, which goes together with the defence of rural Newfoundland as a field of accumulation, appeals to them also.

More immediately, the encouragement by the provincial state in the 1970s of indiscriminate expansion in enterprises supplying raw fish for processing, and of new enterprises in such linked fields as boat-building and marine supplies, was fully compatible with the development of capitalism in inshore fish catching when times were good. Furthermore, the big vertically integrated fish companies represented a common obstacle to the formation of both the new middle class, and the new fish-catching (long-liners) bourgeoisie, though for very different reasons. The former wanted market space, the latter required maximum fish prices.

But the interests of these two fractions of capital did not always coincide, and the provincial state could not always appear to support both, and the whole "inshore" sector as well. This eventually became clear in the federal-provincial dispute of May-September 1983 over the restructuring of the insolvent vertically-integrated fishery in Newfoundland. This conflict began on 17 May 1983 when the federal fisheries minister, Pierre Debané, and James Morgan, the provincial minister, initialled a memorandum of agreement to merge Fishery Products, The Lake Group, the Newfoundland assets of H.B. Nickerson, and several other smaller companies and plants, into a single "supercompany" refinanced and commensurately owned by the federal and provincial states. As part of the agreement processing plants in three different communities were to be closed.

This agreement soon fell apart, being unacceptable to the provincial cabinet. The agreement, Peckford said later when the dispute was made public, was contrary to the provincial government's "all plants open" position on restructuring. And this rejection opened what turned out to be a ten week crisis in federal-provincial relations, highlighted by: the federal government's announcement that it would unilaterally restructure the offshore fishery; the announcement of a provincial restructuring plan in reply; James Morgan's claim that the federal government was "attempt[ing] to take over the fishing industry of poor little weak Newfoundland"; and Fishery Products' charge, when put into receivership by the Bank of Nova Scotia in September 1983, that a conspiracy existed between the Bank and the federal government to force acceptance of the federal plan.

What really surprised many in the course of events, however, was the nature of the agreement finally reached on 26 September 1983. While apparently the product of ten weeks of acrimony, and while touted by Peckford as "the most important agreement the federal and provincial governments had signed since Newfoundland joined Canada in 1949," when the dust settled there seemed to be few substantial differences with the May Debané-Morgan memorandum (*The Globe and Mail*, 21 October 1983; Sinclair, 1985:29-30) and the results seemed hardly to justify the strife. This was even the case regarding plant closures, to which popular politics and Peckford had directed so much attention. While the three plants scheduled for closure were to be reopened, one plant (Grand Bank) was given only an eighteen month reprieve, one (St. Lawrence) was to operate only as an inshore feeder plant and thus (given that the mode of life of the working class was founded on year-round wage employment) might just as well have been closed, and one (Burin) was to engage in secondary processing, a prospect which had been in the offing anyway. The agreement seemed to give credence to those who saw the whole conflict as an exercise in "the politics of smoke and mirrors" by the provincial government (*The Globe and Mail*, 8 July 1983:8).

Yet if the dispute and eventual accord are examined from the perspective of the formation of the new middle class, and close attention is paid to the initial provincial position on restructuring, the May and September agreements are seen to differ significantly. The initial provincial position was set out in two documents presented to the federal government dated 23 March 1983 and 5 May 1983, the latter being the most elaborate (Newfoundland and Labrador, 1983a,b). Both documents called for no less than the complete dismemberment of the offshore sector and the subordination of the remains to the new middle class. First, the separation of the trawler operations from the processing companies and their deployment "under a single consolidated command and management structure" was advocated. The benefits of this would be that "the separate fleet could be used to service the resource short [non-integrated] plant[s] ... and prolong the operating life of their seasonal operations." It would also mean that the "plants of the offshore harvesting companies would not have monopoly control over offshore fish," "raw material could be made available to all processors on a competitive basis" and "[t]here would be no parent company bias in favour of various plants" (1983b:28-29). Second, the "separation of the marketing effort from the processing sector" was called for, so that it could "provide a professional marketing outlet for independent inshore fish processors as well as offshore processors." Marketing would be consolidated into a single company on whose board of directors all plant owners would be "fairly represented" and "the larger trawler-supplied companies ... constrained from exercising a dominant position by voting restrictions" (1983b:27,37). Third, and in sharp contrast to the preceding measures, it was recommended that no consolidation of plant or management in the processing sector should take place: the "essence of the province's position is the retention of a number of different companies of varying sizes in the processing sector." This would promote efficiency and "would preserve a mixture of different size entities in the processing sector which would maintain a range of potential investment possibilities to facilitate divestiture." This "could interest some small and medium-sized investors" (1983b:34-35). Finally, in suggesting in lieu of some plant closures a "social compact" with plant and trawler workers, whose central feature was a "strong wage restraint program" costing workers $25 million over five years, the document seemed to advocate a restructuring in the fishery of the entire "regime of accumulation" in a way that would favour the capital-short new middle class. Rather than a high wage, high productivity, capital intensive, "fordist" accumulation strategy, a low-wage, labour intensive, "pre-fordist" strategy was proposed. "The Social Compact concept ... offers an entirely different perspective for viability. It confronts the growth of wage rates rather than cutting the number of employees and plants" (1983b:21).

This proposal would have effectively subjected vertically integrated capital (to say nothing of the working class) to the requirements of the consolidation of the new middle class, and this is what was at stake in the May-September dispute. For the federal side, this was suggested by a telex on 30 March to Peckford from Donald Johnson, federal Minister of State for Economic and Regional Development, in reply to the March statement of the same program. The telex focused, first and foremost, on the proposal to dismember the offshore industry, and attempted to twist it into an opposite position. On the provincial side, it was just this program which would promote the new middle class that was furthered in the September accord and, from this point of view, made it seem rational for Peckford to proclaim it "the most important federal-provincial agreement." All the 17 May memorandum had said about the dismemberment of the offshore fishery was that the "federal government will endeavour to provide by the end of May a written response to the May 6 [*sic*], 1983 Position Paper" and that "the advisability of the separate Newfoundland offshore fleet, processing and marketing companies will be studied subsequent to the formation of the new company" (Canada and Newfoundland, 1983a:2,3). The "social compact" was included, but so was a provision which immediately gutted it by making the resistance of workers possible: the 17 May memorandum provided that employees who lost their jobs as a result of the proposed plant closures would receive severance pay equal to their 1982 earnings (1983a:2,8). (And Morgan agreed to this! Little wonder that the competence of the provincial Department of Fisheries, *vis a vis* the promotion of the new middle class, has been questioned by House.)

The offensive passage providing severance pay was, at Peckford's behest, deleted. (In a June telex to Peckford from Donald Johnson, reviewing the negotiations, Johnson says: "Mr. Morgan also felt that the guarantee of severance pay, agreed to the day before, should be dropped because it would create a difficult precedent in other layoff situations in your province"). But it was not until the September accord that the position of the new middle class was effectively improved. Unlike the May memorandum, the September accord allowed that two objectives of restructuring would be "to provide new opportunities for independent processors to have access to international markets" and "to have the company internally organized in a way which leaves open the option of a variety of innovative industry structures" (Canada and Newfoundland, 1983b:2). To these ends it was provided that: (1) after the marketing of its own fish, the "second priority" of the restructured company "would be to act as a vehicle through which independent fish companies in Newfoundland ... may market their product upon mutually agreeable terms and conditions," (2) that "in order to ensure the fair and effective working of the marketing system for independent processors a Newfoundland Marketing and Co-ordination Council will be established ...[to give] an opportunity to the independent processors to express their views on marketing strategies and related issues" and (3) that "whenever part of the Company's trawler fleet is not fully utilized and is otherwise available such trawlers will be utilized for the harvesting and supply of fish at [cost] ... to independent plants" (1983b:8-9).

These gains, of course, did not represent anything resembling the full May 5 program. But the point is that for the first time, the new middle class was given a place in the integrated industry itself. But this gain also meant that the interests of the new fish-catching bourgeoisie, already savaged by other policies in favour of integrated capital, were effectively sacrificed to policies of the provincial state which advanced the interests of the new middle class.

As we have already indicated, the fishery union was opposed to the restructuring settlement. What the union found particularly offensive was the "social compact" provision advocated by the provincial state. As soon as it became evident that, as the 5 May provincial position paper had envisaged and the union had warned against, "the social compact mean[t] a way in which to depress wages to workers and prices to fisher[s]" as part of a restructuring of the fishing industry (*inter alia Union Forum*, November 1983:6), a "Unity '84" campaign for improved wages and fish prices was launched. It was in fact soon clear that the whole provincial approach to restructuring the offshore fishery, epitomised by the "Social Compact" and the demands for a decentralized processing sector, directly conflicted with the consolidation of the new fish-catching bourgeoisie, whose interests required a more centralized, capital-intensive, but strictly regulated, offshore fishery.

The position of the fishery union, indeed its very *raison d'être* as a body bringing the trade-union interests of plant and trawler workers together with the demand of inshore fishers for higher prices, was that "too much processing capacity is the root cause of most problems in the fishery," the original source of low fish prices and low wages (*Union Forum*, February 1982:6):

> The fisher[s] themselves, quite often, want to have a fish plant in every cove and want the right to sell in every cove. But it must be understood that if these investments are made, the people who are investing want to have their investments paid for. So when we see a lot of fish plants being built, we have to remember that the people who operate these plants ... know how to pay for their investments. They take it out of the hides of the plant workers and fisher[s].

This capacity of the processors to do this, the union argues, was the primary historical obstacle to commercial inshore fishing in Newfoundland:

> In the old pre-Union days fisher[s] didn't even know what price they'd get until the fall of the year when the fish merchants would pay all their bills, take out a very tidy profit for themselves, and then settle up with the fishermen (*Union Forum*, July-August 1984:7).

And it is also, in the union's view, the restoration of this capacity in fish processing that underlies provincial incomes policy in the fishery:

> What Mr. Peckford and Mr. Morgan and others who think like them are really talking about is a return to the old system, whereby fish companies never went out of business, no matter how badly they were managed, but instead passed all the losses back on to the shoulders of the fishermen and the workers.

In other words, a *highly efficient processing sector* would underpin the continued formation of the new bourgeoisie, and solve the problems of all workers and fishers. Founded on the production of "relative surplus value," such a sector would make possible both higher (nominal) wages *and* fish prices closer to the price of production of capitalist fishers. It was this alternative that the fishery union pursued during the whole period of the restructuring debate (1981-1983), when, in opposition to the provincial government, it supported: a modernized, vertically-integrated fishery concentrated in, and solely in, the traditional twelve offshore communities (*Union Forum*, January 1983:9); a horizontally integrated fishery encompassing both seasonal, inshore-supplied plants and trawler-supplied plants;[16] plus subsidies to inshore plants, on the condition that it be made clear that these were a form of social assistance to the owners and to the unemployed, keeping open relatively inefficient plants which were a drag on the industry and the incomes of fishers and plant workers (*Union Forum*, February 1982:6).

The restructuring of the offshore fishery was by no means the first time the provincial state and the fishery union had clashed over policy positions which had significant implications for class formation. One such issue was the continuing debate over the allocation of the cod stocks off the northeast coast of Newfoundland and Labrador. The provincial state continually sought to have these "northern cod" reserved for processing in the non-integrated (and thus seasonal or, in the provincial government's view, "resource short") plants largely owned by the emerging new middle class (*Evening Telegram*, 11 January 1984:3).[17] These fish would be landed by inshore catching enterprises in summer, and

("Newfoundland for the Newfoundlanders" notwithstanding) *foreign-owned* trawlers in winter. The union, on the other hand, always opposed this proposal, advocating that the northern cod be managed conservatively and reserved to the local inshore catching enterprises, with the excess allocated to trawlers landing in the offshore ports of Newfoundland and the Maritimes. This position once again highlights the neat convergence of trade-union interests with the further formation of the new fish-catching bourgeoisie. First, in the union's view, the provincial program would create a dependence on foreign trawlers, distracting attention from the renewal and modernization of the existing trawler fleet, and Newfoundland "cannot develop a viable industry without an offshore fleet as part of our arsenal" (*Union Forum*, December 1981:23). Second, the program did not represent good resource management: "all of the small plants in Newfoundland cannot have access to offshore fish, especially if we regard them as potential year-round operators. We just don't have enough fish" (23). Third, such an arrangement would betray a trade-off whereby, in return for access to northern cod, Nova Scotia enterprises were excluded from Gulf of St. Lawrence stocks, and these stocks were reserved to mobile-gear equipped longliners and to trawlers owned by the new fish-catching bourgeoisie and the integrated companies respectively (*Union Forum*, January 1980:8-9 and *Union Forum*, September 1977:9).[18] And finally, and most importantly, the provincial position was enunciated "in absence of a comprehensive fisheries policy" which "takes account of the economic needs of the inshore fishermen" (*Union Forum*, December 1981:23), i.e. the necessity of higher prices. Without this the resource-short plant program threatened whatever monopoly power the union possessed: "It works to the disadvantage of fishermen, no doubt about that. A small plant gets a bit of fish in the wintertime, maybe it's not much, but that would still affect his appetite for inshore fish in the summertime"; i.e. by bearing some of the fixed annual costs of production, fish supplied and processed in winter reduced the pressure for meeting all costs in summer production when inshore enterprises supplied the fish (McCurdy, 1985).

The debate over direct, so-called "over-the-side," sales of raw fish by inshore catching enterprises to foreign-owned trawlers was a similar instance of a conflict between the fishery union and the provincial state which had significant implications for class formation. In 1978, and after, the union organized sales of fish to (variously) Swedish, Bulgarian, Japanese and Portuguese trawlers which opened new markets for new species (squid), lengthened the fishing season (mackerel), and maintained sales and fish prices in face of the annual, short-term cod glut caused by the nature of the generally "domestic" trapfishery. These sales clearly offered great impetus to the formation of the new fish-catching bourgeoisie, close as fish prices were at that time to giving good returns to the average longliner enterprise. But in all but one instance such sales also met with the opposition of both processors and the provincial state. According to the provincial government, putting it in a way the stressed the immediate interests of the rural reserve army, over-the-side sales constituted "a dangerous precedent" which threatened shore- based employment by competing unfairly with non-integrated plants and depriving them of raw fish (Close, 1982:7). To put it another way, as the Fisheries Association of Newfoundland and Labrador (FANL) did, the sales "upset the delicate balance of supply and demand" (6) in the Newfoundland raw fish market to the disadvantage of the non-integrated plants generally owned by the new middle class.

The implications of conflicts between the union and the provincial state for class formation was much more transparent in the six-week, union-organized, boycott of the FANL firms by inshore catching enterprises in August 1980. In the course of the boycott the provincial state withdrew social assistance from anyone connected with the inshore fishery, union member or not. As Austin Thorne of the Newfoundland Federation of Labour described it:

> [T]he provincial government has denied social assistance to anyone with any connection to the fishery and this decision can be interpreted as the government showing full support for the fish companies … there are 34 thousand fishermen holding licences … [but] two-thirds are not members of the fishery union. To make matters worse, the government is using [social assistance] to try to turn these people against the fishery union (*Evening Telegram*, 1 August 1980:3).

The move backfired, marking the provincial state as the obvious agent of the "Fish Trades," and raising to new heights the status of the fishery union as the real fighter for all Newfoundlanders. On the other side, the union made an equally strategic error by its campaign in 1980 for restrictive licensing policies and against the pasturing of the reserve army of labour in the inshore fishery, what it called "part-timers," "moonlighters" and "$10 thousand fisher[s]." The union appeared as the self-interested lobbyist of, at best, 10 thousand full-time fishers, and, at worst, a few "rich" fishers. The provincial state, having spent 1977-1980 creating the "$10 thousand fishermen" with the indiscriminate loans of the provincial Fisheries Loan Board, appeared as the representative of the forgotten majority and the regenerator of rural Newfoundland. On close inspection, though, the formation of the new middle class was advanced by the provincial position. According to Morgan, while he was sympathetic to the union's position, "many plants around the province depend on moonlighters to supply raw material to keep the plants operating" (*Evening Telegram*, 1 May 1980:4).

It is clear then that the formation of the new middle class, and the policies of the provincial state which furthered it, constituted obstacles to the formation of the new bourgeoisie. It is certain too that the union—whose positions repeatedly came into conflict with those of the provincial in the late 1970s—in its efforts to resolve the crisis in the 1980s wanted little of Peckfordism, "neo-nationalism" and the "Real Newfoundland":

> The premier ... advocates greater control over Newfoundland by Newfoundlanders, but the question we must ask is what kind of Newfoundlanders. The premier appears to be talking about ... the same elite that has been in power throughout most of our history.... We should remember that it was Newfoundland merchants ... who were mainly responsible for the exploitation of fishermen that was an unfortunate part of our history for so many years. To prevent such exploitation from being a part of our future as well, fishermen and fishplant workers have to continue to press for increased input into the management of the industry which their labour makes possible. In trying to do so one of the biggest problems they will encounter will be the amount of control that's in the hands of a few fish companies, and it won't make much difference whether these companies are based in Newfoundland or Nova Scotia (*Union Forum*, January 1980:11).

The problem for the continued formation of the new bourgeoisie in the conjuncture of the 1980s was that the reverse also held true: the provincial state, as always, wanted little of the fishery union which had hitherto found its influence in the federal state to be sufficient.

The effective consequence of the restructuring by the federal state, and the continuing pre-occupations of the provincial state, and the lack of success of the resistance organized by the fishery union, meant that the economic crisis of the 1980s spelled the reduction of the new fish-catching bourgeoisie to little more than a statistical anomaly and a dream unfulfilled:

> In the last four or five years there has been something like [only] thirty-five new longliners built in Newfoundland, most of them for the Gulf of St. Lawrence.... What's happening is that they're a fleet that is operating strictly on cash-flow.... However they can muck through from one year to the next. No such thing as any return on investment, or depreciation, or putting money aside for a new boat when the old one goes. None of that. Just survival from one year to the next (McCurdy, 1985).

5. Socialism

The preceding analysis of the impact of the actual economic, political, and ideological conditions and struggles of the 1980s on class formation in the Newfoundland fishery might seem to suffer from at least two weaknesses. First, it says little or nothing about the actual intentions of the actual actors, the fishery union, the federal and provincial states, or individuals, in advancing or resisting policy positions which had particular effects of class formation or disorganization. There is none of the certainty, characteristic of "orthodox" (reductionist) class analysis— as in my own previous work, for example—about the real, "objective" motivations behind actors and policy positions. A second, and related, apparent weakness is that the class analysis provided is one-sided and, for this reason if no other, incomplete. It explicitly indicates only the implications of the major struggles over policy for bourgeois class formation. No direct attention is given to the implications of these struggles, *if any*, for the formation of workers and semi-proletarians into classes, or for the long-term amelioration of their life conditions.

Yet these apparent weaknesses are really strengths, I think. First, the lack of specification of the actual motivation of actual actors is as it should be: it is not a theoretical question, but an immediate practical, political question which can only be resolved in the course of open debate and struggle over alternative courses of action. This kind of class analysis points to real and (from the point of view of human liberation) negative or irrelevant implications of actual struggles and policy positions for progressive social development, which had hitherto been conceptualized in an entirely too positive light. Whether there are also more democratic and liberating aspects of these struggles which have been overlooked, or whether there are democratic and liberating alternatives which would be easily accepted by existing social groups and individuals, remains an open question.

As for the one-sidedness of the analysis, this too is as it should be, or as I wish it to be. This is because this one-sidedness poses forcefully (but I think in an open, non-sectarian way) the questions which I never quite succeeded in posing clearly, unfettered by other issues, or in getting a clear answers to. Given their positive implications for *bourgeois* class formation, what precisely was it about some social movements in Atlantic Canada in the 1970s, and what is there in the resistance to restructuring in the 1980s, that might "put socialism squarely and inexorably in our path" (as Williams puts it)? What, if anything, was it about the struggle for higher fish prices and the securing of fishing grounds for vessels under 65-feet in length, that made it "an anti-capitalist, working-class" struggle (as Sacouman called it)? What, if anything, might be done to help ensure that such popular "struggles to organize" (Clement, 1986a) will not effectively be simply yet more "struggles for capitalism"? (Fairley, 1985a)

If the string of defeats of populism and socialism in the twentieth century is to be broken, these are the kinds of questions that socialists will continually need to answer in the Maritimes, Newfoundland and elsewhere.

Notes

1. Bryant Fairley, "Regulation and Industrialisation in Agriculture: The Cases of Canada and the United States." (unpublished Ph.D. dissertation, Queen's University, forthcoming).

2. On the particular example referred to by McCurdy see the issues of *Union Forum* January 1978, (back cover); May 1978, p.19; October 1978, p. 15; April 1979, p. 15; May 1979, (back cover). See also MacDonald, 1979:183n57.

3. Calculated from Canada, Department of Fisheries and Oceans, *Annual Statistical Review of Canadian Fisheries*, Vol. 12-15 (Ottawa, 1981-1984) and *Canadian Fishery Exports*, Vol. 6-7 (Ottawa, 1985) with the change in the implicit price index of Gross National Expenditure (Statistics Canada, *Canadian Statistical Review*, January 1985) as the deflator.

4. These rates of profit are my calculations, calculated in identical fashion to those in "The Struggle For Capitalism," pp. 41-42 (see note 2): from total revenue is deducted operating expenses (repairs, gear replacement, supplies), crew shares to non-owners, an equal crew share for the owner(s) and depreciation (calculated at 8.3 percent of vessel hull and engine, 20 percent of gear and electronic equipment, 33 percent of shore vehicles and 10 percent of shore facilities). The remaining surplus or loss is then divided by the total capital investment which includes the vessel, electronic equipment, gear, shore vehicles and structures and operating capital (equal to operating expenses divided by the number of weeks of operation). This gives the total enterprise rate of profit. The rate of profit for the owner is calculated by first deducting insurance and interest payments from total profit.

5. DFO's surveys of the "Newfoundland Region" exclude both the fixed-gear longliners and the otter-trawl fleet of western Newfoundland which is considered to be part of the "Gulf Region" and has not been as well surveyed. According to a variety of sources, including the fishery union, the otter-trawl fleet remained more or less profitable through the 1980s.

6. These figures assume the same percentage share of revenue for non-owning crew, but a constant labour income for owner(s).

7. Unfortunately data on U.S. consumption of standard quality frozen fillets is not collected. U.S. figures combine fresh fillets, premium frozen fillets and standard frozen fillets which from an analytic point of view is like combining apples, oranges and lemons to determine the consumption or price of apples. This total combined consumption is at record high levels, but by all reports this is owed only to the increased consumption of fresh fillets. What remains clear is that through 1984, the real price of Canadian frozen fillets exported to the U.S. was still 12 percent less than it was in 1978.

8. On the other hand, it was also of increasing importance that other capitalists—notably Dr. Cosmas "Seafood" Ho of St. John's and Clarenville, Newfoundland, and Mr. Hugh Paton of Victoria, Prince Edward Island—found a way to catch fish in waters that contain none, or to bypass water altogether. The former is the owner of a firm which produces imitation crab and scallops (80 percent–90 percent of Canadian production and 33 percent of the Canadian market according to the *Globe and Mail* (12 August 1985:B7). The latter developed a means of raising lobster in captivity (*Globe and Mail*, 12 August 1985:B1).

9. The collective agreements negotiated by the union's leadership with Fishery Products International Limited for trawlermen and plant workers, in February and March 1985, drew significant opposition from among these workers. Ultimately, the plant contract was approved by 71 percent of the relevant membership, and the trawler contract by 76 percent (*Union Forum*, March-April 1985:9-10,13-14).

10. In Fairley (1985b:21) it was suggested that, more than any other, the expansion into the fishing industry *proper*, the catching of fish to be consumed as high-quality seafood, could be seen as a solution to the crisis of the new bourgeoisie, owners of enterprises which with longlines and larger meshed gillnets tended daily, and the capacity to ice and clean fish onboard, could, with the least adjustment, produce the largest and the highest quality fish. One thing at least was clear: the "quality option" is not one for the traditional, artisanal trapfishery. The imposition of quality standards "would probably be hardest on the trapfishery because of the volumes you get in such a short period of time. It's just a commodity, a bulk-volume kind of industry...." (McCurdy, 1985).

11. "The people who were given the job of putting the quality program together, the officials, my Jesus they've been oblivious to the question of the economic consequences of what they're doing. It's become a juggernaut. I don't know how many times I've gone through it, told those guys: 'We ain't interested. Buzz off. Leave us alone. *Unless you....*'"

"They're so convinced of the rightness of what they're doing that maybe they hope that someday we will eventually see the light. Or they've got an empire they'd like to build up. They've just got no recognition that a fellow—you can hardly call him viable—who is just scraping through, you're imposing additional costs for what end?" (McCurdy, emphasis added).

12. Had it applied to the fishing industry, the provincial government's announcement of a swine industry stabilization program in May 1978 would have consolidated the continued formation of the new fishery bourgeoisie once and for all: "It is unreasonable to expect primary producers to remain in production for any extended period if the returns from their business cannot cover production costs and the stabilization program now being offered is a remedial course of action if this situation does, in fact occur [in 1978, as expected]." (Government of Newfoundland *Press Release*, 18 May 1978).

13. The familiar refrain of the Newfoundland provincial government under Peckford was that it "does not have the level of jurisdiction over its most important natural resource which is necessary to economic and social planning and development. The lack of legislative jurisdiction over fisheries for this Province is analogous to a prairie province having no jurisdiction over agriculture" (Newfoundland and Labrador, 1982). [Agriculture is under the concurrent jurisdiction of the provincial and federal states while fisheries is solely under federal jurisdiction.] (Newfoundland and Labrador, Department of Fisheries, *The Fishery: A Business and a Way of Life*, St. John's, 1982). As regards the measures referred to above, however, this is irrelevant. These were implemented under the ambit "Property and Civil Rights" and judicial restriction of the federal "Trade and Commerce" power. In *Carnation Co. Ltd.* vs. *The Quebec Agricultural Marketing Board*, et al. (1968) the Supreme Court of Canada unanimously ruled that the indirect effect of a province's economic regulations on an industry most of whose products are exported—in this case the fixing of prices received by agricultural producers—did not constitute an invasion of federal jurisdiction.

14. "During the period since Confederation a new middle class has developed in Newfoundland. One part of this class, which evolved from the controlling elite of pre-Confederation days, has abandoned its entrenched position in the fish trade for new business opportunities in construction, transportation, communications, and various kinds of merchandising. This class is small and relatively powerless in national and international terms and is clearly dependent on the state and the few basic industries (mainly run by multinationals) that form the productive base of the economy. The other main section of the new middle class consists of what may be called a technocratic function" (Overton, 1979:236ff).

15. The assistance of Leslie Dean (Assistant Deputy Minister, Newfoundland Department of Fisheries), Earle McCurdy (fishery union) and George Perlin

(Department of Political Studies, Queen's University), regarding the owners of the independent fish processing enterprises and their social background is gratefully acknowledged.

16. For example, as in *Union Forum* (December 1981:23), the union often advocated the cross-subsidization of one plant by another. When in 1980 Fishery Products announced that it would keep separate books on, and insist on the individual profitability of, its seasonal plant in St. Anthony, a major longliner port, the union replied that the only justification for centralization in the industry was cross-subsidization—the efficiencies of vertically integrated plants supporting the inefficiencies of major, longliner-supplied, seasonal plants.

17. The 1984 "resource short plant" program involved nineteen enterprises, all independently owned.

18. This trade-off was of critical importance to the growth of the west coast longliner fleet in Newfoundland: "There's a court case in Yarmouth: a fellow is taking the government to court over sector management. If that case is upheld, and the government's right to control who fishes where is lost, the west coast is in tremendous problems ... because there's a big fleet in southwest Nova Scotia that can move right in. That would be reciprocal to some extent, but the most vulnerable ones are on the west coast because that's the best, the most prolific fishing grounds that have been established for otter-trawler [equipped longliners] and additional entrants" (McCurdy, 1985).

Chapter Nine

From Family Farming to Capitalist Agriculture: Food Production, Agribusiness, and the State

Tom Murphy

The recent crisis of agriculture in North America began in 1980. A combination of rapidly declining land values, low farm gate prices, soaring capital debt costs, cheap food imports, and in some places, catastrophic weather conditions, has led some farmers to the extremes of taking their own lives or killing their local bankers or family members (*New York Times*, 1985b:E-5; 1985a). The headlines generated by such personal tragedies, however, often deflect attention from the historical roots of the restructuring which have precipitated this crisis.

In the Maritime provinces, the plight of many farmers has been no less desperate than elsewhere. Potato farmers in New Brunswick and Prince Edward Island have been paid prices below cost of production nearly every year since 1980. Imports of cheap foodstuffs from the United States, Mexico, and other parts of Canada, have made many locally grown or raised products uncompetitive. Plummeting land values in all three provinces have resulted in debt-to-asset ratios that have made both farmers and bankers nervous. Consequently, many farmers have either gone bankrupt, or, more commonly, have quietly left farming altogether.

This deepening crisis in Maritime agriculture is in many respects similar to the situation faced by the Atlantic fishing and forestry industries. There are, of course, important and obvious differences at the intermediate level of analysis, but underlying these is a common political history based on an agenda for restructuring the Atlantic economy. This is no mere accident, but neither is it the product of instrumentally inspired back-room machinations. To understand this structural transformation, it is necessary to explore its origins at an appropriate level of detail.

For this reason, the focus of this paper is on New Brunswick agriculture since the early 1920s. A similar portrait, however, could be painted for any of the Maritime provinces.

1. Some theoretical considerations

Since the early 1970s, there has been a renewed interest in Marxist approaches to the study of Atlantic Canada by social scientists (Sacouman, 1981; Clow, 1984). Within this broad framework, there have been and continue to be numerous debates about the definition, nature, class basis, and transformation of the production systems which have set the groundwork for the socio-economic and historical development of the Atlantic provinces. This paper seeks to contribute to this debate by maintaining that the development of a capitalist agriculture is a product of three major components: the agricultural production process, the presence of agribusiness, and state policies which encourage capitalist relations of production. In other words, we will look at how the "family farm" has evolved over six decades of rapid social and technological change in New Brunswick.

To produce food or natural fibre products—that is, to farm—requires the management and utilization of three essential resources: land on which to grow crops, rear livestock, or construct buildings; capital, which includes not only money with which to purchase such inputs of production as seeds and fertilizer, but also buildings, equipment and livestock; and finally labour, the expenditure of human energy required to manipulate land and capital resources for productive purposes. The production unit (or farm) is the organized composite of these factors.

How the means of production are shaped into a productive unit is a function of the social relations of production. Capitalism is distinguished by a set of social relations in which the owners of the means of production purchase the labour power necessary to utilize these means for productive and profitable purposes. There is a separation between those who own the means of production and those who provide the labour. In capitalist agriculture this separation may be very explicit, as in the case of large-scale corporate farms which hire managers, foremen, and labourers to do all production work. Or it may be more implicit, as in the case of farmers whose families provide much of the labour, but who are heavily in debt to finance or industrial capital, and whose production decisions may be controlled through a contract with an agribusiness concern. In the first instance, we have direct capitalist farms; in the second, we have indirect capitalist farms. In either case, the social relations of production are capitalistic.

An independent commodity production farm production is one in which the land and the capital are directly owned (that is, with little or no debt) and in which most of the labour is provided by the producer and members of the immediate family. The commodities produced from this unit are sold in markets, where other commodities (fertilizer and machinery, for example) are also purchased. It is this unit which has most often been labelled a "family farm."

A third and less relevant category is subsistence production. Subsistence farms are organized to produce only for the immediate consumption needs of the members of the unit; there is no attempt to produce commodities for external sale. The degree to which pure subsistence production has actually existed in Maritime agriculture has been overestimated. For not only have there been numerous channels in local formal economies for the exchange of goods, but as Connelly and MacDonald (1983) have shown, an extensive informal exchange economy exists as well. In short, the isolation implied in subsistence production is a condition rarely met.

Using these categories, how is the structural transformation toward capitalist agriculture to be understood theoretically? Even basic questions pose interpretive challenges to a Marxian approach. Should farmers, for example, be considered members of the capitalist class since they own their own means of production—land, buildings, and machinery? Should they be classified as members of the working class or proletariat since they and the members of their household provide most of the labour that goes into production)? Are there intermediate locations that more suitably designate the class position of farmers?

Friedmann (1982:2) argues that "the majority of farms in advanced capitalist countries are not themselves capitalist in their internal relations. Most agricultural labour is performed by farmers and their families." She refers to this type of farming as "simple commodity production," a concept which she insists is not a mode of production (as is capitalism), but rather, a *form* of production that can only exist *within* a larger capitalist framework. This is because all external relations of the farm enterprise are commodity relations; that is, the farm sells its products and it buys its inputs within the sphere of the capitalist market. Transformation of simple (or independent) commodity production into capitalist production needs, according to Friedmann, a shift in the ownership of the means of production to capitalists; a change from household to wage relations; and capitalist control over the labour process (1982:30).

Davis (1980), on the other hand, contends that capitalist penetration of independent commodity production can occur through the vehicle of a production contract which:

functions as an instrument for the capitalist extraction of surplus value.... Through contract farming and related means, family farming tends to become a capitalist labour process. The family farmer is made an object of capitalist exploitation and the family farm becomes fertile ground for the growth and development of capitalist relations (1980:144,146).

Similarly, Clement (1983:229) maintains that a distinction exists between "independent" and "dependent" commodity production. In the former, the producer is linked with capital through the mechanism of the market; in the latter, the producer "is compelled into a contract or a monopoly relation with capital. Capital directly penetrates the relations of production by dominating economic ownership, while the direct producer retains formal ownership and possession."

Buttel (1982), Friedmann and others are correct in noting that the majority of farms in Canada are still not capitalist enterprises. But to conclude from this that Canadian agriculture is therefore not capitalist would be quite wrong. In almost every major commodity, with the notable exceptions of dairy and grain farms, a significant percentage of production originates with a very small percentage of farms, and this kind of concentration is increasing (see Ehrensaft and Bollman, 1983). In general, even though in 1986 there are still many non-capitalist "family farmers" in Canada, agriculture has become much more capitalist in this sense, and in its forward and backward linkages to capital regardless of the "class location" of individual farmers and their families.

In order to appreciate the current crisis in farming, we must look at the dynamics of structural change, both historically and in the present. To do so does not assume a transformative process which is complete, nor one which has had a uniform outcome. Apparent contradictions, anomalous class locations, and other puzzling phenomena will be encountered. But by focusing on processes of change, we may be able to resolve some of the apparent anomalies of our empirical terrain.

2. Data and methodology[1]

In order to understand better the structural characteristics of New Brunswick agriculture, the Province's fifteen counties were collapsed into five regions of three counties each which have been labelled Regions "A" to "E" (see Figure 1). One working hypothesis, based on preliminary evidence, was that the three major potato-producing counties—Carleton, Madawaska and Victoria—had experienced the greatest degree of agricultural industrialization, and that the three counties in the northeast— Northumberland, Restigouche and Gloucester—had experienced the

Figure 1

The five regions of New Brunswick

Region A:
Carleton, Madawaska, and Victoria

Region B:
Restigouche, Gloucester, and Northumberland

Region C:
Kent, Westmorland, Albert

Region D:
York, Sunbury, and Queens

Region E:
Kings, St. John, and Charlotte

least. Thus these counties were grouped into regions "A" and "B" respectively. Since maintaining geographical contiguity and preserving the obvious character of the regions of the Province were also of concern, the three counties in the southeast of the Province were grouped together as Region "C" and the three most southerly counties became Region "E". This left the three remaining, more centrally located, counties as Region "D". Comparing the structural profiles of these five regions in 1951 and 1981 shows how the dynamics of centralization, concentration, and uneven development have affected the character of the Province.

3. A profile of New Brunswick agriculture

Historically, the forest industries have been the dominant primary resource activity of New Brunswick, but both fishing and agriculture have played important supplementary roles in the rural economy. At the turn of the century most farms were unspecialized farming operations which provided most of the household food as well as small cash surpluses for commodities such as tea, sugar, molasses, and nails (Sinclair, 1984a). Trapping, hunting, fishing, and woodcutting provided many who farmed with additional means of support. The informal domestic economy was at least as important as the gradually emerging market economy in many areas of the Province.

For at least the last sixty years, total farm-gate receipts show that potatoes have been New Brunswick's most important and most commercialized agricultural product; the dairy sector has always been second in importance, followed by livestock, poultry and eggs, and finally, fruits, vegetables, and other field crops (New Brunswick, Department of Agriculture, 1967-1982). But despite this stability in commodity patterns, major shifts have occurred in agricultural structure, as Table 1 shows. Between 1921 and 1951 there was a gradual but consistent decline in the number of farms and the amount of land farmed; the more rapid disappearance of farms apparently allowing those that remained to become much larger. Similarly, whereas prior to 1951 mechanization and use of hired labour was quite uncommon throughout the Province, by 1981 the remaining farms were, for the most part, heavily mechanized and the use of wage-labour had increased dramatically.[2]

Hidden within the province-wide data are more startling developments which are only revealed by further disaggregation. By controlling for farm size and region of the province, it can be concluded that between 1951 and 1981:

1. The number of small (10 to 69 acres) and medium (70-239 acres) farms rapidly declined; conversely, the number of farms greater than 240 acres increased.

Table 1
A comparison of agriculture in New Brunswick in 1921, 1951 and 1981

Attribute	1921	1951	1981
Number of farms	36,655	26,430	4,063
Total farm area ('000)	4,270	3,470	1,082
Improved acres ('000)	1,368	1,006	474
Acres per farm	116.5	131.3	266.3
Improved acres per farm	37.3	38.1	116.7
Number of farm horses	67,705	31,019	2,972
Horses per farm	1.85	1.17	.73
Trucks per farm	—	.18	1.12
Tractors per farm	—	.21	1.73
Weeks hired labour per farm	n.a.	3.6	24.7
Lbs. fertilizer used per acre	—	119	244

Source: Censuses of Agriculture, 1941, 1951, 1981 and Agricultural Statistics, 1967, 1973

2. There was an increasing separation between hired labour and capital, especially on the largest farms. By 1981, 20 percent of the province's farms sales were accounted for by the 1.5 percent of the farms which hired more than five person-years of labour (Ehrensaft and Bollman, 1983:Table 19).

3. Mechanization has also occurred most rapidly on the largest farms and more rapidly in Region "A" than any other region.

4. Mixed farming has been replaced by an increase in specialization. By 1981, 94.8 percent of all New Brunswick farms were specialized (defined as having more than 50 percent of all receipts from one commodity sector). By far the most specialized territory was Region "A".

5. In terms of capital value, between 1951 and 1981 Region "A" increased its degree of concentration (based on Gini coefficients) relative to the other regions by 107 percent in terms of machinery and equipment, and 27 percent for land and buildings.

This increase in the capitalization of the fewer remaining farms was possible because of the heavier debt loads assumed by farm operators who based their credit on the euphoric rise in land values which occurred from the mid-1970s until 1981. By 1982, however, land values began to deflate (due in part to the pressure exerted by the numbers leaving farming) which had a negative effect on the equity of those remaining. Debt-to-asset ratios worsened rapidly after 1980, creating the climate of crisis which still persists. As Table 2 indicates, by 1985 the average New Brunswick farm was burdened by a debt amounting to 52.4 percent of assets. Since some wealthier, generally older farmers are fairly debt free, this means that others have debt loads that may be 80, 90, or even 100 percent of their farm assets. There is little to indicate that this situation will improve in the near future.

There have also been regional variations in the depth of the crisis. The most capitalized area, Region "A", has, of course, suffered the largest effects of deflation and debt interest charges. This is one of the consequences of the centralization of capital in New Brunswick agriculture which, in turn, is a result of the restructuring which has taken place over the past thirty years. In 1951, the amounts of farmland and capital within New Brunswick's five regions were much more evenly distributed than they are today. This must not be overlooked. Although some changes had occurred earlier, the fact remains that in 1951, as Table 3 shows, agriculture was still an important activity in most areas of the Province.

Table 2

The capital and debt structure of New Brunswick Farms, 1976-1985

(in constant 1981 dollars)*

Year	Total Capital	Land & Buildings	Total Debt	Total Equity	Debt/Asset Ratio
1976	557.1	369.5	121.5	435.6	.279
1977	545.1	361.7	131.8	413.3	.319
1978	591.1	390.9	141.7	449.4	.315
1979	630.2	406.2	158.5	471.7	.336
1980	653.2	418.1	164.6	488.6	.337
1981	669.4	440.6	180.6	488.8	.369
1982	593.5	380.1	167.1	426.4	.392
1983	553.3	355.8	153.5	399.8	.384
1984	537.0	337.0	163.1	373.9	.436
1985	515.2	323.6	177.1	338.1	.524

Source: Computed from Statistics Canada, 1986:1-9

* Constant values have been computed using the Consumer Price Index for Saint John, N.B.

Table 3

Degree of comparability of New Brunswick's five regions 1951 and 1981*

Variable	1951					
	A	B	C	D	E	Prov.
Farmland	22	21	21	21	15	(100%)
Land & buildings	23	29	20	16	13	(100%)
Equipment	30	17	21	17	15	(100%)
Total capital	24	26	20	16	14	(100%)
	1981					
Farmland	34	9	21	18	19	(101%)
Land & buildings	33	10	21	18	19	(100%)
Equipment	44	9	18	14	15	(100%)
Total capital	36	10	20	17	17	(100%)

Source: Computed from Censuses of Agriculture, 1951 and 1981

* Each figure represents that region's percentage of the provincial total for that year. Due to rounding error, some rows may not add to 100 percent.

By 1981, however, Regions "A" and "C" were dominant, while Region "B", which had the most farm capital in 1951, had by far the least in 1981!

Potato agriculture in particular (see Table 4) gradually concentrated in Region "A", leaving virtually no significant production anywhere else in the Province by 1961. Does this suggest that these three counties are more agronomically suitable? Two major agronomic factors to consider are quality and fertility of soil and weather patterns. Recent weather data (New Brunswick, Department of Agriculture, 1982a:25-28) show that climate does not particularly favour Region "A"; it is not favoured in either the number of frost-free days nor in the number of growing-degree days. Similarly, although Region "A" does have more acres of Class 2 soils than any other region (there is no Class 1 land in the Province), most of the Province's agriculture takes place on Class 3 and Class 4 lands which are quite suitable for potatoes and other vegetable crops. The fact that in 1910 potato production was almost evenly distributed over Regions "A" to "D" tends to support the view that agronomic factors cannot explain today's concentration in Region "A".[3]

A better explanation might be the historic location and growth of potato shipping firms. By 1921, firms located in Region "A" (notably

Table 4
The percentage of New Brunswick's potato acreage In each of its regions, 1910-1981*

Year	A	B	C	D	E	Acreage
1981	95	3	2	1	-	53,793
1976	96	2	1	1	-	55,517
1971	96	2	1	1	-	59,421
1966	90	4	2	2	1	64,901
1961	83	7	5	4	2	54,165
1956	72	13	8	6	3	46,190
1951	60	17	11	8	4	38,123
1941	48	22	16	11	6	44,092
1931	46	22	16	11	5	60,260
1921	42	19	20	12	7	62,769
1910	26	26	23	16	9	40,433

Source: Computed from Censuses of Agriculture, 1951 to 1981, and New Brunswick, 1962.

* Some rows contain rounding errors.

those owned by Guy Porter and Andrew McCain) had secured supply contracts with Cuba which spurred potato production in the area (Canada, 1925). Yet this historic fact does not seem to be sufficient. Until 1951 further concentration of production in Region "A" was only very slight. It is only in the 1970s and 1980s that these three counties have come to virtually monopolize potato production. Furthermore, concentration and centralization of production has occurred *within* Region "A" itself. By 1976, 77 percent of the Province's potato acreage was concentrated into two relatively small areas of only a few parishes each (Senopi, 1980:5), one around the town of Florenceville, the other borders on the town of Grand Falls.

The explanation of the concentration and centralization of potato production is in reality considerably more complex. First, we cannot understand these structural shifts without looking at the social relations of production. Second the presence or absence of agribusiness is crucial— a commodity sector which is dominated by an agribusiness will be more rapidly restructured than a sector which is not (Florenceville and Grand Falls are home to large potato processing plants). Finally, the facilitating role of the state in economic restructuring cannot be overlooked.

4. Structural transformation and the potato production process

The period between 1951 and 1981 saw the most significant technical changes that have ever occurred in the production of potatoes in New Brunswick. A review of the manner in which potatoes were grown in 1851, for example, would only have to be slightly modified to portray accurately the production methods most farmers used in 1951. The techniques of 1981, however, bear little resemblance to those of 1951 and before. In the intervening period, a range of entirely new machines and biochemical innovations was developed to facilitate the efficient cultivation of potatoes. By 1981, one can see the effects that extensive mechanization (and concurrent capital-intensiveness) have had in the development of potato agriculture in New Brunswick, as well as the particular forms of social relations that have evolved as a consequence of these changes in production techniques.

Potatoes were grown as a crop on over 20 thousand farms in New Brunswick in 1951, but 93 percent of these units grew fewer than 7.3 acres of potatoes. Only two percent of the farms at that time had potato acreages greater than 22.4 acres, and very few units had more than 30 acres. This was because 1951 production techniques limited a given farmer to planting and harvesting no more than the available labour pool would permit. The development of capital-intensive and mechanized farming changed potato production practices drastically. By 1981, there were only 740 potato farmers remaining in the Province, and of these, over 55 percent had more than 33 acres of potatoes. The largest 71 of these farmers (less than 10 percent of all potato farmers) produced 40 percent of total potato production. At the other end of the spectrum, the 45 percent of farmers with less than 33 acres in potatoes together accounted for only three percent of the Province's total production (Bollman, 1983). Clearly potatoes are no longer a small producers' game.

The potato production process has six major steps. A brief examination of each of these shows how the social relations of potato production have changed from 1951 to 1981.

Assembling materials and inputs

With the smaller acreages of 1951 farms, assembling seed, manure, storage containers and so on was not, for most farmers, a major chore. By 1981, the task of preparing for a commercial potato crop required considerable managerial expertise. The variety and quantities of materials being handled have put much of this work outside the sphere of family labour.

Field preparation

Ploughing, harrowing, spreading lime and manure, and rock picking were all tasks that the majority of 1951 farmers would have done with the aid of horse-drawn implements. The 20 percent of farms with tractors used them to increase the efficiency of their own labour rather than the size of their potato acreage. But by 1981 a powerful tractor could plough in 30 to 40 minutes what in 1951 would have taken a long day for a man and a team of horses.

Planting

Planting involves both seed cutting and actual planting. In 1951, seed cutting was a very labour-intensive operation, and one which might have involved the use of some hired labour. Simple seed planters were used on some larger farms to space plants evenly. With the larger acreages of 1981, even a seed cutting device still required labour, but investment in two- and four-row planters helped alleviate the problem of getting a crop into the ground within the relatively narrow climatic planting "window."

Cultivation and Maintenance

Horsehoeing and cultivation, with some weeding by hand, were the major horticultural practices in 1951. By 1981, applications of chemicals were being made to the crop almost on a weekly basis. This has entailed the purchase of specialized spraying equipment, as well as the chemicals. Chemicals have changed the nature of cultivation from being labour-intensive to capital-intensive.

Harvesting

Of all of the stages of production, the harvest was the most labour-intensive in 1951, and would have been the crucial factor limiting expansion. One might be able to prepare more field area, cut more seed, and even weed and cultivate a larger crop, but if the labour is not available to harvest another ten or twenty acres, there's little point in planting it.

By 1981, the mechanical harvester had dramatically changed the shape of the harvesting process. A harvester commits the farmer to a wholly new way of completing the final stages of the potato production process. Under the older system of using diggers and pickers (which are still used by some farmers, especially in Victoria county), the process is paced so that one can, with existing flatbed trucks and lower-powered tractors, transport the tubers in containers to the storage buildings. With the harvester, however, there is considerable economic pressure to operate the machine at its highest capacity to conserve fuel and labour. One harvester could, in an average three-week effective harvest period, reap between 150 and 195 acres of potatoes. For a harvester (and the related equipment it entails) to be economically justified, a farmer would have to plant at least seventy acres in potatoes.

Though harvesters reduce the need for labour, they do not eliminate it entirely. The conventional harvester requires a seven- or eight-person trained crew; the vacuum harvester can be operated with half as many workers. The drama of the harvest is an occasion in which one most clearly sees a reflection of developing capitalist social relations of production. In all of the harvesting operations that I have witnessed, either the grower or his son operated the harvester and the windrower while those who drove the trucks and worked on the harvester belt were wage-workers.

Storage and grading

Neither storage nor grading were serious problems in 1951 for most farmers. By 1981, with acreages and yields vastly increased, climate-controlled buildings were essential to protect a crop. Furthermore, the task of grading potatoes became even more involved as government regulations, processors and wholesalers demanded more uniform quality standards.

What clearly emerges from an overview of the changing process of production is that the employment of technical innovations in the potato production process permitted producers to rearrange social relations of production to cope with labour scarcity especially during the harvest period. The solution—the harvester—had the impact, however, of leading to further capital expenditure and land acquisition which then enlarged the scale of the rest of the production process to the degree where it was necessary to maintain a relatively constant pool of wage- labour. Thus, the 1981 potato production process has, in most cases, led to highly developed capitalist social relations of production.

5. Production relations in other commodities

Most New Brunswick farms were not highly specialized operations in 1951. Even the larger potato and dairy operations seldom relied exclusively on one commodity. In 1956, 99 percent of all New Brunswick farms had poultry and at least a few pigs, with many farms having a dozen or more. Collectively, these small operations accounted for nearly all of the Provincial production in these commodities.

By 1981, both hogs and poultry had become much more concentrated industries. Indeed, the 13 percent of hog producers who had more than 178 head controlled 85 percent of the Province's production. And in poultry, 99 percent of all meat-bird production was in the hands of the seven percent of producers who had more than 972 birds. In fact, the average flock size for these larger producers was 36,610 chickens. Egg production was only slightly less concentrated.[4]

Neither the dairy nor the beef sectors have shown such extreme tendencies toward concentration. In 1981 about 66 percent of the Province's dairy production took place on the 45 percent of farms which had between 13 and 62 cows. Beef production is slightly more concentrated in operations with somewhat larger herds. Furthermore, unlike potatoes, which became very geographically centred, other commodities have exhibited only minor tendencies toward geographical concentration. Region "E", for example, and especially Kings County, is more noted for dairy production, but all regions have a viable dairy sector.

Changes in production technologies have altered the social relations of production more in the poultry and hog sectors than they have in either dairy or beef. Pigs and chickens have moved from the barnyard to the biofactory, but there are differences between them. Very few hog operators hire much wage-labour, which suggests that the technology of even quite large hog production units permits the operators and their families to do most of what is required. Capital formation in the poultry sector, however, has been very extreme. In New Brunswick's modern facilities, one person over one year can maintain a flock of 20 thousand to 25 thousand laying hens (United States, 1980:148), yet despite this, the poultry sector used more paid labour per farm than any other commodity sector in the Province.

Neither dairy nor beef have been able to replicate the biofactory model of poultry and hogs within the province, though there is now at least one feedlot operation for beef cattle (owned by the potato processor McCains). Thus far, production still involves maintaining an extensive land base (for pasture, and producing hay and forage) and thus there are few realistic opportunities for expanding operations without expanding the land base (which can be prohibitive). The introduction of such technologies as milking machines and refrigerated bulk storage tanks has certainly encouraged a modest increase in the average dairy farm size, but neither innovation is strongly scale-biased. Thus dairy and beef farming remain the stronghold of family farm operations in New Brunswick.

The above analysis suggests several conclusions regarding production processes and social relations. First, the advent of mechanization does not, in itself, lead to changed social relations of production. In fact, a certain degree of mechanization (such as smaller tractors and associated implements) may reinforce independent commodity relations rather than automatically lead to capitalist ones. This occurs when mechanization allows production to be expanded using only the labour of the farm family.

Second, if new technology has a uniform impact over the entire production process, and it is not scale-biased, it is less likely to alter the social relations of production. The introduction of milking machines has not significantly altered social relations within the dairy industry. If, however, some part of the production cycle is put out of phase by the introduction of new technology, then the alteration of social relations is likely to occur. The potato harvester pushed potato agriculture toward capitalist relations, and the introduction of confinement technology in the poultry sector has virtually wiped out any independent commodity poultry production.

Third, there are two conflicting relationships between land and capital penetration. For commodities requiring a land base (that is, all plant products and pastured livestock) capitalist penetration will result in an increase in the area of land cultivated and controlled. For commodities that were formerly land based, but whose production does not now directly require land (poultry, hogs), capitalist penetration is indicated by the degree to which there has been a separation of production from the land base. This does not mean that the owners of the means of production no longer own farmland; rather, production no longer directly requires farmland. When agricultural production can be transferred indoors, the possibilities for factory-like industrialization open up. All cost factors can be strictly controlled, and profit margins can be closely calculated. Such circumstances are ideal from a capitalist perspective. In addition, the land that was formerly used for production can be put to other, more profitable purposes.

Fourth, because mechanization and bio-chemical techniques are external inputs from the capitalist sphere, their utilization lessens the degree of input control by producers, and capitalist social relations of production tend to be reinforced. Conversely, when producers are more self-sufficient in terms of inputs, independent commodity relations tend to be reinforced.

Fifth, dramatically increasing the size of an operation or introducing sophisticated machinery or production techniques increases the requirement for a pool of full-time and reliable skilled labour which is qualitatively different from seasonal labour. Hiring a few part-time workers at peak production periods is unlikely to undermine the essentially independent commodity relations of most family-labour farms. Hiring regular full-time wage-labour will, however, result in a stronger tendency toward the formation of capitalist relations.

In sum, introducing new mechanization or production techniques will facilitate the formation of capitalist social relations of production when: (a) a limiting factor in the production process is encountered, and (b) some effort is made to overcome this condition, and, most importantly, (c) success in overcoming it leads to the emergence of other limiting factors.

Capitalist social relations of production will tend not to develop from the independent commodity form if limiting factors do not emerge in the production process. The more severe the limiting factors, and the more frequently they occur, the more rapid the possible transition from independent commodity production to capitalist production. Whether such a transition will actually occur, however, is dependent upon several external factors:

1. The technical means to overcome the limiting factor must exist. The potato harvester was the technical solution that did not exist locally until many years after the "limiting factor" emerged. Once the harvester was introduced, new limiting factors quickly emerged, and the efforts to overcome these by consolidating land, acquiring other machinery, and so on, propelled potato production rapidly into the capitalist sphere.

2. The financial means are also crucial. The producer must either have the capital, or access to the capital, to permit the purchase of the new technology. In the case of the poultry sector, the capital

demands were so high that few could actually meet them. Consequently, production rapidly concentrated in the hands of the few that did. Any independent commodity production that existed in poultry was virtually decimated overnight.

3. The presence of sufficient markets in which to sell the larger quantity of products produced per grower is essential. In a given market area, command of sufficient markets may only occur if enough other growers stop producing. In the potato sector, potato acreage remained relatively constant over the past seventy-five years, even though the number of growers declined radically.

Beyond the production process, however, there are two other very important factors to consider, the roles of agribusiness and the state. The analysis which follows shows that it is the interplay between these three matrices—the production process, agribusiness and the state— which ultimately determines the rate of transformation from independent commodity to capitalist relations in a given commodity sector.

6. Agribusiness and structural transformation in agriculture

Although the term "agribusiness" was originally defined to include all economic activities associated with the production of food, for purposes of this analysis, I have adopted a more common and restrictive use of the term to refer only to those firms whose primary business activity is in either the inputs industries (fertilizers, seeds, chemicals, machinery), the outputs industries (shipping, wholesaling, food processing), or both. Though direct production may be a part, perhaps even a significant part of certain agribusinesses, it is the control exerted by the forward and backward linkages on "independent" producers which is of concern here.

Specifically, what needs to be determined are the types of social and economic relations that exist between the agribusiness sector and potato farmers, and how these relations have influenced the form of agricultural production and, ultimately, the restructuring of New Brunswick agriculture. It is my contention that as agribusiness dominance over a particular commodity sphere increases, a structural pressure is exerted which encourages the transformation from the independent commodity pre-capitalist form of production to one embodying a more capitalistic character.

No New Brunswick agricultural product was "commercialized" earlier than the potato. By 1910, several of the larger growers had formed shipping companies to market potatoes in the United States. This market collapsed with the passing of the import-restricting Fordney Act in 1922, and a new market was developed in Cuba. By this time the shippers, notably the Porter and McCain groups—who were often in unscrupulous competition with one another—had become quite sophisticated in their marketing practices. By colluding, they got a high price on the Cuban market while paying a very low price to the growers. Eventually this was discovered, and the very first Federal investigation under the 1921 Combines Investigation Act was conducted. The 1925 report gives detailed and chilling evidence on the manner in which growers were manipulated and exploited by these shipping consortiums (Canada, 1925).

Though there were a couple of potato starch companies in New Brunswick in the late 1940s, there was actually little in the way of processing. Thus agribusiness relations with potato growers from 1910 to 1956 were restricted to marketing and shipping. These relations took place primarily with those growers who were physically near the shippers who, in turn, had ready access to the original American market. This geographical proximity had the effect of commercializing potato production in Region "A" but it had only a minimal effect on transforming independent commodity production into capitalist production. Indeed, shippers preferred to deal with many smaller growers not only because it made price manipulation easier, but because it also stymied potential competition.

In January 1957 the entire situation changed with the opening of the first McCains plant processing potatoes into frozen french fries. The twenty-five years from 1957 to 1982 have seen the company grow from 30 employees to over 6,600; from one potato plant to thirteen in seven different countries; from potatoes and peas to twelve varieties of frozen potato products, nineteen vegetables, twenty-six desserts, six varieties of frozen pizza, and eight lines of juices; and from one potato processing plant to holdings in transportation, cold storage, fertilizer, machinery, beef feedlots, meat processing plants, large scale farms, wholesaling and retailing. It has also seen sales grow from $152,678 in 1957 to $47.7 million in 1971 and $695 million in 1981. McCains is now the largest producer of frozen french fries in the world, and one of the three or four largest frozen food processors (Kimber, 1982:86).

There are four ways in which McCains is able to influence the shape of potato agriculture. First, it is able to exert control in the area of agricultural inputs, such as seed and fertilizer. Both can be obtained from McCains' subsidiary operations. In exchange for buying equipment from other McCains-owned companies, McCains will arrange credit, which, of course, can be repaid through contract provisions.

Second, because of its ownership of land, it is also able to compete in the sphere of agricultural production. McCains owns at least 15 thousand acres in Carleton and Victoria counties, of which 6 thousand acres are prime agricultural land. By directly competing with other producers,

McCains is able to exert a downward pressure on the price of the commodities it produces.

Third, since McCains is now the major market for potatoes, it is able to wield its influence as a processor. It virtually sets the price it will pay to farmers in the Province despite the fanfare created by the powerless potato marketing board.

Finally, through its contracts with producers, McCains is able to legalize a set of social and economic arrangements with producers that are advantageous to the company. One of the most obvious implications of the contract is the manner in which decision making is transferred from the producer to the processor. No longer does the farmer have the say in what variety to plant, when to sow and when to reap, or how much fertilizer and how many chemicals to use. The horticultural practices, the methods of storage—in essence, all factors having to do with the production of contracted potatoes—are dictated to the grower.

When we look at how agribusiness has affected land, labour, and capital, the evidence suggests that the presence of a vertically integrated agribusiness in a commodity sector will alter the social relations of production in that sector. Farm-owners essentially become propertied surrogate-labour for agrobusiness. Through agribusiness's control and marketing of specialized and scale-biased equipment, some workers are displaced, while others are required to obtain new skills, a development which alters the structure of the labour force. Finally, when an agribusiness locates in a rural area, it tends to proletarianize those in the region by incorporating formerly independent commodity producers into facets of agribusiness production. In terms of its impact on labour, then, it is clear that agribusiness has facilitated the transformation of independent commodity production into full capitalist production.

It would be wrong to create the impression that only the potato sector has been affected by the growth of agribusiness. In New Brunswick, it is certainly the most obvious example of agribusiness domination, but no agricultural commodity is exempt from its influence. As more food products are processed; as wholesale and retail channels of distribution become more corporately concentrated; as the production of inputs becomes more widely integrated into vertical and horizontal business structures; so too, will other commodity sectors become increasingly penetrated and controlled by agribusinesses, given present conditions.

7. State policy and the restructuring of agriculture

The state has been a vitally important actor in the restructuring of New Brunswick agriculture. One of the important roles that the apparatus of the state plays in capitalist society is supporting the accumulation of capital. That is, state policies and programs should create a climate of "business confidence," and they should encourage economic linkages between different sectors of the economy. In agriculture, capital accumulation is facilitated by programs and policies which encourage the growth of larger farm units, which provide incentives for agribusiness development, and which encourage numerous economic linkages between farmers and agribusinesses. In order to create and maintain the conditions of social harmony, the state must legitimize these actions, which, in agriculture, it does by appealing to the ideological sentiments attached to the concept of the "family farm."

Neither the provincial nor the federal government has pursued a singular and consistent course of action with respect to agricultural policy and programs. Indeed, in reviewing policies of the past thirty years or so, the ambivalence of strategy and the contradictory implementation of programs is striking. The contradictions, however, are more apparent than real; the differences lie primarily at the level of detail. If one looks at agricultural policies and programs analytically, one may discern a development which is consistent with the role of the state in capitalist society.

The Rationalization of Agriculture

In the context of agriculture, rationalization implies a concern with developing profitable, efficient enterprises that will result in a reasonable income for the farmer's labour as well as a return on investment. Marginal(traditional) production units that have no prospect of achieving these "rational" goals are to be discouraged. There is little doubt that rationalization has been an emergent theme of state agricultural policy between 1951 and 1981. The Whalen Report (New Brunswick, 1962) on the New Brunswick potato industry, for example, expressed concern about the large number of small, inefficient farms, the shortage of working capital, the deterioration of markets, and the lack of mechanization. In the 1970 report of a Federal task force on agriculture the commissioners stated:

> The organizational structure of agriculture both in the government and private sectors should be rationalized. Management by objectives, program planning and budgeting, cost-benefit analysis and other modern management techniques should be adopted. Every public policy should embrace these principles and procedures (Canada, 1969:10).

These reports were often converted into programs at both levels of government which have attempted to inculcate the notion of "rational" agriculture.

The Emergence of Agricultural Linkages

A further way of promoting rationalization is to encourage the development of economic linkages to and from the sphere of production. Agricultural policies and programs in the 1950s did not explicitly stress the importance of linkages. The production sector was very much treated in isolation from other economic activities, with the exception of the export of seed and table potatoes. But by the 1960s, a distinct change was beginning to occur in state policy which coincided with the early appearance of agribusiness in New Brunswick. Though the production sector was still viewed as separate, the notion of linkages to the processing sector was more common. One study (New Brunswick, 1962:176-181) warned producers that profitable potato farming would be intimately connected to the success of the processing sector. Similar linkages were made in other reports with reference to other commodities. But perhaps the biggest impetus to viewing the agricultural sector in more integrated terms came with the passing of the Federal Agricultural Rehabilitation and Development Act, commonly referred to as ARDA. The first general agreement with New Brunswick under this act was signed in 1962. In essence, this agreement tied rural development to the expansion of the forest, fisheries and agricultural sectors by linking primary with secondary development (New Brunswick, 1966:8-9).

By the 1970s, government agricultural policy was couched in terms of "food systems." Programs were designed to make these systems operate efficiently. If the processing sector needed a reliable and steady supply of farm products, state policies and programs would be created to assure that farm production met these systemic goals.

The "system" concept was only a step away from the present context for the articulation of federal and provincial agricultural policy. Essentially, all of the "systems" have been amalgamated into one giant "agri-food sector" which includes "suppliers, farmers, distributors, retailers, and governments" (Agriculture Canada, 1981:4). By thinking in terms of an all-encompassing "agri-food sector," policies are formulated for farming that seek to adapt it to the strengthening of the necessary linkages between the various components of the sector. Indeed, the fundamental premise of the "agri-food strategy" is to create programs which will "maximize its [the agri-food sector's] contribution to the growth and development of the Canadian economy and play an enhanced and more effective role internationally" (Agriculture Canada, 1981:4). In particular, the strategy is designed for "optimizing value-added in the agri-food system" (Agriculture Canada, 1981:8). The production and provision of food for society, or the gainful employment of people in agriculture— once primary goals of the state—are now seen merely as vehicles for the larger goal of economic growth within the capitalist system.

Technology Transfer in Agricultural Production

Another way of encouraging rationalization in agriculture is to promote the introduction of technology designed to save labour costs and increase production efficiency. This has proved to be an enduring and favourite theme of agricultural policy makers. The push for mechanization began in the 1950s by wedding the idea of self-sufficiency to tractor technology. The worries of the early 1960s about having an inadequate technological base were quieted by state policies, and by the later 1960s new programs were dealing with the adjustment problems of an agricultural sector that had become quite highly mechanized. Eventually, however, the farm machinery industry fell into troubled times, and in order to protect the holistically conceived agri-food sector, new initiatives stressing "technology transfer" were undertaken. At no time between 1951 and 1981 did state policies and programs ever veer away from the basic commitment to an increasingly technological agriculture.

Pledging Allegiance to the Family Farm

In the 1950s, when most farm products originated on family farms, there was little need to reaffirm allegiance to this particular form of organization. But as corporate and large scale farms became increasingly dominant, statements reflecting commitment to the notion of the family farm became more common. What appears as a contradiction vanishes when one realizes that the definition of a family farm has not remained constant, but has been routinely redefined to parallel the development of the above themes, so that, by 1981, a "viable" family farm is seen as one which operates solely on the principles of economic rationalization. In turn, the most favourable state programs and credit packages are restricted to these "viable" family farm entities—usually large-scale and highly specialized operations.

There are four ways in which both the provincial and federal states have supported accumulation in the New Brunswick agricultural context. They have created a favourable fiscal climate, especially for export crops such as potatoes. They have underwritten private risks at public expense. McCains, in particular, has been the recipient of over 25 million dollars in grants, bonds, guarantees, forgivable loans, and interest-free payable loans. They have tried to create a capitalist labour market. And they have supported the development of technical infrastructures. Agricultural research, for example, is a major expense to both federal and provincial governments. Yet most of the research which is conducted at these experimental stations is designed not for the "family farm," but rather, large corporate farms and agribusiness.

The truth is that in the thirty years between 1951 and 1981, the state has supported agribusiness and capital accumulation more frequently, and with greater intensity, than it has the "family farm," despite all professed sentiments to the contrary.

8. Conclusion

The restructuring of New Brunswick agriculture can be analyzed as the product of three interacting factors. First, certain technical innovations have been introduced into some commodity production processes that have changed not only the efficiency of production, but also the social relations within those commodity sectors. Second, agribusiness has facilitated the development of capitalist relations. Commodity sectors lacking a dominant agribusiness fulcrum have not as easily been able to make the intersectoral linkages which promote capitalist production. Finally, state policy has gradually but insistently created programs that have rewarded rationalized agriculture while penalizing alternatives.

For those who cling to the idea of the "family farm" this analysis, at first glance, is pessimistic. It is, I believe, too late to "save" the family farm. It is a unit of social organization which is no match for capitalism. Despite the ritualistic and predictable assertions by government and others about the health and vigour of the family farm in Canada, the reality is that the family farm, by any usual definition, is terminally ill. What is alive is the ideology and the rhetoric of the family farm; pledging allegiance to the concept creates and fosters the political illusion that farming is still in the hands of farmers. The dominance of this ideology has effectively obfuscated the actual social and economic relations within agriculture. Although small farms are numerically dominant, the actual control of most agricultural production has passed, or is in the process of passing, into the hands of larger-than-family and corporate farms which form a small elite. Even this elite does not operate with full autonomy, for it too must work by the imperatives of the dominant players in the agro-food complex—the processors, wholesalers, retailers, inputs suppliers, machinery manufacturers, financial institutions, and various state agencies. This is not the historical context in which the traditional family farm unit previously existed, and it is not a context in which it can now survive.

Does this mean that the role of the family in agriculture has no future? It does not. The traditional family farm was able to operate as an autonomous and atomized unit only so long as the capitalist forces of concentration and centralization were kept in check. Once the balance tipped unequivocally to capitalist strength, the atomized and isolated units simply could not survive. The family, however, may still have a place in farming if radical social reorganization occurs. I believe that we must cease thinking about the family farm, and start concerning ourselves with the "family-in-farming."[5] Essentially, this concept implies reorganization of the farm unit so that the family still plays a central and fundamental role in actual production of food and fibre. Such a reorganization may involve "group" farming arrangements whereby several families pool their resources and their labour to form a strong economic and social unit that is able to counter the proletarianization of capitalist penetration. Several experiments have been conducted already in Canada, mostly in the Prairies, and these have realized many advantages, such as reduced machinery costs and access to larger, specialized equipment; greater possibility for enterprise diversification and for experimentation with new technology and techniques; increased access to credit and financial management; security in case of illness or incapacity; reduced isolation, stress, and physical risk due to the sharing of work and responsibilities (Gertler and Murphy, 1987). Such ventures could also enhance the possibilities of more equitable roles for women. The traditional farm unit has not recognized the central role that women have played in its sustenance, and this chauvinism still persists. With new structures which emphasize the centrality of the family in farming, the redefinition of sex roles may give women the credit they have long deserved in farming enterprises.

In traditional farm units, stewardship of the land through sensitive and ecological agricultural practices has had to take second place to the reality of survival in a capitalist context. With new forms of co-operative farming ventures, stewardship could resume its rightful preeminence, for there can be no agriculture without fertile land. Nor can there be agriculture for long without "true" farmers. If such farmers are able to organize production in co-operative units, they may incidentally produce among themselves people with leadership skills, enthusiasm, and the free time necessary to revitalize and rebuild other community institutions. The success of such efforts might allow us to look to the future of farming with hope rather than despair.

Notes

1. Much of the data used in the structural analysis component of this paper is derived from the Censuses of Agriculture of 1921 to 1981. Other sources of data include interviews and discussions with farmers, particularly potato producers in Carleton and Victoria counties, numerous government reports and documents, and specialized statistical publications. The Censuses of Agriculture were taken at ten year intervals from 1921 to 1951, and at five year intervals since then. Any errors in the collection and analysis of information

necessarily become the errors of those who use the Census, but the fact that the Census polls the entire agricultural population considerably enhances its reliability and validity.

2. The importance of 1951 is dictated by Census data. In actuality, it is the two decades between 1941 and 1961 during which much of the demographic and technological change takes place in New Brunswick agriculture. Thus 1951 appears to be a demarcation point and it is used as such throughout this paper. It is, however, somewhat artificial.

3. Cavendish Farms, the Irving-owned potato processing plant based on Prince Edward Island, has considered plans for promoting potato agriculture in Kent County (in Region "C"). This area has soil conditions similar to Prince Edward Island which are particularly suitable for potato production.

4. The figures in this section have been calculated from the 1981 Census of Agriculture unless otherwise noted.

5. For a more detailed discussion of this concept, see Michael Gertler and Thomas Murphy, "The Social Economy of Canadian Agriculture: Family Farming and Alternative Futures," in Eugene Wilkening and Boguslaw Galeski (eds.), *Comparative Family Farming in Europe and America* (Boulder: Westview Press, 1987).

Chapter Ten

Pulpwood Producer Marketing Organizations in New Brunswick

Peter deMarsh

Pulpwood producers in New Brunswick began a process of developing marketing organisations more than twenty years ago. This experience of collective marketing is now far enough advanced to permit some tentative generalizations about the results obtained by these organizations and the limits within which they function. Discussion of these is preceded by a brief description of the socio-economic context within which the experience has developed, and of the organizing strategy adopted. Some suggestions are also made concerning the future prospects of the small woodlot sector in New Brunswick. The recommendations of a 1983 provincial government study of the private woodlot resource not only reflect the current political "weight" of the marketing organizations, but help define some of the future challenges they and their members confront. Also discussed is the somewhat different agenda for small woodlots proposed by the 1984 Nova Scotia Royal Commission on Forestry which brings the implications of the New Brunswick Study into sharper focus.

1. The socio-economic context

The landholdings of New Brunswick's 35 thousand "small woodlot owners" originated in the pattern of land grants to European settlers which involved small allotments of almost exclusively forested land. The proportion of cleared land on these original grants is now well below the maximum reached in the 1890s, the and average size of holdings remains quite small, reflecting limited tendencies to concentration of land ownership. As a result, the 35 thousand woodlot owners control one-third of the province's forested land in parcels whose average size is about 50 hectares.

The dominant industry in New Brunswick is pulp and paper. Six companies own ten mills and also control two-thirds of the less important saw-milling industry. Pulpwood sold to the industry has been an important cash-crop for New Brunswick's rural population throughout this century. Of the industry's total supply, private woodlots continue to provide nearly one-third. Most of the remainder comes from Crown lands owned by the province.

The market for woodlot-owner pulpwood is quasi-monopsonistic due to the geographic dispersal of mills (pulpwood cannot be economically transported by truck for distances much over 125 kilometres) and the concentration of mill ownership. In addition to the companies' ability to fix pulpwood prices, the position of small producers was further weakened by government policies which provided industry with virtually unlimited supplies of Crown land wood. As a result, small producers were faced with a situation in which prices barely covered costs of production with no return on the product itself, and in which the market for this cheap wood was chronically unstable due to uninhibited access to the Crown resource, in conjunction with the cyclical character of the industry.

Creating marketing organizations to offset company market power, and mobilizing the sizeable number of woodlot owners in order to gain some political influence over government policies regarding access to Crown land pulpwood, would appear—in the circumstances just described—to be fairly straight-forward courses of action. In practice, several factors ensured that producers who sought to organize were faced with a complex and challenging task. While the overall numbers of owners, total production, and their share of the resource are all substantial, the average size of industrial woodlot holdings means that for most individuals, the share of their income derived from pulpwood production and hence their motivation to organize, is small. Furthermore, the 35 thousand owners are by no means a homogeneous group. One-quarter at most conform to the traditional image of the rural primary producer who combines farming, fishing and some seasonal wage work. The remainder are distributed in approximately equal proportions among blue-collar and white-collar workers and pensioners. Of the 35 thousand only about 10 thousand produce pulpwood in a given year. Finally, while land ownership has remained widely dispersed, there is nonetheless considerable concentration of actual production. In 1970, 2 percent to 3 percent of producers controlled about one-third of the total volume produced. This small group emerged, before the period of widespread organizing efforts, as a result of the mechanization of harvesting and the growing number of non-producing owners from whom standing wood could be purchased. Members of this group own the trucks which transport pulpwood to the mills, and also act as buyers from smaller producers.

2. The organizing strategy

The earliest pulpwood marketing organization in New Brunswick emerged in 1962. Most activity occurred during the 1970s and by 1983 more than 90 percent of pulpwood from small woodlots was being sold through contracts negotiated by seven regional organizations which cover the entire province. Most dealings with industry are through the regional bodies, while efforts to influence government policy are coordinated through a provincial federation of the seven.

Organization of marketing on a regional basis within the province was clearly an important feature of the strategy. This approach reflected linguistic, social, and economic differences within the province. It was also thought that organization should not exceed a scale that allows democratic control by producers. A second key feature of the strategy was the choice of a "common front" approach, bringing together both large and small producers in order to achieve maximum political impact, to control a significant proportion of total production, and to make it less easy for companies to attempt to play some groups off against others. Thirdly, the initial goals of the organization were clear and simple: "fair" prices and stable deliveries. The presence of two external targets (companies and government) further assisted initial mobilization. Finally, a choice was made to use existing provincial agricultural marketing legislation as the legal basis for collective bargaining.

3. Results

In terms of initial goals, the organizing effort was fairly successful. During the period 1973-1984 price increases were on average about 10 percent above increases in the cost of living. Stability of deliveries improved considerably. Both gains were based largely on success in achieving changes in provincial Crown lands legislation: the industry is now required to negotiate contracts with the seven marketing organizations before it receives its annual allotment of Crown wood.

The likely consequences of these changes can be summarized as follows. The outflow of economic surplus from rural areas has been modestly reduced and as a consequence, standards of living have improved somewhat, and some related spin-off development has probably occurred. In turn, disintegration of the rural sector as a whole in terms of land concentration has slowed. As suggested above, the trend was already a limited one within the rural population and has probably been weakened even further. A second type of concentration, that of land purchases by industry, has been sporadic in the past, although it reached significant proportions in some areas. It is very limited at the present time, due at least in part to the contribution made by better pulpwood prices to higher land values.

A further effect is increased husbandry by small woodlot owners of the forest resources under their control. This is due both to improved incomes and to efforts by the organizations to promote improved forestry practices and to obtain an increased share of public funds devoted to the improvement of forest resources. Finally, the organizations have also provided several thousand rural New Brunswickers with an opportunity for direct and long-term participation in relatively democratic organizations, and have given a more intense experience of dealing with government and industry to several hundred of them.

Within very limited terms, the organizing strategy chosen by woodlot owners in New Brunswick has been modestly successful. However the strategy has been largely defensive, and disintegrative trends have by no means been fully offset. The pressure to mechanize has not been reduced. As well, the positive results in terms of price increases have themselves had a mixed effect, at least in terms of social differentiation. Improved prices have meant that a greater proportion of smaller producers have survived than would otherwise have been the case. On the other hand price increases have at the same time contributed to the efforts of some large producers to get larger, not in this case through concentration of land ownership, but through increased mechanization and control of a growing proportion of production. Four to five per cent of all producers now control 60 percent of production. The battle to halt or at least slow internal differentiation is fought out in each of the seven organizations and is the dominant issue in their internal politics. In a few exceptional cases, small producers, on the strength of their numbers, have won an improved share of the market.

4. Future prospects

The ability of producers to use the marketing organizations as a means of strengthening their economic position is limited by several factors. The first of these is the effect of success in price negotiations on the tendency to differentiation just discussed. As a large producer continues to get larger, at some point in the process of capitalization his or her allegiance to the "common front" will be threatened. Internal cohesiveness is also weakened by fluctuations in the larger economy which usually involve periods of reduced demand for paper and therefore for pulpwood. The marketing organizations have succeeded in reducing the amplitude of the swings in pulpwood purchases, but not in eliminating them. Since 1970, the number of years of relatively low pulpwood demand in New Brunswick has exceeded the number of years with average or high demand. Enormous pressure is placed on the common front as organizations attempt to distribute reduced volumes as fairly as possible. Further aggravating this situation is the tendency for reduced demand for wood to coincide with increased supply as woodlot owners who are normally employed elsewhere fall back on the woodlot during periods of temporary unemployment. The "recovery" level of 10 percent official unemployment reached in the larger economy by 1985 suggests that this burden is now chronic. In that year, the organizations reported up to twice the usual number of individuals seeking a share of wood deliveries.

A further cause of concern is the current state of the pulp and paper industry in New Brunswick. Competition on world markets is increasing and New Brunswick mills face a deteriorating position due to inadequate capital investment and rising wood costs. Concern over wood costs has led to a growing campaign in New Brunswick in support of increased public investment in forest management. In conjunction with these efforts to arouse concern over "a future wood shortage," industry and government are paying increased attention to gaining greater control over the private woodlot resource. Recent studies in New Brunswick and Nova Scotia propose quite different strategies for gaining such control.

5. The Private Woodlot Resource Study

The problem as defined in the New Brunswick Government's *Private Woodlot Resource Study* (1983) is one of devising policies which will ensure that private woodlots play the fullest possible role in minimizing a medium-term wood shortage. They are seen as playing a potentially crucial role in overcoming the predicted shortages, but will do so only if the "interactions" among owners, industry, and government are improved. The proposed means of achieving these goals is the scheduling of harvesting so that mature and overmature lots receive harvesting priority. The suggested vehicles for such planning are the seven existing owner organizations which are urged to assume these broader responsibilities in the context of a more co-operative relationship with industry and government.

Two principles are the basis for the Study's proposals. The present structure of collective bargaining through the seven existing organizations is acknowledged as legitimate, and the right of individual owners to manage their resources as they see fit is accepted as valid. Efforts to convince owners to comply with regional harvesting plans must, the Study says, be based on persuasion and education through their own organizations, and coercive legislation of a direct or indirect nature is explicitly ruled out.

6. The Nova Scotia Royal Commission on Forestry

The Nova Scotia Royal Commission (1984) also defines the basic problem as one of a future wood shortage, and policy proposals focus on achieving levels of harvesting in line with the resource's full, and currently unrealized, potential. The strategic position of private woodlots in terms of medium-term wood supply is again identified. Scheduling of harvesting and a greatly expanded reforestation program based on public funds are the Commission's central recommendations. However, the two principles noted as the basis for the New Brunswick Study's proposals are absent. While the Commission hopes that the individual owner will voluntarily accept government-imposed management and harvesting plans for his or her woodlot, legislation making such compliance obligatory is not ruled out. Immediate action to impose punitive taxation levels on the unco-operative and a program to expand provincial Crown lands are both suggested, hinting indirectly, at very least, at a policy of creeping expropriation. The present glutted pulpwood market offers a further means of inducing owner co-operation: those accepting government management plans will be guaranteed a market. The marketing prospects for non-compliers are not addressed. The need for reasonable wood prices is noted, but the means proposed to establish such prices are unconvincing (a government pricing commission, and unspecified efforts to develop expanded markets). The existence of present owner marketing organizations is barely acknowledged and their future role as bargaining agents is said to be "unclear."

7. Conclusion

The "hard-line" approach of the Nova Scotia Commission leaves no place for collective owner action, and removes control by owners over management and harvesting decisions. The political basis for the differences between the recommendations of the Commission and the Study could be usefully analyzed. Differences in the strength of organizations in the two provinces is certainly one factor. The willingness of governments and industry to entertain more or less "progressive" policies could also be considered. A comparison of the two sets of proposals is particularly useful from the New Brunswick perspective because it suggests an obvious danger facing owners, the prospect that their own organizations will be used to achieve the same transfer of control of their resource that in Nova Scotia would be obtained by more direct means. The challenge is to use the New Brunswick Study's recommendations as a means of ensuring greater and more stable access to markets, and of continuing the legitimate work of gaining an increased share of publicly-funded forest management programs, and on more flexible terms, while avoiding the transformation of owner organizations into mere appendages of the pulp and paper industry.

Comment on deMarsh

James Cannon

DeMarsh's assessment is rather more optimistic than that presented in the chapters by Macdonald and Connelly, and Murphy on independent commodity producers in other primary sectors. This raises the question of why small-scale woodlot producers should have been more successful than their counterparts in fishing and agriculture in their struggle with integrated corporate producers. Three possible lines of explanation seem worth commenting upon: the nature of the commodity; the configuration of class interests underlying the production of primary products; and the nature of the relation between the state and primary producers.

1. The nature of the commodity

Does timber possesses any attributes which contribute to small-scale wood producers having greater success in their struggle with integrated producers than in other sectors of primary production such as fishing or agriculture? With respect to marketing, the preliminary response seems to be in the affirmative. It would appear to be easier for woodlot owners to secure more stable or predictable production than is the case in agriculture or fishing which are more susceptible to short term output changes attributable to biological or climatological fluctuations. Wood supply can be more accurately forecast through time and the harvesting schedule can be modified much more easily than in the other sectors. However, supply management could also be practised by corporate sector producers. Thus, while supply management might be expected to stabilize and increase returns to producers, it is not obvious that this circumstance would differentially favour smaller producers.

The nature of a commodity can also affect the way in which production is organized. Recent research has stressed the potential for production of a particular commodity to be undertaken using very different technical and labour processes (Piore, 1984). If commodities can be produced using either small-scale, flexible production methods or large-scale mechanized processes, both types of production systems may co-exist. The economic viability of the small-scale producer will be determined by the relative balance of costs and output compared with the corresponding balance for the large-scale producer.

While the reality of this trade-off in particular sectors of primary production is a subject for empirical investigation, it seems plausible to suggest that wood producers may not have as great a burden of fixed costs as agriculturalists, yet may also be able to achieve relatively higher levels of productive efficiency than small boat fishers. If these hypotheses are sustainable, small-scale production may be better able to compete with large-scale producers in wood harvesting than in fishing or agriculture.

Moreover, the nature of wood as a commodity invites not only alternative harvesting processes but also alternative management regimes. The application of silviculture makes the contemporary forest susceptible to intensive management. However, debates about the appropriateness of alternative management practices reveal strong differences of opinion on many matters. One of the most visible concerns conflicting views on the use of herbicides and pesticides. Such differences can reinforce distinctions between corporate and small-scale approaches to management of the resource and produce a politics of forest management which transcends and compounds more typically economic matters affecting the relative strengths of large- and small-scale wood producers (Howard, 1980).

In summary, the attributes of a primary product may in part determine the technical and social relationships which are adopted in producing the commodity. Analysis of the Saskatchewan experience with potash supports the view that the nature of the commodity can influence the relations of production which are adopted with subsequent implications for social outcomes (Kirk Laux and Appel Molot, 1979; 1981). However, while the nature of the commodity may facilitate certain strategies, it by no means determines outcomes. This suggests that it is also necessary to look in other directions to explain the relative success of the woodlot owners.

2. Configuration of class interests in wood production

Individualism and diversity of interest have always confounded attempts to promote common interests among independent commodity producers. As deMarsh stresses in his chapter, a priority of the Federation of Woodlot Owners has been to establish a "common front" embracing all producers. Internal cohesion has been facilitated by restricting attention to the marketing of unprocessed wood and by a regionalized organizational structure which has allowed for local interests to be accommodated at the grass roots level.

However, as deMarsh indicates, the organization's success is also contributing to increased differentiation among its ranks which is likely to present challenges to the group's cohesion in the future. Thus the question of class interest involves an important internal dynamic as well as the relationship between woodlot owners and the corporate sector. In general, the reasons for the Federation's cohesion are not self-evident and merit further study.

3. Relation between the state and primary producers

The importance of examining the state's role in establishing policy regulating primary production and mediating the relationship between small- and large-scale producers is a theme common to all the sector cases studied in this book. In discussing the relation of the state to primary production, it is important to distinguish between its proprietary and regulatory roles. Moreover, the roles of the federal and provincial states must also be separated. Whereas the federal state is more central in considering the fishery and agriculture, the provinces are much more important in a discussion of wood production. Although private ownership of forest land is high in New Brunswick, the state exerts significant control through its ownership of almost 50 percent of provincial forest land. However, the way in which the state chooses to exercise control can vary considerably as is illustrated by the contrasts between the policies proposed in New Brunswick and Nova Scotia (compare New Brunswick, 1983 with Nova Scotia, 1982). In short, New Brunswick has elected to work within structures which have emerged from within the wood producing sector while the recent Nova Scotia Royal Commission on Forestry reveals an apparent distrust of woodlot producers, a bias in favour of the corporate sector and a clear intention to centralize and streamline bureaucratic control of forest operators.

In New Brunswick, woodlot owners have been able to win concessions from the provincial government. The political implications of the priority of provincial jurisdiction in forestry seem clear. Whereas the federal government might choose to ignore the plight of small-scale fishers or farmers who constitute small electoral groups on the national scene, a provincial government with direct jurisdiction over forest activities is less likely to ignore a group which has the electoral significance of the woodlot owners on the provincial stage.

However the differences in the ability of Nova Scotia and New Brunswick woodlot owners to influence public policy merit further attention. In view of the difficulties that independent potato producers have experienced in New Brunswick in attempting to strengthen their position in relation to corporate producers, there does not appear to be any basis for arguing the New Brunswick government always adopts a more populist stance. Rather the need to examine concrete situations in their appropriate historical context appears all the more important.

4. Conclusion

The relative success of the New Brunswick Federation of Woodlot Owners is attributable to a constellation of factors. These would seem to include as a minimum the nature of the commodity, the cohesion of wood producers around a common interest and the response of the provincial state to the specific producer group.

Clearly other avenues for explaining the relative success of the woodlot owners need to be investigated. For example, the specific nature of the relationship between the corporate and independent producer sectors needs to be explored. This would appear to be an important avenue of enquiry in view of recent research on segmented markets and would guard against a one-way reading of the power relation between the corporate and independent producer sectors. In addition, more detailed examination of the mobilization strategies employed by the leadership of the woodlot owners would also appear to be in order.

However, in conclusion we need to ground discussion in the realization that the gains made by the woodlot owners remain modest and any euphoria regarding their relative success needs to be tempered by the realization that the per cord price of wood received by woodlot owners in Atlantic Canada is only about 20 percent to 25 percent of that received by similar small-scale operators in European countries where private ownership of woodlots dominates the forest sector. This observation offers both hope and frustration.

Conclusions

Restructuring, Class Conflict and Class Alliances: Some Theoretical and Practical Conclusions

R. James Sacouman

The accelerating destruction of the material basis for small "peasant"/ semi-proletarianized agricultural production over the last twenty years in Atlantic Canada has now been well documented. In agriculture, work by Murphy (1983; and this volume) and Sinclair (1984a), for example, has provided the empirical basis for arguing that the land-based "farmstead" household, the reproductive basis for subsistence, petty commodity and semi-proletarian primary production, has been dramatically eroded both in relative and absolute terms. Thousands of households have been made productively landless, have been proletarianized, or (more often) "lumpenized"; a few have made the transition to corporate farms in their own right or to commodity production fully dominated by huge expanding corporations. The structure of class conflict in agriculture is, in other words, quickly being transformed and simplified.

Those "on the margins" who do not leave "cope" by drawing upon and reproducing "symmetries of gender and community relations" (de Vries and MacNab-de Vries, 1986) which continue to provide tenacious reproductive support. However, *in the absence* of an alliance between "lumpen," petty producer and working-class primary producers and households that will explicitly serve the interests of each class and gender segment against the needs of capitalist accumulation, the possibility and necessity of collective resistance are seldom perceived beyond the level of the household and the immediate community.

In forestry, as with the destruction of the farmstead base, it is becoming apparent that corporate control over pulp and paper manufacturing including woodlot production is being extended, and that the structure of class conflict is being transformed in similar ways and sometimes by the same huge corporations. Since the relatively early growth of vertically integrated pulp and paper production between the last two world wars (Cote, 1977; Hiller, 1982), the pulp and paper industry, like the situation in the agriculture *and* in the fishery, has tended to rely on small- and medium-sized woodlot owners for about one-half the production of softwood, its crucial raw material. Recent indications are that this 50 percent - 50 percent tradition is being eroded by provincial and federal state initiatives, in alliance with large corporations and the larger woodlot owners, in favour of facilitating the growth in constant and variable capital of the big corporations at the expense of the semi-proletarianized small woodlot owners (see, deMarsh in this volume; and Nova Scotia, Royal Commission on Forestry, 1984). Lumpenization of the many, direct proletarianization of the few, and expanded capital reproduction for the very few is, again, the trend.

Woodlot owner associations, especially in New Brunswick, are attempting to battle this trend not only in their negotiations with companies over the price of pulpwood but also through the formation of marketing and woodlot-owner controlled co-operatives. Again, in the absence of any real alliances between these mostly male producers and all other forestry-related lumpenized and proletarianized households, the trend towards expanded capital accumulation will continue, though some of the co-operators may survive and expand.

Turning to the Atlantic fishery, it is certainly not by chance that it has continued to receive close analytical attention. Besides its clear centrality to the regional economy and culture, the Atlantic fishery has become, at long last, the leading primary production industry in terms of the transformation of the structure of class conflict towards expanded capital reproduction for the few and the lumpenization/proletarianization of the many, led by large capital and the state.

Over the last twenty years, state policy has appeared to shift three major times, though all the shifts are interrelated (see for example Barrett and Davis, 1983; Canada, Task Force on the Atlantic Fisheries, 1982; Clement, 1983; 1986a; Fairley, 1983; 1985a; and this volume; Grady and Sacouman, 1984; Kearney, 1984; Overton, 1979; Sinclair, 1985a; 1985b; Winson, 1983). Active federal and provincial attempts to destroy the basis for petty production through the enforced relocation of households, and thus to lumpenize or proletarianize them, really began in the 1960s. Under an ideology of social concern, federal policies appeared to shift during the 1970s to attempts at creating and supporting a petty bourgeoisie in particular branches of the fishery (such as the longliner groundfishery and scallop dragging): through favourable economic and political incentives during "the Romeo LeBlanc years," on the one hand, and simultaneous increase in enforcement/control by the Department of Fisheries and Oceans over petty fisheries activity on the other. Meanwhile provincial fishery policy combined financial incentives to boat builders and processors with heavy gifts to large capitals.

With the specific capitalist crisis of overproduction in the fisheries in the late 1970s and 1980s (see, especially, Barrett and Davis, 1983; Fairley, 1985b; Grady and Sacouman, 1984; Williams, 1984; and Williams and Theriault in this volume), state policy has apparently returned to its more normal stance of open support for large capital against both small-scale and medium-scale petty production. What is new about this support is its determined drive to facilitate, economically and politically, the real subordination of the petty fisheries and of small and medium-sized fish processing (see Apostle, et al., 1983) to the requirements of expanded reproduction in two supercompanies. What large capital alone failed to do in fifty years of class struggle, the state in alliance with large capital is currently doing: transforming the industry into fully capitalist production for all but the most luxurious of luxury species, by creating and capitalizing a virtual state capitalist monopoly/monopsony in Newfoundland and a private, but highly subsidized, virtual monopoly/monopsony in Nova Scotia. In both provinces, these capitals are now able to transform the 50 percent–50 percent tradition in favour of direct investment in capital intensive production, culminating in the recent introduction of freezer-trawlers.

Now, clearly, defensive "organized resistance" (Clement, 1986a) in the fisheries to capitalist development/restructuring reflects both the complexity of these variations and the actual and emergent diversity of the class alliances formed between workers, small and medium-sized independent producers, processors and marketeers. There now exists in the Atlantic fisheries an almost overwhelming confusion of union, associational, co-operative, community and *ad hoc* organizations for struggle (Clement, 1986a; also Boyd, 1983; Cameron, 1977; Fairley, 1985a; and this volume; Grady and Sacouman, 1984; Neis, 1984; *New Maritimes*, 1982-now; Sinclair, 1985b; Williams, 1979). These diverse and divergent organizations have few links among themselves, seldom support each other, and often tend to be silent on inequalities between the sexes. Yet female analysts of the East Coast fisheries have demonstrated that the sexual division of labour must be integrated fully into our understanding of the changing structure of class conflict and of diverse, particular struggles in the fisheries and, by extension, in other primary production sectors (see, e.g. Boyd, 1983; Connelly and MacDonald, 1983 and in this volume; McFarland, 1980; Neis, 1984; Porter, 1985). Porter's general call (1986) for a Marxist-feminist political economy of struggles in Atlantic Canada is entirely apposite.

Faced with this history of the expansion of corporate capitalism and the defeats and disunity among those most affected, it would be easy to adopt a fatalistic, defeatist stance; or alternatively, to argue that the way forward now lies in a purely "proletarian" socialist strategy based first and foremost on the organizations of those who have been integrated as wage-workers into purely capitalist production. The latter seemed, at least, to be the political implication of many of the critiques of *Underdevelopment and Social Movements in Atlantic Canada*, and especially of my own contribution. However, there are good theoretical and practical (and orthodox Marxist) reasons for declining to draw any such conclusions.

"Classical" Marxism needs to be and can be renewed in order to provide a valid and creative theory of the development of capitalism and of class struggles today. Marx did not develop a full-fledged theory of global, national or regional uneven development, he merely assumed it. Nor did Marx ever develop a full-fledged theory of any of the forms of "unevenness" of capitalism except for the crucial unevenness of class formation and class conflict in social, commodity production.

"Primitive accumulation"—the historical process of separating the direct producers from their means of production, proletarianizing them—required not just economic coercion but also intense violence. For Marx, the history of the expropriation of small property holders "is written in the annals of mankind in letters of blood and fire" (1976:875). Yet "[t]he history of this expropriation assumes different aspects in different countries, and runs through its various phases in different orders of succession, and at different historical epochs. Only in England, which we therefore take as our example, has it its classic form" (1976:876). Thus, while Marx fully expected primitive accumulation to be a bloody battle lost by smallholders, he did recognize that it would take different forms at different times and in different places, and be the focus of different kinds of class struggles.

Within capitalist production proper, on the other hand, the central class struggles are between capital (and its state) and the workers over ways of increasing the rate of exploitation. In this connection Marx saw as the necessary product of necessarily increasing exploitation (if capitalism is to survive it must expand) the making redundant for social production of a necessarily increasing vast reserve army of labour. This "normally" produced, expanding relative surplus population—surplus to capitalism but not of course to humanity—was regularly joined, in times of capitalist crisis, by the normally employed proletariat.

The struggle between labour and capital, Marx saw, is often deflected to a struggle between workers. The struggle for socialism, for Marx, requires the entire army of the exploited and unemployed in the struggle; socialism requires the refocusing of struggles between worker and worker, and between worker and near-worker, onto the conflict between capital and labour.

Yet because Marx tended to take a (Euro)centrist and linear/evolutionary view of capitalist development, he tended to reduce class struggles to a two-class model, instead of a two-*bloc* reality (and most often argued for socialism emerging first from within the most advanced nation-states).

It was, in fact, these difficulties with Marx that Lenin addressed in his final analysis of the Russian situation after 1905, when he called for a worker-*led*, peasant-supported socialist revolution that would spark successful socialist revolutions in the imperialist countries. These revolutions in the imperialist countries either failed to occur, or occurred and failed, and the Soviet Union proceeded not to socialism but to Stalinism and statism. Nevertheless Lenin's commitment to the necessity and possibility of socialist revolution in non-imperialist countries based on worker-led alliances among all the exploited and oppressed has better captured twentieth century experience than any Marxism that waits for the final total dominance of the capitalist-worker relation, and/or for socialist revolution in the imperialist centres.

Lenin's central insight, based on Russian reality, that the successful struggle for socialism will always require an alliance between the proletariat and other pre-capitalist elements not yet eliminated by primitive accumulation, has been taken up in recent times most creatively by S. Amin. Like Marx and Lenin, Amin bases his analysis of the development of capitalism on a world scale on the class formation of class conflict through social production. But unlike some of the Marx of *Capital*, Amin does not assume, indeed he denies, that social production can be understood as if labour-capital-state relationships were reducible to the exploitation of a fully proletarianized working class.

Amin's argument is classically Marxist in so far as it develops, on a global scale, Marx's own "absolute general law" of the necessity of a continually (but not continuously) increasing relative surplus population which becomes increasingly immiserated and oppressed. But unlike Marx, Amin does not assume that wages are paid at a socially and historically defined level of subsistence of labour power. On the contrary, Amin argues, a crucial feature of the expansion of capitalism on a global scale has been the drive to push and maintain wages for the majority of human beings below the currently accepted level of subsistence. And this crucial process of expanding the rate of exploitation by decreasing wages below the means of subsistence is not merely—or at times even primarily—brought about through strictly economic coercion but has often required, and still does, state and ideological violence against the working class as a whole, the relative surplus population in particular, and especially the female sector of that relative surplus population. Analyses of development must therefore comprehend not only the "economic" aspect but also the social-cultural-political-coercive aspect of capitalist accumulation. Moreover, Amin understands history as global and "always the history of unequal development"(1980:2). Amin's central thrust is to argue the political centrality of the global "periphery."

Amin does not theorize the role of struggles in the peripheries inside imperialist countries (such as Atlantic Canada), nor does he recognize the importance of women's struggles in both the imperialist centres and the various "peripheries." He does, however, show that any tendency to dismiss the struggles in peripheries such as Atlantic Canada as not being "inherently" socialist is erroneous, and that whatever the difficulties and differences of interest, levels of organization, etc., it is the *linking* of the remaining independent primary producers, the marginalized and "lumpenized" semi-employed and unemployed, and employed workers, that is the central task. The socialist or even the anti-capitalist nature of the organizations and projects in which they are mobilized is not given by the structures in which these people find themselves, but by organization and struggle. Class struggle, indeed, never occurs purely. It is always linked to the formation of class blocs between and within class fragments and is always linked to other movements that are across-class, but not beyond-class, struggles, such as nationalism/regionalism and feminism.

These theoretical considerations suggest that the way forward with respect to the thorny issue of the kinds of alliances actually and potentially emergent from the restructuring of primary production in Atlantic Canada does not lie in abandoning the struggles of those who are being marginalized and "lumpenized" by capitalist restructuring, but in trying to link these struggles with those of all others, including wage workers and women, who are struggling against exploitation and oppression. For example, to take the fishery again, like all primary commodities, the production and circulation of fish and fish products are organized globally under capitalist (and masculine) dominance. The federal and provincial branches of the Canadian capitalist state have both become increasingly directly involved in dealing with both the imperium's increasing protectionism and our own (e.g. the fish tariffs conflict with the U.S.), and in setting the terms and conditions of entry, with the extended 200-mile limit, of selected peripheral states (e.g. Cuba).

This "rationalizing" of global, inter-state, and intra-state relations in the fishery during the entire period of the current global crisis of capitalism, from the late 1960s to the present day, finds its *central* material basis in the increasing convergence of the capitalist state with monopoly "private" and state capital in the fishery. On the one hand, this convergence has resulted in an increase during the entire period of crisis in "primitive"/ primary accumulation. Primitive accumulation has been facilitated not only through "normal" economic coercion in the form of unequal exchange with small producers but also through legal co-optative mechanisms (especially the expansion of restrictive Department of Fisheries and Oceans guidelines and some financial carrots to a few "new bourgeoisie"), ideological attacks on part-timers, and legalized, if often technically illegal, coercive assaults on small producers and small-producer organizations which refuse to be exterminated as a class fragment. The direction here is towards the "lumpenization"/proletarianization of entire populations in the region as a necessary base for expanded capitalist accumulation by, primarily, the two supercompanies in Newfoundland and Nova Scotia.

Expanded reproduction in the fishery has thus been directly linked to the state's facilitation of primitive accumulation, of that central condition for expanded capitalist reproduction, the creation and reproduction of a productive but propertyless "surplus" population of formerly smallholders. That other central condition for expanded reproduction, the creation of large enough capital pools to expand definitively "high-tech" constant capital, has also been the object and result of the increased convergence of monopoly capital and the state. The specific crisis of the fishery in the 1980s has been the occasion for the state's creation, through financial handouts and coercive laws restricting workers' control over terms and conditions of employment, of two large enough pools to begin what capitalism had failed to do from the 1910s to the late 1960s, i.e. fully proletarianize the remaining workforce.

In this respect, the recent introduction of factory trawlers represents the clear *social* direction of the dominant state bloc. Factory trawlers do indeed "rationalize" the fishery. Their introduction will mean the unification of catching and processing under strictly capitalist-working class relations: the loss of 140 or so worker-years per factory trawler, the end of the 50 percent–50 percent tradition of fish inputs from directly and indirectly controlled sources of production, the radical altering of conditions of work (40 to 60 days at sea per trip), the direct assault, given the prevailing sexual division of labour in both production and human reproduction, on women's and family's proletarianization (most women processors, who are the current majority, and also some married men will not be allowed or will not choose to be away from home for 40 to 60 days). A very few rural locales (e.g. Lunenburg) may benefit, but most will become productively redundant.

The task is to bring together all those who are bearing the brunt of this attack, *including* the region's wage workers, in an alliance for an alternative project that will conserve and enhance the society and communities to which they belong. This is not utopian but necessary, as it always has been, for the formulation and achievement of a popular democratic form of socialism.

• • •

The 1980s ended with the permanent closure of numerous fish processing plants in Atlantic Canada and drastically shortened operating seasons for most others. The capital concentration and centralization pursued through the 1980s have led to drastic declines in fish stocks. This crisis of "overfishing" has, of course, been uneven, but in general the communities, households, and individuals most affected have been those that were most dependent on the fishery for paid economic activity.

As the chapters in this volume by Veltmeyer, Murphy and Overton show, this latest turn of the screw is not an accident but results from the logic of capitalism, with its inexorable pressure towards larger-scale, more capital-intensive, labour-"saving," profit-making forms of efficiency, supported by the state under the influence of now this, and now that, segment of capital itself. And whereas a hundred or even fifty years ago, the growth of still relatively labour-intensive manufacturing offered at least the younger generation of the primary-producing population the alternative of wage employment—and in smaller countries, such as those of Western Europe, one that did not even necessarily force them to migrate out of their regions, and could lead to the transformation rather than the mere decay of rural communities (Franklin, 1969: chs. 1 and 7)—this is not the case today, least of all in the Atlantic Provinces. Nor can these citizens hope that the Canadian state will fashion a dignified and worthwhile alternative, through programs of income support, let alone state-led projects for regional recovery. In the name of market efficiency (combined, ironically, with populist appeals to "small is beautiful") the state is renouncing all responsibility of this kind (including even a contribution to unemployment insurance).

The Atlantic Provinces will survive as self-regenerating, self-governing, self-respecting communities, only to the extent that collective popular opinion and social organization crystallizes around a recognition of these facts, and a shared alternative project of regional development and social transformation. To put it another way: does a future of long-term redundancy or, at best, a further casualization and seasonalization of work and life chances, confront most petty *and* most proletarianized primary producers in Atlantic Canada? Does it just mean the end of all those irritating and contradictory gender-and-class fragments, and all those little dots on the map? If so, will this be accepted? Or does the process of restructuring offer a material basis for political unity among all petty producers and workers, employed and unemployed, male and female, young and old, against capital and for socialism?

The debate continues, as do protests by affected wage workers, small producers, and their communities. Having set the agenda for closure and destruction, capitalists and capitalist state policy appear to have the upper hand. Plant workers strive to save "their" particular processing plants. Small fish producers attempt to find alternative foreign markets for their produce. There is no regional or even provincial movement of resistance. "Divide and rule" prevails, not least through the exacerbation of real and imagined differences between and within classes, genders, generations, areas.

As we have seen, the effects of restructuring primary production are always uneven; it can even happen that while petty producers are being destroyed in one area, others are expanding in the same sector of primary production in another area. Similarly, the use of women's paid labour has always been unequal by sector and area, and has notably different political and ideological effects in different contexts. This volume shows the need for careful analysis of these differences by class, by gender, by age, and by locale. This is particularly clear in the chapters by MacDonald and Connelly, which focus not only on gender and class but also on the processing as well as the growing and/or harvesting of the primary product. They make it clear that understanding the differences (real and imagined) and also the *links* between "producers" and "processors" within the food industry is central to any alliance for resistance and change. This is true whether we consider differences within unionized labour, or between unions and unorganized workers, or between workers, petty producers and processors, or within households, or within communities.

Coming to grips with all these and other differences among primary producers is, in the last analysis, the central concern of this volume. All the contributors share the view that without good theoretical and empirical work on this question, effectively communicated, the bases for unity in the effort to build a popular and democratic project of regional reconstruction will be misconceived, and grounds for effecting opposition will be missed.

For the central issue is whether or not there can be united movement towards a popular democratic, socialist alternative to the present path of marginalization and decay. Others have argued that this is the central issue for all of the Americas (e.g. Burbach and Nunez, 1988). Wherever we focus our attention, however, a progressive solution requires not just analysis but a political movement. Such a movement is so far painfully absent in Atlantic Canada, as well as in Canada as a whole. However, periods of popular defeat, when a degree of fatalism tends to develop, are succeeded by periods of resistance and the generation of new goals and projects both of reform and transformation. Laying the groundwork for such a period of regeneration and advance in favour of social transformation is the task to which this book has sought to contribute.

Bibliography

Acker, Joan, 1988, "Class, Gender, and the Relations of Distribution," *Signs* 13(3) (Spring).

Adkin, L. and C. Hyett, 1984, "'Convergence' in Popular Movements in Latin America and Canada," Paper presented to the Workshop on Development in the 1980s: Canada in the Western Hemisphere, Queen's University.

Aguiar, Neume, 1983, "Household, Community, National, and Multinational Industrial Development," in J. Nash and M.P. Fernandez-Kelly (eds.), *Women, Men and the New International Division of Labour*, Albany: State University of New York Press.

Alexander, David, 1974, "Development and Dependence in Newfoundland, 1880-1970," *Acadiensis* 4(1).

Alexander, David, 1976, "Newfoundland's Traditional Economy and Development to 1934," *Acadiensis* 5(2).

Alexander, David, 1978, "Economic Growth in the Atlantic Region, 1880-1940," *Acadiensis*, 8(1).

Alexander, David, 1983, *Atlantic Canada and Confederation: Essays in Canadian Political Economy*, Toronto: University of Toronto Press.

Allain, G. and S. Coté, 1984, "Le Developpement regional, l'etat et la participation de la population: La vie courte et mouvement des conseils regionaux d'amenagement du Nouveau Brunswick, 1964-1980," *Egalite*, Automne/Hiver.

Amin, Samir, 1977, *Imperialism and Unequal Development*, New York: Monthly Review Press.

Amin, Samir, 1978, *The Law of Value and Historical Materialism*, New York: Monthly Review Press.

Amin, Samir, 1980, *Class and Nation: Historically and in the Current Crisis*, New York: Monthly Review Press.

Amin, Samir, 1982, "Crisis, Nationalism and Socialism," in S. Amin et al., *Dynamics of Global Crisis*, New York: Monthly Review Press.

Andersen, R. and C. Wadel, 1972, *North Atlantic Fishermen: Anthropological Essays on Modern Fishing*, St. John's: Institute of Social and Economic Research (ISER), Memorial University of Newfoundland.

Antler, Ellen, 1981, "Fishermen, Fisherwomen, Rural Proletariat: Capitalist Commodity Production in the Newfoundland Fishery," Unpublished Ph.D. Dissertation, University of Connecticut.

Apostle, Richard, Gene Barrett, Anthony Davis and Leonard Kasden, 1985, "Land and Sea: The Structure of Fish Processing in Nova Scotia: A Preliminary Report," Project Report Series No. 1-85, Halifax: Gorsebrook Research Institute, Saint Mary's University.

Armstrong, Pat, 1984, *Labour Pains: Women's Work in Crisis*, Toronto: The Women's Press.

Armstrong, Pat and Hugh Armstrong, 1983a, *A Working Majority: What Women Must Do For Pay*, Ottawa: Canadian Advisory Council on the Status of Women.

Armstrong, Pat and Hugh Armstrong, 1983b, "Beyond Sexless Class and Classless Sex: Towards Feminist Marxism," *Studies in Political Economy* 10.

Armstrong, Pat and Hugh Armstrong, 1984, *The Double Ghetto: Canadian Women and their Segregated Work* (Rev. Ed.), Toronto: McClelland and Stewart.

Athanasiou, Tom, 1977a, "Compost and Communism: Part 1," *UnderCurrents* 24.

Athanasiou, Tom, 1977b, "Compost and Communism: Part 2," *UnderCurrents* 25.

Atlantic Consulting Economists Limited, 1986, *Business and Job Creation*, Background Report for Newfoundland and Labrador, Royal Commission on Employment and Unemployment, St. John's: Queen's Printer.

Baldursson, Einar Baldwin, 1984, "Work Stress in the Fishing Transformation Plants," in Jean-Louis Chaumel (ed.), *Labor Development in the Fishing Industry*, Canadian Special Publication of Fisheries and Aquatic Sciences 72, Ottawa: Fisheries and Oceans Canada.

Banaji, J., 1976, "Chayanov, Kautsky, Lenin: Considerations Towards a Synthesis," *Economic and Political Weekly*, October 2.

Barrett, G., 1976, "Development of Underdevelopment and the Rise of Trade Unions in the Fishing Industry of Nova Scotia, 1900-1950," Unpublished M.A. Thesis, Dalhousie University.

Barret, G., 1977, "Notes on a Monopoly," Halifax: Research Co-op.

Barret, G., 1979, "Underdevelopment and Social Movements in the Nova Scotia Fishing Industry to 1938," in R.J. Brym and R.J. Sacouman, *Underdevelopment and Social Movements in Atlantic Canada*, Toronto: New Hogtown Press.

Barret, G., 1980, "Perspectives on Dependency and Underdevelopment in the Atlantic Region," *Canadian Review of Sociology and Anthropology*, 17(3).

Barret, G., 1983, "Uneven Development, Rent and the Social Organization of Capital. A Study of the Fishing Industry of Novia Scotia, Canada," Unpublished dissertation, University of Sussex.

Barret, G., 1984, "Capital and the State in Atlantic Canada: The Structural Context of Fishery Policy between 1939 and 1977," in Lamson and Hanson (eds.), *Atlantic Fisheries and Coastal Communities*, Halifax: Ocean Studies Program, Dalhousie University.

Barrett, G. and R. Apostle, 1985, "Labour surplus and local labour markets in the Nova Scotia fish processing industry," Gorsebrook Research Institute for Atlantic Canada Studies, Saint Mary's University (December).

Barrett, G. and A. Davis, 1983, "'Floundering in Troubled Waters: The Political Economy of the Atlantic Fishery and the Task Force on Atlantic Fisheries,"*Journal of Canadian Studies*, 19(1).

Barss-Donham, P., 1981, "The Nickerson's Empire," *Atlantic Insight* (October).

Bassler, Gerhard P., 1986, "'Develop or Perish': Joseph R. Smallwood and Newfoundland's Quest for German Industry, 1949-1953", *Acadiensis* 15(2).

Beckmann, B., 1981, "Imperialism and the National Bourgeoisie," *Review of African Political Economy* 22.

Beneria, Lourdes, 1979, "Reproduction, Production and the Sexual Division of Labor," *Cambridge Journal of Economics* 3.

Beneria, Lourdes and Gita Sen, 1982, "Class and Gender Inequalities and Women's Role in Economic Development—Practical Implications," *Feminist Studies* 8(1) (Spring).

Beneria, Lourdes and Martha Roldan, 1987, *The Cross Roads of Class and Gender. Housework, Subcontracting and Household Dynamics in Mexico City*, Chicago: University of Chicago Press.

Bickerton, James, 1982, "Underdevelopment and Social Movements in Atlantic Canada: A Critique," *Studies in Political Economy* 9.

Bickerton, J. and A.G. Gagnon, 1984, "Policy in Historical Perspective: The Federal Role in Regional Economic Development," *American Review of Canadian Studies* (1).

Blomstrom, Magnus and Bjorn Hettne, 1984, *Development Theory in Transition*, London: ZED Books.

Bollman, Ray, 1983, "Special Tabulation" prepared by Bollman from Agricultural Census data.

Booth, General, 1890, *In Darkest England and the Way Out*, New York: Funk and Wagnalls.

Boserup, Ester, 1970, *Women's Role in Economic Development*, London: George Allen and Unwin.

Boyd, Mary, 1983, "The Irish Moss 'Strikes' in Prince Edward Island," Wolfville: Regional Centre for the Study of Contemporary Social Issues, Acadia University.

Britten, Nicky and Anthony Heath, 1983, "Women, Men and Social Class," in Eva Garmarnikow et al. (eds.), *Gender, Class and Work*, Heinemann Educational Books Limited.

Brown, Rosemary et al., 1976, *Small Business: Strategy for Survival*, London: Wilton House.

Brox, Ottar, 1972, *Newfoundland Fishermen in the Age of Industry*, St. John's: ISER.

Brunton, R., J. Overton and J. Sacouman, 1981, "Uneven Underdevelopment and Song: Culture and Development in Atlantic Canada," in L. Salter (ed.), *Communication Studies in Canada*, Toronto: Butterworth.

Brym, R.J. and R.J. Sacouman, 1979, *Underdevelopment and Social Movements in Atlantic Canada*, Toronto: New Hogtown Press.

Bulloch, John, 1984, "Guest Editorial: Small Business Policies for the 1980s—Guidelines for Governments," *Journal of Small Business* 2(2).

Burbach, R. and O. Nunez, 1988, *Fire in the Americas*, New York: Monthly Review Press.

Burrill, Gary, 1985, "The Great Debate," *New Maritimes* 3(8).

Burrill, Gary, 1986, "Purchase and Patch," *New Maritimes* 4(7).

Buttel, F.H., 1982, "The Political Economy of Agriculture in Advanced Industrial Societies," *Current Perspectives in Social Theory* 3.

Buttel, F.H. and H. Newby (eds.), 1980, *The Rural Sociology of the Advanced Societies*, Montclair: Allanhel Osmun.

Byres, T.J., 1979, "Of Neo-Populist Pipedreams: Daedalus in the Third World and the Myth of Urban Bias," *Journal of Peasant Studies* 6(2).

Cameron, Silver Donald, 1977, *The Education of Everett Richardson*, Toronto: McClelland & Stewart.

Canada, 1925, *Investigation into Alleged Combine Limiting Competition in the Marketing of New Brunswick Potatoes*, Ottawa.

Canada, 1926, *Report of the Royal Commission on Maritime Claims*, Ottawa.

Canada, 1957, *Report of the Royal Commission on Canada's Economic Prospects*, Ottawa.

Canada, 1985, *Report of the Royal Commission on the Economic Union and Development Prospects for Canada*, 3 vols., Ottawa.

Canada, Agriculture Canada, 1981, *Challenge for Growth, An Agri-Food Strategy for Canada*, by Eugene Whelan, Ottawa.

Canada, Department of the Environment, 1976, *Policy for Canada's Commercial Fisheries*, Ottawa.

Canada, Department of Fisheries and Oceans, 1981, *Returns to Labour and Capital in 1979 for Selected Fisheries in Newfoundland*, St. John's.

Canada, Department of Fisheries and Oceans, 1984a, *An Economic Assessment of the Newfoundland Nearshore Fixed Gear Groundfish Fishery—1979*, by G.P. Brocklehurst, St. John's.

Canada, Department of Fisheries and Oceans, 1984b, 1984c, *Costs and Earnings of Selected Inshore and Nearshore Enterprises in the Newfoundland Region, 1982 and 1983*, St. John's.

Canada, Employment and Immigration, 1981a, *Labour Market Development in the 1980s*, Ottawa: Supply and Services Canada.

Canada, Employment and Immigration, 1981b, *Unemployment Insurance in the 1980s*, Ottawa: Supply and Services Canada.

Canada, Statistics Canada (formerly Dominion Bureau of Statistics), 1921-, *Censuses of Agriculture*, Ottawa.

Canada, Statistics Canada, 1983, *Provincial Economic Accounts*, Cat. 13-213, Ottawa.

Canada, Statistics Canada, 1985, *Provincial Economic Accounts*, Cat. 13-213. Ottawa.

Canada, Task Force on Canadian Agriculture, 1969, *Canadian Agriculture in the Seventies*, Ottawa.

Canada, Task Force on the Atlantic Fisheries, 1982, *Navigating Troubled Waters: A New Policy for the Atlantic Fisheries*, Ottawa: Canadian Government Publishing Centre.

Canada and Newfoundland, 1983a, "Memoranda of Understanding between Mr. Morgan and Mr. Debane" (May).

Canada and Newfoundland, 1983b, "Agreement between the Government of Canada and Government of Newfoundland Concerning the Restructuring of the Newfoundland Fishery," (September).

Canadian Dimension, 1985, Special Section on Atlantic Canada, 19(1).

Canning, Stratford, 1974, "The Illusion of Progress: Rural Development Policy Since 1949," *Canadian Forum* 53(6).

Cannon, James, 1984, "Explaining Regional Development in Atlantic Canada: A Review Essay," *Journal of Canadian Studies*, 19(3).

Carachedi, Guglielmo, 1975, "On the Economic Identification of the New Middle Class," *Economy and Society* 4(1).

Cardoso, F.H. and E. Faletto, 1979, *Development and Underdevelopment in Latin America*, University of California Press.

Carter, R., 1983, *Something's Fishy: Public Policy and Private Corporations in the Newfoundland Fishery*, St. John's, Nfld.: Oxfam Committee.

Chevalier, J. M., 1982, "There is nothing simple about simple commodity production," *Studies in Political Economy* 7.

Chossudovsky, M., 1983, "China and the International Division of Labour," *Studies in Political Economy* 10.

Chilcote, Ronald, 1983, "Introduction: Dependency or Mode of Production? Theoretical Issues," in Chilcote, R. and D. Johnson (eds.), 1983, *Theories of Development: Mode of Production or Dependency?*, California: Sage Publications.

Chilcote, R. and D. Johnson (eds.), 1983, *Theories of Development: Mode of Production or Dependency?*, California: Sage Publications.

Chinchilla, Norma Stoltz, 1983, "Interpreting Social Change in Guatemala: Modernization, Dependency, and Articulation of Modes of Production," in Chilcote, R. and D. Johnson (eds.), 1983, *Theories of Development: Mode of Production or Dependency?*, California: Sage Publications.

Clancy, P., 1985, "Caribou, Fur and the Resource Frontier: A Political Economy of the NorthWest Territories to 1967," Unpublished Ph.D. thesis, Queen's University.

Clement, Wallace, 1983, *Class, Power and Property: Essays on Canadian Society*, Toronto: Methuen.

Clement, Wallace, 1986a, *The Struggle to Organize: Resistance in Canada's Fishery*, Toronto: McClelland & Stewart.

Clement, Wallace, 1986b, "The Limits of Cooperation: Strategies for Fisheries Development," draft copy (March) of paper presented to the International Working Seminar on Social Research and Policy Formation in the Fisheries: Norwegian and Atlantic Canadian Experiences, June 16-20, Institute of Fisheries, University of Tromso, Norway.

Close, D., 1982, "Unconventional Militance: Union Organized Fish Sales in Newfoundland," *Journal of Canadian Studies*, 17(2).

Clow, Michael, 1984a, "Politics and Uneven Capitalist Development: The Maritime Challenge to the Study of Canadian Political Economy," *Studies in Political Economy* 14.

Clow, Michael, 1984b, "The Struggle with Orthodoxy: Maritime Political Economy in the 1970s and 1980s," paper presented at the annual meeting of the Atlantic Association of Sociologists and Anthropologists, University of New Brunswick.

Collison, R., 1982, "Have the Interventionists Lost Their Nerve?" *Canadian Business* 55(1).

Connelly, Patricia, 1978, *Last Hired, First Fired: Women and the Canadian Work Force*, Toronto: The Women's Press.

Connelly, Patricia, 1984, "Women's Work, the Family Household and the Canadian Economy: A Conceptual and Methodological Approach," paper presented at the Second International Interdisciplinary Congress on Women, Gronigin, The Netherlands.

Connelly, M.P. and M. MacDonald, 1983, "Women's Work: Domestic and Wage Labour in a Nova Scotian Community," *Studies in Political Economy* 10.

Connelly, M.P. and M. MacDonald, 1986, "Workers, Households, Community: A Case Study of 'Restructuring'in the Nova Scotia Fishery," paper presented to the International Working Seminar on Social Research in the Fisheries: Norwegian and Atlantic Canadian Experiences, University of Tromso, Norway.

Connelly, M.P. and M. MacDonald, forthcoming, "The Impact of State Policy on Women's Work in the Fishery," in *Women and the State, H. Armstrong* (ed.): McGill-Queens Press.

Copes, Parzival, 1972, *The Resettlement of Fishing Communities in Newfoundland,* Ottawa: Canadian Council on Rural Development.

Copes, Parzival, 1975, "Ethical Issues in Policy Research: A Comment," *Canadian Public Policy* 1(4).

Copes, Parzival, 1978, "Canada's Atlantic Coast Fisheries: Policy Development and the Impact of Extended Jurisdiction," *Canadian Public Policy* 4.

Coté, Serge, 1977, "Origins of the Owners of the First Pulp and Paper Mills in New Brunswick," paper presented at the annual meeting of the Atlantic Association of Sociologists and Anthropologists, Memorial University of Newfoundland.

Coulson, Margaret, Blanka Magas and Hilary Wainwright, 1975, "The Housewife and Her Labour Under Capitalism—A Critique," *New Left Review* 89.

Courchene, T., 1978, "Avenues of Adjustment: the Transfer System and Regional Disparities," in Michael Walker (ed.), *Canadian Confederation at the Crossroads,* Vancouver: Fraser Institute.

Courchene, T., 1981, "A Market Perspective on Regional Policy," *Canadian Public Policy* 7(4).

Courchene, T., 1984, "Entitlements versus Efficiency," *Policy Options* 5(4).

Cousineau, Jean-Michel, 1979, "Unemployment Insurance and Labour Market Adjustments," in *Income Distribution and Economic Security in Canada*, Vol. 1, Background Paper prepared for the Royal Commission on the Economic Union and Development Prospects for Canada, Toronto: University of Toronto Press.

Croll, Elizabeth J., 1981, "Women in Rural Production and Reproduction in the Soviet Union, China, Cuba and Tanzania: Socialist Development Experiences," *Signs* 7(2).

Davis, Anthony, 1975, "Organization of Production and Market Relations in a Nova Scotian Inshore Fishing Community," *Papers in Anthropology* 15, Winnipeg: University of Manitoba.

Davis, Anthony, 1984, "Property Rights and Access Management in the Small Boat Fishery: A Case Study of Southwest Nova Scotia," in C. Lamson and A. Hanson (eds.), *Atlantic Fisheries and Coastal Communities*, Halifax: Ocean Studies Program, Dalhousie University.

Davis, John Emmeus, 1980, "Capitalist Agricultural Development and the Exploitation of the Propertied Labourer," in F.H. Buttel and H. Newby (eds.), *The Rural Sociology of the Advanced Societies*, Montclair: Allanhel Osmun.

Deere, Carmen Diana, 1976, "Rural Women's Subsistence Production in the Capitalist Periphery," *Review of Radical Political Economics*, 8(1).

Deere, Carmen Diana and Magdalena Leon de Leal, 1981, "Peasant Production, Proletarianization, and the Sexual Division of Labour in the Andes," *Signs* 7(2).

de Leal, Magdalena Leon and Carmen Diana Deere, 1979, "Rural Women and the Development of Capitalism in Colombian Agriculture," *Signs*, 5(1).

Delphy, Christine, 1984, *Close to Home*, London: Hutchinson and Co.

Delphy, Christine, 1984, *The Main Enemy*, London: The Women's Research and Resources Centre.

Denis, Wilfred B., 1979, "Exploitation in Canadian Prairie Agriculture, 1900-1970," a paper presented to the annual meeting of the Canadian Sociology and Anthropology Association, Saskatoon, 1979.

deRoche, Constance P., 1985, "The Village, The Vertex: Adaptation to Regionalism and Development in a Complex Society," *Occasional Papers in Anthropology* 12, Halifax: Department of Anthropology, Saint Mary's University.

de Vries, P.J. and G. MacNab-de Vries, 1986, "Coping on the Periphery: A Cape Breton Example," paper presented at the annual meeting of the Atlantic Association of Sociologists and Anthropologists, Acadia University.

Economic Council of Canada, 1977, *Living Together: A Study of Regional Disparities*, Ottawa: Supply and Services Canada.

Economic Council of Canada, 1979, *A Promise of Abundance*, by George Munroe, Ottawa.

Economic Council of Canada, 1980, *Newfoundland: From Dependency to Self-Reliance*, Ottawa: Supply and Services Canada.

Economic Council of Canada, 1981a, "Fiscal Arrangements: Federal-Provincial Discussion Raises Some Key Issues," *Au Courant* 11(2).

Economic Council of Canada, 1981b, "The Economic Implications of Migration to Newfoundland," by R. Boadway and A.G. Green, Economic Discussion Paper No. 189, Ottawa.

Edwards, Richard, 1979, *'Contested Terrain': The Transformation of the Workplace in the Twentieth Century*, New York: Basic Books.

Ehrenreich, Barbara and John Ehrenreich, 1978, "The Professional-Managerial Class," in Pat Walker (ed.), *Between Labour and Capital*, Montreal: Black Rose Books.

Ehrensaft, Philip and Ray Bollman, 1983, "Structure and Concentration in Agriculture," a paper presented to the Vancouver meetings of the Canadian Sociology and Anthropology Association.

Elliott, Brian and David McCrone, 1982, "The Social World of Petty Property," in P.G. Hollowell (ed.), *Property and Social Relations*, London: Heinemann.

Fabian Colonial Bureau, 1945, *Co-operation in the Colonies*, London: George Allen and Unwin.

Fairley, Bryant D., 1983, "The Development of Capitalism in the Fishing Industry in Newfoundland: A Critique of Narodism in Atlantic Canada," Unpublished M.A. thesis, Queen's University.

Fairley, Bryant D., 1984, "The Metaphysics of Dualism and the Development of Capitalism in the Newfoundland Fishery," *Occasional Paper* 84-101, Programme of Studies in National and International Development, Queen's University.

Fairley, Bryant D., 1985a, "The Struggle for Capitalism in the Fishing Industry in Newfoundland," *Studies In Political Economy* 17.

Fairley, Bryant D., 1985b, "Looking For Solutions: Towards a Political Economy of Fishing in Newfoundland in the 1980s," Programme of Studies in National and International Development, Queen's University, *Occasional Paper* No. 85-101.

Figueroa, Miguel, 1986, "Right diagnosis, wrong prescription," *Canadian Tribune*, November 10.

Freeman, Milton M.R. (ed.), 1969, *Intermediate Adaptation in Newfoundland and the Arctic: a Strategy of Social and Economic Development*, St. John's: ISER.

Fox, Bonnie (ed.), 1980, *Hidden in the Household: Women's Domestic Labour Under Capitalism*, Toronto: The Women's Press.

Frank, Andre Gunder, 1967, *Capitalism and Underdevelopment in Latin America*, New York: Monthly Review Press.

Frank, David, 1976, "Class Conflict in the Coal Industry: Cape Breton 1922," in Gregory Kealey and Peter Warrian (eds.), *Essays in Canadian Working Class History*, Toronto: McClelland and Stewart.

Franklin, S.H., 1969, *The European Peasantry: the Final Phase*,London: Methuen.

Friedmann, Harriet, 1980, "Household Production and the National Economy," *Journal of Peasant Studies* 7(1).

Friedmann, Harriet, 1982, "The Family Farm in Advanced Capitalism: Outline of a Theory of Simple Commodity Production in Agriculture," Working Paper Series No. 33, Structural Analysis Programme, Department of Sociology, University of Toronto.

Frobel, Folker, Jurgen Heinrichs, and Otto Kreye, 1977, *The International Division of Labour*, Cambridge: Cambridge University Press

Gardiner, J., 1975, "Women's Domestic Labour," *New Left Review*89.

Gertler, Michael and Thomas Murphy, 1987, "The Social Economy of Canadian Agriculture: Family Farming and Alternative Futures," in Eugene Wilkening and Boguslaw Galeski, *Comparative Family Farming in Europe and America*, Boulder, Colorado: Westview.

Gerzon, G.M., 1977, "Counterculture Capitalism," *The New York Times*, June 5.

Gillis, Valda, 1985, "Structure of Maritime Agriculture with Specific Reference to Farmwomen and the Role of Off-farm Work," Unpublished M.A. Thesis, University of Guelph.

Glenday, D., 1983, "The 'Dependencia' School in Canada: An Examination and Evaluation," *Canadian Review of Sociology and Anthropology* 20(3).

Goldthorpe, John, 1983, "Women and Class Analysis: In Defence of the Conventional View," *Sociology* 17(4) (November).

Gore, Charles, 1984, *Regions In Question: Space, Development Theory and Regional Policy*, London: Methuen.

Gorz, A., 1982, *Farewell To the Working Class*, London: Pluto Press.

Grady, D.J. and R.J. Sacouman, 1984, "'Piracy', the Capitalist State and Proactive Struggle: The Woods Harbour Experience," paper presented at the annual meeting of the Canadian Sociology and Anthropology Association, University of Guelph. (An earlier version was presented at the Fifth Conference on Workers and Their Communities, Ontario Institute for Studies in Education.)

Gunnlaugsdottir, Sigurlaug Sara, 1984, "Restraint in Workers Situation as Determined by Organization of the Labor Process in the Fishing Industry in Iceland," in Jean-Louis Chaumel (ed.), *Labor Development in the Fishing Industry*, Canadian Special Publication of Fisheries and Aquatic Sciences 72, Ottawa: Fisheries and Oceans Canada.

Hall, Stuart, 1983, "The Problem of Ideology—Marxism without Guarantees," in Betty Matthews (ed.), *Marx 100 Years On*, London: Lawrence & Wishart.

Hanson, Arthur and Cynthia Lamson, 1984, "Fisheries Decision Making in Atlantic Canada," in C. Lamson and A. Hanson (eds.), *Atlantic Fisheries and Coastal Communities*, Halifax: Ocean Studies Program, Dalhousie University.

Hanson, Arthur, Leonard Kasden and Cynthia Lamson, 1984, "Atlantic Coastal Communities: Problems and Prospects," in C. Lamson and A. Hanson (eds.), *Atlantic Fisheries and Coastal Communities*, Halifax: Ocean Studies Program, Dalhousie University.

Harding, Neil, 1977, *Lenin's Political Thought*, Atlantic Highlands, N.J.: Humanities Press

Harris, José, 1977, *William Beveridge: A Biography*, Oxford: Clarendon Press.

Harris, Nigel, 1983, *Of Bread and Guns: The World Economy in Crisis*, Harmondsworth: Penguin.

Harrison, John, 1978, *Marxist Economics for Socialists: A Critique of Reformism*, London: Pluto Press.

Harrison, Paul, 1980, *The Third World Tomorrow: A Report from the Battlefront in the War Against Poverty*, Harmondsworth: Penguin.

Hawken, Paul G., 1980, "What's Economical?" *Coevolution Quarterly* 26.

Hawken, Paul G., 1981, "Disintermediation," *Coevolution Quarterly* 29.

Hedley, M.J., 1981, "Relations of Production of the Family Farm: Canadian Prairies," *Journal of Peasant Studies* 9(1)

Hill, Judah, 1975, *Class Analysis: United States in the 1970s,*San Francisco: Synthesis Publications.

Hiller, James, 1982, "The Origins of the Pulp and Paper Industry in Newfoundland," *Acadiensis* 11(2).

Hoggart, K.. 1979, "Resettlement in Newfoundland," *Geography* 64(3).

Holmes, J. and C. Leys (eds.), 1987, *Frontyard, Backyard: The Americas in the Global Crisis*, Toronto: Between The Lines.

Howard, Ross, 1980, "Blind faith in chemicals: the spruce budworm aerial spraying program in New Brunswick," in Ross Howard, *Poisons in Public: Case Studies in Environmental Pollution in Canada*, Toronto: Lorimer

Howland, R.D., 1957, "Some Regional Aspects of Canada's Economic Development," a study prepared for the Royal Commission on Canada's Economic Prospects.

Humphries, Jane, 1977, "The Working Class Family, Women's Liberation and Class Struggle: The Case of Nineteenth Century British History," *The Review of Radical Political Economics* 9(3).

Humphries, Jane and Jill Rubery, 1984, "The Reconstitution of the Supply Side of the Labour Market: The Relative Autonomy of Social Reproduction," *Cambridge Journal of Economics* 8.

Illich, Ivan, 1973, *Tools For Conviviality*, London: Calder and Boyars.

Inglis, G., 1985, *More Than Just a Union*, St. John's: Jesperson.

Jéaquier, Nicholas, 1983, "Small is Beautiful... and becoming big," *Appropriate Technology* 10(3).

Johnson, Dale, 1983, "Class Analysis and Dependency," in R. Chilcote and D. Johnson, *Theories of Development: Mode of Production or Dependency?* California: Sage Publications.

Johnstone, R., 1981, "In Praise of Peckford," *This Magazine* 15(1).

Jones, W. D. and P. Tung, 1977, "A Regional Comparison of Structural Change and Resource Use in the Canadian Farm Industry: 1961 to 1971," *Canadian Farm Economics* 12(5).

Kaplinsky, R., 1979, "Capitalist Accumulation in the Periphery," *Review of African Political Economy*.

Kaluzynska, Eva, 1980, "Wiping the Floor With Theory—A Survey of Writings on Housework," *Feminist Review* 6.

Kautsky, Karl, 1971, *The Class Struggle*, New York: Norton.

Kay, G.B., 1975, *Development and Underdevelopment: A Marxist Analysis*, London: Macmillan.

Kearney, John F., 1984, *Working Together: A Study of Fishermen's Response To Government Management of the District 4a Lobster Fishery*, Pointe-de-l'Eglise: Presses de l'Université Sainte-Anne.

Kelly, Maria Patricia Fernandez, 1981, "Development and the Sexual Division of Labour: An Introduction," *Signs* 7(2).

Kerans, Pat, 1986, "Bad News for Atlantic Canada," *Perception* 9(3).

Kimber, Stephen, 1982, "Spud Wars," *Canadian Business*, (September).

Kindersley, R., 1962, *The First Russian Revisionists*, London: Clarendon.

Kirk Laux, Jeanne and Maureen Appel Molot, 1979, "*The politics of nationalization*," *Canadian* Journal of Political Science 13(2).

Kirk Laux, Jeanne and Maureen Appel Molot, 1981, "The Potash Corporation of Saskatchewan," in Alan Tupper and Bruce Doern (eds.), *Public Corporations and Public Policy in Canada*, Montreal: Institute for Research on Public Policy.

Kitching, Gavin, 1982, *Development and Underdevelopment in Historical Perspective*, London: Methuen.

Laclau, E., 1971, "Feudalism and Capitalism in Latin America," *New Left Review* 67.

Laclau, E., 1977, *Politics and Ideology in Marxist Theory*, London: New Left Books.

Lamson, C. and A. Hanson (eds.), 1984, *Atlantic Fisheries and Coastal Communities*, Halifax: Ocean Studies Program, Dalhousie University.

Laxer, Robert M., 1973, *Canada Ltd.*, Toronto: McLelland & Stewart.

Leacock, Eleanor and Helen Safa (eds.), 1986, *Women's Work: Development and the Division of Labour*, New York: Bergin and Garvey.

Lebowitz, Michael A., 1982, "The General and the Specific in Marx's Theory of Crisis," *Studies In Political Economy* 7.

Lenin, V.I., 1960a, "What The Friends Of The People Are And How They Fight The Social Democrats," in *Collected Works*, Vol. I, London: Lawrence and Wishart.

Lenin, V.I., 1960b, "On The So-called Market Question," in *Collected Works*, Vol. I, London: Lawrence and Wishart.

Lenin, V.I., 1960c, "The Development of Capitalism in Russia," in *Collected Works*, Vol. III, London: Lawrence and Wishart.

Levitt, K., 1970, *Silent Surrender: The Multinational Corporation in Canada*, Toronto: Macmillan.

Lewis, W.A., 1966, *Development Planning*, New York: Harper and Row.

Leys, Colin, 1977, "Underdevelopment and Dependency: Critical Notes," *Journal of Contemporary Asia* 7(1).

Leys, Colin, 1978, "Capital Accumulation, Class Formation and Dependency: The Significance of the Kenyan Case," *Socialist Register*.

Leys, Colin, 1982, "Kenya: What does 'Dependency' Explain?" in M. Fransman (ed.), *Industry and Accumulation in Africa*, London: Heineman.

Levy, B. and R.J. Sacouman, 1986, "Socialism, Masculine Domination, and Women's Struggle for Human Development in Cuba: A Review Essay," Unpublished manuscript.

Lipietz, A., 1987, "The Globalisation of the General Crisis of Fordism, 1967-1984," in J. Holmes and C. Leys (eds.), *Frontyard, Backyard: The Americas in the Global Crisis*, Toronto: Between The Lines.

Lithwick, N.H., 1982, "Regional Policy: A Matter of Perspectives," *Canadian Journal of Regional Science* 5(2).

Lummis, Trevor, 1984, *Occupation and Society: The East Anglian Fisherman 1880-1914*, Cambridge: Cambridge University Press.

MacDonald, D., 1980, *Power Begins at the Cod-end*, St. John's:ISER.

MacDonald, Martha, 1979, "Women in the Workforce: Meeting the Changing Needs of Capitalism," Halifax: Institute of Public Affairs.

MacDonald, R.D.S., 1979, "Inshore Fishing Interests on the Atlantic Coast," *Marine Policy* (July).

MacDonald, R.D.S., 1984, "Canadian Fisheries Policy and the Development of Atlantic Coast Groundfisheries Management," in Lamson, C. and A. Hanson (eds.), *Atlantic Fisheries and Coastal Communities*, Halifax: Ocean Studies Program, Dalhousie University.

MacKay, R.A., 1946, *Newfoundland: Economic, Diplomatic, and Strategic Studies*, Toronto: Oxford University Press.

Mahon, R., 1977, "Canadian public policy: the unequal structure of representation," in L. Panitch (ed.), *The Canadian State*, Toronto: University of Toronto Press.

Mallory, J.R., 1986, "The Macdonald Commission," *Canadian Journal of Political Science* 19(3).

Mandel, Ernest, 1968, *Marxist Economic Theory*, New York: Monthly Review Press.

Mandel, Ernest, 1973, *Capitalism and Regional Disparities*, Toronto: New Hogtown Press.

Mansell, Robert and Lawrence Copithorne, 1984, "Canadian Regional Economic Disparities: A Survey," in K. Norrie (ed.), *Disparities and Interregional Adjustment*, Toronto: University of Toronto Press.

Maritime Fishermen's Union, 1985, *Background Study and Proposals for a Group Insurance Plan and/or Pension Plan for Inshore Fishermen: A Report Submitted to the Department of Fisheries and Oceans*.

Maritime Fishermen's Union, 1986, *Fatalities and Injuries in the Inshore Fishing Industry: A Report Submitted to the Department of Fisheries and Oceans.*

Martin, Cabot, 1975, "Newfoundland's Case on Offshore Minerals: A Brief Outline," *Ottawa Law Review* 7(1).

Marx, Karl, 1967, *Capital*, 3 Vols., New York: International Publishers.

Marx, Karl, 1976, *Capital*, Vol. I, Harmondsworth: Penguin Books.

Marx, Karl, 1978a, *Capital*, Vol. II, Harmondsworth: Penguin Books.

Marx, Karl, 1978b, *Capital*, Vol. III, Harmondsworth: Penguin Books.

Marx, K. and F. Engels, 1976, *The German Ideology*, Moscow: Progress Publishers.

Mattera, Philip, 1980, "Small is not Beautiful: Decentralized Production and the Underground Economy in Italy," *Radical America* 14(5).

Mattera, Philip, 1985, *Off the Books: The Rise of the Underground Economy*, London: Pluto Press.

Matthews, Ralph, 1975, "Ethical Issues in Policy Research: The Investigation of Community Resettlement in Newfoundland," *Canadian Public Policy* 1(2).

Matthews, Ralph, 1976, *'There's No Better Place Than Here': Social Change in Three Newfoundland Outports*, Toronto: Peter Martin.

Matthews, Ralph, 1977, "Canadian Regional Development Strategy: A Dependency Theory Perspective," *Plan Canada* 17(2).

Matthews, Ralph, 1979, "The Smallwood Legacy: The Development of Underdevelopment in Newfoundland, 1949-1972," *Journal of Canadian Studies* 13(4).

Matthews, Ralph, 1980a, "Class Interests and the Role of the State in the Development of Canada's East Coast Fishery," *Canadian Issues* 3(1) (Spring).

Matthews, Ralph, 1980b, "Two Alternative Explanations of the Problem of Regional Dependency in Canada," *Canadian Public Policy* VII(2).

Matthews, Ralph, 1983, *The Creation of Regional Dependency*, Toronto: University of Toronto Press.

Maxwell, Judith, 1978, *A Time For Realism*, Montreal: C.D. Howe Research Institute.

McAllister, Ian, 1980, "How to Re-make DREE," *Policy Options* 1(1).

McCay, Bonnie J., 1979, "'Fish is Scarce': Fisheries Modernization on Fogo Island, Newfoundland," in R. Andersen (ed.), *North Atlantic Maritime Cultures: Anthropological Essays on Changing Adaptations*, The Hague: Mouton.

McCracken, F.D. and R.D.S. MacDonald, 1976, "Science for Canada's Atlantic Inshore Fishery," *Journal of the Fisheries Research Board of Canada* 33(9).

McCurdy, E., 1985, Personal Interview with Earle McCurdy, Secretary-Treasurer, United Food and Commercial Workers International Union, Local 1252—Fishermen's Union, by Bryant Fairley (20 June).

McFarland, Joan, 1980, "Changing Modes of Social Control in a Fish Packing Town," *Studies in Political Economy* 4.

McKay, Ian, 1982, "Review of *Underdevelopment and Social Movements in Atlantic Canada,*" *Labour/Le Travail* 10.

McNiven, James D., 1986, "Regional Development Policy in the Next Decade," *Canadian Journal of Regional Science* 9(1).

Mitrany, D., 1951, *Marx Against the Peasant*, London: Weidenfeld and Nicolson.

Montgomery, LeeAnn, 1986, *Overview of the Canadian Jobs Strategy, Background Report for Newfoundland and Labrador, Royal Commission on Employment and Unemployment*, St. John's: Queen's Printer.

Morton, Suzanne, 1986, "Labourism and Independent Labor Politics in Halifax, 1919-1926," Unpublished M.A. Thesis, Dalhousie University.

Muir, Bryce and Margaret Muir, 1981, "'Where've You Been, Stranger?': Disintermediation in the Maritimes," *Coevolution Quarterly* 30.

Munroe, C. and J. Stewart, 1981, "Fishermen's Organizations in Nova Scotia: The Potential for Unification," Halifax: Institute for Public Affairs, Dalhousie University.

Murphy, Thomas R., 1983, "The Structural Transformation of New Brunswick Agriculture From 1951 to 1981," Unpublished M.A. Thesis, University of New Brunswick.

Nash, June and Maria Patricia Fernandez-Kelly (eds.), 1983, *Women, Men, and the International Division of Labor*, Albany: State University of New York Press.

Nash, June and Helen Icken Safa (eds.) 1980, *Sex and Class in Latin America: Women's Perspectives of Politics, Economics and the Family in the Third World*, South Hadley, Massachusetts: J.F. Bergin Publishers.

National Council of Welfare, 1985, *1985 Poverty Lines*, Ottawa: Supply and Services Canada.

Neis, Barbara, 1981, "Newfoundland Merchants and Fishermen," *Studies in Political Economy* 5.

Neis, Barbara, 1984, "'Gus! It's Time to Surrender': Women and Resistance in Burin, Newfoundland," paper presented at the annual meeting of the Atlantic Association of Sociologists and Anthropologists, University of New Brunswick.

Newfoundland, 1938a,b, *Papers Relating to a Long Range Reconstruction Policy in Newfoundland* (Interim Report of J.H. Gorvin), 2 Vol., St. John's.

Newfoundland, 1940, *Explanation of the Sections of the Special Areas Development Bill*, 1940, St. John's.

Newfoundland and Labrador, 1967, *Report of the Royal Commission on the Economic State and Prospects of Newfoundland and Labrador*, St. John's: Queen's Printer.

Newfoundland and Labrador, 1981, *Report of the Royal Commission To Inquire into the Inshore Fishery of Newfoundland and Labrador*, St. John's: Queen's Printer.

Newfoundland and Labrador, 1983a, *Presentation to the Federal Cabinet Committee on Fisheries Restructuring* (23 March).

Newfoundland and Labrador, 1983b, *Restructuring the Fishery: A Detailed Presentation to the Government of Canada* (5 May).

Newfoundland and Labrador, 1983c, *Submission of the Government of Newfoundland and Labrador to the Royal Commission on the Economic Union and Development Prospects for Canada*, St. John's: Queen's Printer.

Newfoundland and Labrador, 1986a, *Building on our Strengths: Report of the Royal Commission on Employment and Unemployment*, St. John's: Queen's Printer.

Newfoundland and Labrador, 1986b, *Education for Self-reliance: A Report on Education and Training in Newfoundland, Education Report of the Royal Commission on Employment and Unemployment*, St. John's: Queen's Printer.

New Brunswick, 1983, *Private Woodlots: What Does the Future Hold?*, Fredericton.

New Brunswick, Department of Agriculture, 1962, *Report of the Royal Commission on the New Brunswick Potato Industry*, by H. Whalen, Fredericton.

New Brunswick, Department of Agriculture, 1966, *Annual Report of the New Brunswick Department of Agriculture*, Fredericton.

New Brunswick, Department of Agriculture, 1967- , *Agricultural Statistics*, Fredericton.

New Brunswick, Department of Agriculture, 1982, *New Brunswick Agricultural Development Strategy*, Fredericton.

New York Times, 1985, "The Squeeze on Agriculture Makes 'Crisis' Sound Too Mild," (November 10).

New York Times, 1985b, "The Hands of Anger, Frustration, Humiliation," (December 15).

Nicholson, P.J., 1984, "Restructuring the Fishing Industry in Atlantic Canada: Interplay of Analysis and Politics," paper presented in Washington, D.C. (6 August).

Nova Scotia, 1982, *Report of the Royal Commission on Forestry*, Halifax.

Nun, José, 1969, "Superpoblacion relativa, ejército industrial de reserva y masa marginal," *Revista Mexicana de Sociologia* 5(2).

Offe, C., 1984, *Contradictions of the Welfare State*, Boston: MIT Press.

O'Neil, B. and J. Overton, 1981, "Will the Real Brian Peckford Please Stand Up?", *This Magazine* 15(4).

Overton, James, 1977, "Unemployment, Social Unrest and Social Control: The Politics of Make-Work Schemes," Unpublished report, Centre for the Development of Community Initiatives, Memorial University, St. John's.

Overton, James, 1978, "Uneven Development in Canada: The Case of Newfoundland," *Review of Radical Political Economy* 10(3).

Overton, James, 1979, "Towards a Critical Analysis of Neo-nationalism in Newfoundland," in Brym, R.J. and R.J. Sacouman, 1979, *Underdevelopment and Social Movements in Atlantic Canada*, Toronto: New Hogtown Press.

Overton, James, 1980, "Promoting 'The Real Newfoundland': Culture as Tourist Commodity," *Studies in Political Economy* 4.

Overton, James, 1985a, "Progressive Conservatism? A Critical Look at Politics, Culture and Development in Newfoundland," in *Ethnicity in Atlantic Canada*, Social Science Monograph Series, Volume 5.

Overton, James, 1985b, "Living Patriotism: Songs Politics and Resources in Newfoundland," *Canadian Review of Studies in Nationalism* 12(2).

Overton, James, 1985c, "Peckford and Anti-Dependency in Newfoundland," *Canadian Dimension* 19(1).

Overton, James, 1986a, "Oil and Gas: The Rhetoric and Reality of Development in Newfoundland," in R. Clark (ed.), *Contrary Winds: Essays on Newfoundland Society in Crisis*, St. John's: Breakwater Books.

Overton, James, forthcoming, "The Politics of Culture and Ecology in *A Whale for the Killing*", *The Journal of Canadian Studies*.

Overton, James, forthcoming, "A Newfoundland Culture?", *Journal of Canadian Studies*.

Overton, James, forthcoming, "Riots, Raids, and Relief, Police, Prisons, and Parsimony: The Political Economy of Public Order in Newfoundland in the 1930s," in E. Leyton, W. O'Grady and J. Overton (eds.), *Violence and Popular Anxiety: A Canadian Case*.

Overton, James and Lee Seymour, 1977, "Towards Understanding Rural Social Change: A Critique of *There's No Better Place Than Here*", *Our Generation* 12(1).

Paine, R.P.B., Skolnik, M.L. and C. Wadel, 1969, "Intermediate Adaptation— Rural Development as an Alternative to Rural Immiseration," in M.M.R. Freeman (ed.), *Intermediate Adaptation in Newfoundland and the Arctic, St. John's:* ISER.

Palmer, Christopher, 1986, *Perspective on the Newfoundland Labour Market, Background Report for the Royal Commission on Employment and Unemployment, Newfoundland and Labrador*, St. John's: Queen's Printer.

People's Commission on Unemployment, 1978, *'Now That We've Burned Our Boats'*, St. John's: Newfoundland and Labrador Federation of Labour.

Peterson, Rein, 1977, *Small Business: Building A Balanced Economy*, Erin,Ontario: Press Porcepic.

Phillips, Anne, 1987, *Divided Loyalties: Dilemmas of Sex and Class*, London: Virago Press.

Piore, Michael J., 1984, *The Second Industrial Divide: Possibilities For Prosperity*, New York: Basic Books.

Poetschke, L.E. and T. Shovciw, 1974, "Activity Status Report—Regional Communities Development: Managing the Development Process, Newfoundland and Labrador," Canada, Department of Regional Economic Expansion, Contract Number 2106.

Polése, Mario, 1985, "Patterns of Regional Economic Development in Canada: Long-Term Trends and Issues," paper presented at the Conference Still Living Together, School of Public Administration, Dalhousie University (October).

Pollert, Anna, 1983, "Women, Gender Relations and Wage Labour," in Eva Gamarnikow et al. (eds.), *Gender, Class and Work*, London: Heinemann Educational Books Limited.

Pollock, K. and T. Miller, 1982, "Memorandum on Corporate Concentration in the Canadian Fishing Industry," New Democratic Party Caucus, House of Commons, Ottawa.

Porter, Marilyn, 1983a, "Women and Old Boats: The Sexual Division of Labour in a Newfoundland Outpost," in E. Garmarnikow (ed.), *The Public and the Private*, London.

Porter, Marilyn, 1983b, *Home, Work and Class Consciousness*, Manchester: Manchester University Press.

Porter, Marilyn, 1985a, "'She was Skipper of the Shore-Crew': Notes on the History of the Sexual Division of Labour in Newfoundland", *Labour/Le Travail* 15.

Porter, Marilyn, 1985b, "'A Tangly Bunch': The Political Culture of Outport Women in Newfoundland," *Newfoundland Studies* 1(1).

Porter, Marilyn, 1986, "Peripheral Women: Towards a Feminist Analysis of the Atlantic Region," paper presented at the annual meeting of the Atlantic Association of Sociologists and Anthropologists, Acadia University.

Poulantzas, Nicos, 1973, *Political Power and Social Class*, London.

Pratt, C.C., 1959, "A Greater Self-sufficiency among Newfoundlanders," *The Newfoundland Journal of Commerce* 26(2).

Przeworski, Adam, 1977, "Proletariat into a Class: The Process of Class Formation from Karl Kautsky's *The Class Struggle* to Recent Controversies," *Politics and Society* 7(4).

Quijano, Anibal, 1974, "The Marginal Pole of the Economy and the Marginalised Labour Force," *Economy and Society* 3.

Rainnie, Al, 1985, "Small Firms, Big Problems: The Political Economy of Small Businesses," *Capital and Class* 25.

Reilly, Nolan, 1980, "The General Strike in Amherst, Nova Scotia, 1919," *Acadiensis* IX.

Roche, P., 1985a, "Adrift on a Cruel Sea," *Report On Business Magazine* (April).

Roche, P., 1985b, "Newfoundland Offers a Variety of Aid Programs," *Globe and Mail*, May 10.

Ross, Alexander, 1977, "How to Join the March to the New Politics," *Quest* 8(1).

Rostow, W.W., 1960, *The Stages of Economic Growth: A Non-communist Manifesto*, Cambridge: Cambridge University Press.

Royce, D.M., 1985, *Creating Troubled Waters: Public Policy-making and the Task Force on Atlantic Fisheries*, Unpublished M.A. thesis, Queen's University.

Sacouman, R. James, 1980, "Semi-Proletarianization and Rural Underdevelopment in the Maritimes," *Canadian Review of Sociology and Anthropology* 17(3).

Sacouman, R. James, 1981, "The 'Peripheral' Maritimes and Canada-Wide Marxist Political Economy," *Studies in Political Economy* 6.

Sacouman, R. James, 1983a, "Regional Uneven Development, Regionalism and Struggle," in J.P. Grayson (ed.), *Introduction to Sociology: an Alternate Approach*, Toronto: Gage.

Sacouman, R. James, 1983b, "Nationalism and Regionalism in Capitalist Democratic Middle Powers: A Renewed Marxist Approach to the Canadian Case," paper presented to the Conference on the Structure of the Canadian Capitalist Class, University of Toronto.

Sacouman, R. James, 1985a, "Atlantic Canada," in D. Drache and W. Clement (eds.), *The New Practical Guide To Canadian Political Economy*, Toronto: Lorimer.

Sacouman, R. James, 1985b, "Broken-up Canada and Breaking-up Britain: Some Comparative Lessons in Uneven Development, Regionalism and Nationalism During the Current Crisis," in G. Rees et al. (eds.), *Political Action and Social Identity: Class, Locality and Ideology*, London: The Macmillan Press.

Sacouman, R. James, 1985c, "Uneven Capitalist Development in the 'Third World' and in Atlantic Canada," paper presented at the annual meeting of the Canadian Association for International Development Studies, Université de Montreal.

Safa, Helen, 1981, "Runaway Shops and Female Employment: The Search for Cheap Labor," *Signs* 7(2).

Saffioti, Heleieth, 1977, "Women, Mode of Production, and Social Formations," *Latin American Perspectives* IV (1 and 2).

Schumacher, E.F., 1974, *Small Is Beautiful: A Study of Economicsas if People Mattered*, London: Abacus.

Schumacher, E.F., 1982, "On Technology for a Democratic Society," in G. McRobie, *Small Is Possible*, London: Abacus.

Science Council of Canada, 1977, *Canada as a Conserver Society: Resource Uncertainties and the Need for New Technologies*, Ottawa.

Sen, Gita, 1980, "The Sexual Division of Labor and the Working Class Family: Towards a Conceptual Synthesis of Class Relations and the Subordination of Women," *Review of Radical Political Economics* 12(2).

Senate Standing Committee on Finance, 1982, *Government Policy and Regional Development*, Ottawa.

Senopi Consultants Ltd., 1980, "A Report on the Situation of New Brunswick Potato Farmers," prepared for the National Farmers Union.

Shanin, Teodor, 1972, *The Awkward Class*, London: Oxford University Press.

Shanin, Teodor, 1983, *Late Marx and the Russian Road: Marx and the 'Peripheries' of Capitalism*, New York: Monthly Review Press.

Simoni, Arnold, 1982, "Three Steps to a No-Growth Economy," *The Nation* 234(22).

Sinclair, Peter R., 1984, "From Peasants to Corporations: The Development of Capitalist Agriculture in Canada's Maritime *Provinces*," in *J.A. Fry (ed.)*, *Contradictions* in Canadian Society, Toronto: John Wiley and Sons.

Sinclair, Peter R., 1984b, "Fishermen of Northwest Newfoundland," *Journal of Canadian Studies* 19(1).

Sinclair, Peter R., 1985a, "The State Goes Fishing," [*Research and Policy Papers*. No. 1, St. John's: ISER.

Sinclair, Peter R., 1985b, *From Traps to Draggers: Domestic Commodity Production in Northwest Newfoundland, 1850-1982*, St. John's: ISER.

Sinclair, Peter R., 1985c, "Reproducing Petty Capital: State Policy and the Dragger Fleet in Northwest Newfoundland," paper presented to the Annual Meeting of the Canadian Association of Sociology and Anthropology, Montreal.

Shortall, D., 1985, personal interview with David Shortall, Senior Trade Officer (Fisheries), Department of Regional Industrial Expansion of Canada, by Bryant Fairley (19 June).

Skolnik, M.L. (ed.), 1968, *Viewpoints on Communities in Crisis, St. John's:* ISER.

Skolnik, M.L. and Cato Wadel, 1969, "Intermediate Adaptation in Newfoundland," in M.M.R. Freeman (ed.), *Intermediate Adaptation in Newfoundland and the Arctic*, St. John's: ISER.

Smith, Dorothy, 1987, "Feminist Reflections on Political Economy," draft copy of a paper presented to the Political Economy Sessions, Canadian Political Science Association, Learned Societies Conference, McMaster University, Hamilton.

Squires, C., 1985, "Awareness of Women in the Fishery—Statistics for Cape Breton Island," Beaton Institute, University College of Cape Breton.

Stanworth, Michelle, 1984, "Women and Class Analysis—A Reply to John Goldthorpe," *Sociology* 18(2) (May).

Stepniak (S. Kravchinskii), 1888, *The Russian Peasantry*, 2 Vols., New York: Swan Sonnenschein, Lowrey & Co.

Stewart-Patterson, David, 1985, "Opportunities abound for aggressive, flexible firms," *Globe and Mail*, May 10.

Storey, Keith and Roger Bayter, 1978, "Adjustment and Regional Development Policies in Newfoundland, 1965-1978," paper presented at the Annual Meeting of the Association of American Geographers, New Orleans.

Sunkel, Osvaldo, 1973, "Transnational Capitalism and National Disintegration in Latin America," *Social and Economic Studies* 22.

Teeple, G.(ed.), 1972, *Capitalism and the National Question in Canada*, Toronto: University of Toronto Press.

Thornton, Patricia A., 1986, *Jack of All Trades*, Technical Consultation Report prepared for Newfoundland and Labrador, Royal Commission on Employment and Unemployment, St. John's.

United States, Department of Agriculture, 1980, *Poultry and Eggs:Another Revolution in U.S. Farming?*, by G.B. Rogers, U.S.D.A. Economic Report No. 441.

United States, Department of Agriculture, 1983, *The U.S. Poultry Industry*, by F.A. Lasley.

United States, Department of Commerce, 1968, *Food Fish Market Review and Outlook, 1968-1981*, Washington.

United States, Department of Commerce, 1979, *Fisheries of the United States, 1978-1984*, Washington.

Utechin, S.U., 1963, *Russian Political Thought*, London: Dent.

Veltmeyer, Henry, 1979, "The Capitalist Underdevelopment of Atlantic Canada," in R.J. Brym and and R.J. Sacouman, 1979, *Underdevelopment and Social Movements in Atlantic Canada*, Toronto: New Hogtown Press.

Veltmeyer, Henry, 1980, "A Central Issue in Dependency Theory," *Canadian Review of Sociology and Anthropology* 17(3).

Veltmeyer, Henry, 1983, "Surplus Labor and Class Formation on the Latin American Periphery," in R. Chilcote and D. Johnson (eds.), 1983, *Theories of Development: Mode of Production or Dependency?*, California: Sage Publications.

Veltmeyer, Henry, 1986, *Canadian Class Structure*, Toronto: Garamond Press.

Vernon, Gary C., 1980, "The Canadian Fisheries: Present and Future," *Canadian Issues* 3(1) (Spring).

Wadel, Cato, 1969, *Marginal Adaptations and Modernization in Newfoundland*, St. John's: ISER.

Walby, Sylvia, 1986, *Patriarchy at Work*, Cambridge: Polity Press.

Walicki, A., 1969, *The Controversy Over Capitalism*, London: Oxford University Press.

Wallerstein, I., 1979, *The Capitalist World Economy*, Cambridge: Cambridge University Press.

Wallerstein, I., 1974, *The Modern World-System Capitalist Agriculture and the Origins of the European World-Economy in the Sixteenth Century*, New York and London: Academic Press.

Warren, B., 1973, "Imperialism and Capitalist Industrialisation", *New Left Review* 81.

Warren, B., 1980, *Imperialism: Pioneer of Capitalism*, London: New Left Books.

Weeks, Ernie and Leigh Mazany, 1983, *The Future of the Atlantic Fisheries*, Montreal: The Institute for Research on Public Policy.

Williams, Raymond, 1979, *Politics and Letters*, London: New Left Books.

Williams, Raymond, 1986, "Too Many Socialisms", *Socialist Review* 85.

Williams, R., 1977, "Fish or Cut Bait," *This Magazine* 11(2).

Williams, R., 1978, "Fish at my Price or Don't Fish," *Canadian Dimension* 13(2).

Williams, R., 1979, "Inshore Fishermen, Unionization, and the Struggle against Underdevelopment Today," in R.J. Brym and R.J. Sacouman, 1979, *Underdevelopment and Social Movements in Atlantic Canada*, Toronto: New Hogtown Press.

Williams, R., 1982, "Implications of Political Economic/Class Position of Inshore Fishermen For Development of the Maritime Fishermen's Union," unpublished paper.

Williams, R., 1983, "The Kirby Report—Machiavelli Strikes Again," *New Maritimes* 1(7).

Williams, R., 1984, "The Restructuring that Wasn't," *New Maritimes* 2(7).

Winson, Anthony, 1983, "The Atlantic Fisheries Dilemma: Implementing the Kirby Commission Recommendations," Gorsebrook Research Institute, Saint Mary's University.

Winson, Anthony, 1985, "The uneven development of Canadian agriculture: farming in the Maritimes and Ontario," *Canadian Journal of Sociology* 10(4).

Wood, Barbara, 1985, *Alias Papa: A Life of Fritz Schumacher*,Oxford: Oxford University Press.

Wright, Erik O., 1976, "Class Boundaries in Advanced Capitalist Societies," *New Left Review* 98.

Wright, Erik O., 1978, *Class, Crisis and the State*, London: New Left Books.

Wrobel, M., 1981, "The H.B. Nickerson/National Sea Products Group," Ottawa: Economics Division, Research Branch, Library of Parliament.

Young, Kate, 1978, "Modes of Appropriation and the Sexual Division of Labour: A Case Study from Oaxaca, Mexico," in A. Kuhn and A. Wolpe (eds.), *Feminism and Materialism: Women and Modes of Production*, London: Routledge and Kegan Paul.